What Works in Inclusion?

What Works in Inclusion?

Edited by Christopher Boyle and Keith Topping

Open University Press

Open University Press
McGraw-Hill Education
McGraw-Hill House
Shoppenhangers Road
Maidenhead
Berkshire
England
SL6 2QL

email: enquiries@openup.co.uk
world wide web: www.openup.co.uk

and Two Penn Plaza, New York, NY 10121–2289, USA

First published 2012

A catalogue record of this book is available from the British Library

ISBN-13: 978-0-33-524468-3 (pb)
ISBN-10: 0-33-524468-8 (pb)
eISBN: 978-0-33-524469-0

Library of Congress Cataloging-in-Publication Data
CIP data applied for

Typesetting and e-book compilations by
RefineCatch Limited, Bungay, Suffolk
Printed in the UK by Bell & Bain Ltd, Glasgow

Fictitious names of companies, products, people, characters and/or data that may
be used herein (in case studies or in examples) are not intended to represent any
real individual, company, product or event.

MIX
Paper from
responsible sources
FSC
www.fsc.org   FSC® C007785

The *McGraw·Hill* Companies

The great aim of education is not knowledge, but action.

(Herbert Spencer)

Contents

List of tables and figures

Figures

Tables

List of contributors

Editors

Dr Christopher Boyle is a Lecturer in Psychology and Inclusive Education in the Faculty of Education at Monash University, Melbourne. His main research interests are in the area of teacher perceptions of inclusion and students' attributions for success and failure in learning. Previously Chris has worked as a secondary school teacher and as an educational psychologist in Scotland. He is currently editor of the *Australian Educational and Developmental Psychologist* and he has published widely in psychology and education.

Keith Topping is Professor of Educational and Social Research in the School of Education at the University of Dundee. His research interests include peer learning, parents as educators, problematic behaviour and social competence, computer-assisted learning and assessment, and inclusion. He has produced over 300 publications in 12 languages, including 21 books and 160 journal papers. Further details are at www.dundee.ac.uk/eswce/people/kjtopping.htm.

Contributors

Adrian Ashman is Emeritus Professor in the School of Education at the University of Queensland, former Head of School. He has doctoral degrees in cognitive educational psychology and also creative writing. Professor Ashman has produced numerous books, journal articles and chapters in the areas of special education, inclusive education and disability over 35 years.

Robert Conway is Professor and Dean of Education at Flinders University. His background is as a teacher in both regular and special education. His interests include the adaptation of learning and teaching to support the inclusion of students with special needs. He is a Fellow of the Australian College of Educators and holds a Distinguished Service Citation from the Australasian Society for the Study of Intellectual Disability.

Joanne Deppeler is Associate Professor and Associate Dean of Research Degrees in the Faculty of Education at Monash University. She has extensive experience in leading research projects in areas of inclusive education, school reform, and the professional learning of teachers. In particular, she is interested in finding new and innovative ways of researching the complexity of professional practice and learning in order to improve teacher quality and the outcomes of schooling for a range of students. She publishes widely and contributes to the professional and policy domains in Australia and internationally.

Laurel M. Garrick Duhaney is Associate Provost for Academic Affairs and Dean of the Graduate School at the State University of New York at New Paltz. She is an Associate Professor of Special Education in the Department of Educational Studies at New Paltz, and has held a range of teaching and administrative positions in Jamaica. Her research interests include inclusion of students with disabilities in general education classrooms, meeting the educational needs of students from culturally and linguistically diverse backgrounds, assessment of student learning, and responsive teacher education for a diverse society. She has published widely in the areas of inclusive education and multicultural education.

Dr Roberta Fadda is a senior research fellow at the University of Cagliari, Italy. Her main research interests focus on social and cognitive development in typically developing children and in children with autism spectrum disorders. Recently, she has been actively involved in a national project, funded by the Italian Ministry of Education, which aims to promote the inclusion of children with special needs in mainstream classes.

Dr Fraser Lauchlan is currently a Visiting Professor at the Università di Cagliari, Italy, where he is researching the cognitive benefits of bilingualism in children who speak minority languages. He is an educational psychologist and works as a consultant for local authorities in the UK (www.fraserlauchlan.com). He is also an Honorary Lecturer at the University of Strathclyde in Scotland. He has published extensively in many areas of educational psychology.

Margo Mastropieri is Professor at George Mason University in Fairfax, Virginia. She is interested in how students with disabilities learn in school and much of her research has focused on cognitive strategies designed to promote learning and retention of school-related information. She is editor with Tom Scruggs of *Exceptional Children*, the flagship journal of the Council for Exceptional Children.

Kim M. Michaud is completing her PhD in Special Education from George Mason University and a MA in Special Education from Marshall University. Kim has spent 15 years involved in teaching students with special needs at both the elementary and secondary levels. She collaborated to successfully design and implement a special education programme for the parochial schools in West Virginia.

Brahm Norwich is Professor of Educational Psychology and Special Educational Needs at the Graduate School of Education, University of Exeter. He has worked as a teacher and as a professional educational psychologist, and researched and published widely in these fields. His books are *Moderate Learning Difficulties and the Future of Inclusion* (Routledge 2005), *Special Pedagogy for Special Children: Pedagogies for Inclusion* (with Ann Lewis, Open University Press 2005); *Dilemmas of Difference, Disability and Inclusion: International Perspectives* (Routledge 2008) and *SEN: A New Look* (with Mary Warnock and Lorella Terzi, *Continuum Publishers 2010*).

Diane Richler, CM, has been advocating for the rights of persons with disabilities and their families for over 40 years. She was President of Inclusion International and Chair of the International Disability Alliance. She has been a consultant with the World Bank, the Organization for Economic Co-operation and Development and United Nations agencies and was an Erasmus Mundus Visiting Academic.

Richard Rose is Professor of Inclusive Education at the University of Northampton. He is Director of Project IRIS, a longitudinal study into special education in Ireland. Richard previously taught in schools in several parts of England and has done consultancy and research in many countries. His publications include *Confronting Obstacles to Inclusion: International Responses to Developing Inclusive Education* (Routledge 2010).

Dr Spencer J. Salend is a Professor of Educational Studies at the State University of New York at New Paltz. He is the author of *Creating Inclusive Classrooms: Effective and Reflective Practices* (Pearson Education 2010) and *Classroom Testing and Assessment for All Students: Beyond Standardization* (Sage Publications 2009). His scholarship addresses inclusive education practices, students from diverse backgrounds, educational assessment and model teacher education programmes.

Tom Scruggs is Professor at George Mason University in Fairfax, Virginia. His research interests include instructional and cognitive strategies for students with disabilities. His most recent book is *The Inclusive Classroom: Strategies for Effective Differentiated Instruction* (Prentice Hall 2010). Dr Scruggs is currently editor (with Margo Mastropieri) of the Council for Exceptional Children journal, *Exceptional Children*.

Roger Slee is Professor and the inaugural Director of the Victoria Institute for Education, Diversity and Lifelong Learning at Victoria University. He previously held the Chair of Inclusive Education at the Institute of Education, University of London. Roger is the founding editor of the *International Journal of Inclusive Education*. He has been the Deputy Director General of the Queensland Education Ministry. His most recent book is *The Irregular School* (Routledge 2010).

Dr Jacqueline Thousand is Professor in the School of Education at California State University San Marcos and the coordinator of the special education teacher preparation and graduate programmes within the school. A prolific author of books, chapters and articles on universal design, co-teaching and inclusive schooling, she is actively involved in international teacher education and serves on the editorial and advisory boards of several national and international journals.

Dr Richard Villa has worked with governmental and non-governmental agencies, advocacy organizations, and thousands of teachers and administrators in schools throughout the world, to develop and implement organizational and instructional support systems for educating all students within general education settings. He has co-authored 14 books and over 100 articles and book chapters regarding inclusive education, differentiated instruction, collaborative planning and teaching, and school restructuring. Further information is available at ravillabayridge.com

Dr Catharine Whittaker is a Professor of Educational Studies and the co-ordinator of the Special Education Program at the State University of New York at New Paltz. She is the co-author of *Bridging Multiple Worlds: Case Studies of Diverse Educational Communities* (Pearson Education in 2008). Her research addresses instructional strategies for secondary students with disabilities, differentiating instruction, case studies in teacher education and teacher preparation.

Foreword

When I put 'inclusion special education' into Google scholar there are well over one million hits. It thus seems timely to create a volume about what is known from this evidence base of scholarly articles. 'Inclusion' has become a buzz word – which means it is often used, but not always with the same meaning, same intent, or same impact on students. It seems a mistake to have used a noun to denote this important process, as nouns can too readily lead to 'inclusion' being about a thing or a place. There is, too often, a sense that if the child is 'included' (i.e. 'they are there') then all is well; job done.

In his chapter, Slee reminds us that there may be many problems hiding behind nice words like inclusion. By concentrating on 'placement' (where these students are to be placed) it can allow us to look away from 'the tragedy of exclusion'. It can also allow us to say 'we have done our best' and then attach blame to those who suffer most; indeed he sees schools becoming incubators of exclusion. He argues that inclusive education 'is not a project wherein we update and rehouse special education. Nor is it about inviting different groups to participate in an unreconstructed regular education. Inclusion requires far more thought and effort.' Inclusion requires building trust and negotiation, asking what can sometimes be awkward questions, bringing multidisciplinary teams to the table, inviting schools to be concerned about the learning of *all* students, and valuing many who previously were less valued by and in schools.

So who are these students?

The answer seems to be a moving target. Certainly there are now more of these students simply because the population of students is increasing. The proportions, however, may have changed less – although they remain hotly contested. The percentage ranges from 4 per cent to 100 per cent, with the latter argument being that all students are 'diverse' and need inclusion – which surely defeats the point of the notion of Inclusion and Diversity (although Ashman argues that 'truly inclusive classrooms exist because they do away with the concept of special learning needs; because *every* child has a special learning need'). Richler notes that 10–15 per cent of the world's population have a disability, and many of these students do not go to schools; many are hidden, many are never identified, and many are caused by war, illness and poverty. Inclusion more recently also relates to homeless children, gender differences, and so on go the classifications.

The question needs to be asked why so many want 'inclusion' and who are those that do not? Salend and Whittaker noted the over-identification (in the US) of students with socially constructed disabilities being served in special education, Lauchland and Fadda noted that teachers tend to express greatest concern about students with emotional and behavioural difficulties, and Conway noted the (almost unbelievable) increase in students with autism spectrum disorder in mainstream schools. Topping shows the evolving nature of inclusion, from the early days of special schools and classes to its current wide sense. He hints at the tension between sufficient funding, the ethical imperatives and the societal claims for *all* to participate in education without exclusionary consequences.

A major reason for this increase in 'who is included' relates to the apportionment of resources. This has led to much more effective diagnoses, with the (desirable) intent to then couple this diagnosis with appropriate treatment. As the pool of money is never enough, so success at labelling, seeking diagnosis, and advocacy for 'new' needs are ever present. It seems that children no longer have reading difficulties; instead they have dyslexia, ADHD, Aspergers or OCD. The medicalization of education continues apace – not because these 'diagnoses' are correct or not, but so often labelling is the only way to advocate for the scarce resources. This money-labelling model favours those with advocacy skills, assists schools to seek more resources, helps parents to argue for entitlement for their children, and once again those often in most need of the resources are the losers. The other down side of labelling is that it is being used by parents and teachers to explain why a child cannot learn, why a teacher cannot teach, why special provision should be made for the lack of learning, and so on. So, we have a tension – there is a need for better diagnosis to allow the best evidence-based treatment to be implemented (and optimize access to scarce resources), but the very act of classification can become the major barrier to the student learning! This leads to the contradiction that 'all' may well be *included* but the funds are apportioned to those who can best or loudest demonstrate special needs! What an opportunity to come up with a teaching model that welcomes better diagnosis (and classification) but does not lead to the classification then becoming the barrier to optimal teaching and learning.

Resolving the problems in the regular (mainstream) classroom

One of the other dilemmas is that we have invented a place called 'classrooms' and for historical reasons we fill these with 25–30 students and one teacher. We then expect this teacher to be excellent in teaching all students. When there was less variability in the school population this was not too daunting a task, but there is an increased diversity among students (in terms of their cultural, developmental, emotional, home, intellectual backgrounds) plus so much more knowledge about how to best diagnose and educate students with specific learning issues. Expecting all teachers to be expert for all students is a big ask.

Teacher expertise relates to their attitudes, efficacy and proficiency in teaching all students. Throughout so many chapters it is noted that the attitudes of teachers, peers, parents and school leaders are critical to making inclusion successful for students. Conway is very clear: successful inclusion is dependent on the attitude of teachers, their recognition of the child's right to participation, and their efficacy to teach these students along with all others in their class. Mastropieri and Scruggs also comment, 'Teachers are the main players in the inclusion arena and they are clearly resourceful and not against inclusion, as has been shown in several studies.' The good news is that the majority (66 per cent) of teachers express a willingness to teach students with disabilities. But one third are still not so willing (Mastropieri and Scruggs), and these teachers cite the constraints of time, training and support for inclusion.

It is unlikely that 'all' teachers can become expert at inclusion and know the evidence base outlined in this book. It seems ironic that one of the advantages of special schools is that expertise is less spread and more concentrated. There have been experts available to schools but they are often too thin in availability, take the problem away from the teachers and thus leave little behind, and the evidence in this book is not particularly supportive of the 'bring in the experts' model. An alternative is to have at least one teacher in a school responsible for having access to the evidence, expertise in knowing best evidence-based practice and the responsibility of working with all teachers to ensure that there are positive impacts on students (learning, acceptance, social, attitude, character etc.) in the school and (as Rose notes) on families and communities. This model presumes collaboration among teachers, and this has proved difficult to implement as it is changing two centuries of working alone in 'lone classrooms'.

Resolving the problem via specifying standards

More recently many systems have implemented national curricula and national testing in a move to support *all* students. These seems to be a desire for *all* students to be at or above these standards. There is a reality: given a normal distribution in most achievement domains, there will always be a percentage of students that will find it difficult to attain the 'standards' (no matter how good the teaching). Not all students can be above the average (and the standards are usually set at, or above, the average). Hence, the more recent claims are that 'schools are failing' as not all teachers can get students to master the standards!

Once again, those well below the average will be deemed to have 'failed' to reach these standards. But, if the standards were rephrased as growth standards – that all students need to make at least a year's growth for a year's input – then it is possible for any student to reach this standard (regardless of where they start the year). Of course, those who start below the curricular standards need more than a year's achievement growth per year. Those then gaining less than a year's growth could be classified as being in most need of additional resources. This could lead to a different notion of disability – I was fascinated with the footnote in Lauchlan and Fadda, in which they suggest that in Italy disability refers not to a symptom or classification but to 'children who have additional support needs'.

It is not as if there is not a surfeit of resources – but they tend to be spent on matters that have little effect. The cost of reducing class sizes has been incredibly substantial with little evidence of any changes to students' learning, engagement, or attitude; there have been many curricular reforms and implementation of assessment regimes with similarly little evidence of improvement in student outcomes; and many professional development programmes are costly, with the same lack of evidence of effect. It seems there is a love of spending on structures, on 'things', and then mandating policies to ensure teaching is even more impactful in these structures. We place demands on teachers but spend more resources providing them with things, rather than investing in the greatest untapped potential in our system: teacher expertise.

Exciting developments

One of the major features of the book is the descriptions of many evidence-based effective methods. Salend and Whittaker outline the response-to-intervention system, which has already engendered a lot of success. The first meta-analysis of RTI by Tran, Sanchez *et al.* (2011) based on 13 studies has a very large average effect size of 1.07. Ashman outlines responsive teaching based on teachers knowing each student, focusing on the teaching–learning environment, developing instructional strategies and techniques that accommodate learner diversity, and involving deliberate planning, data collection and lesson presentation that accommodate all students' learning needs.

Deppeler describes 'innovation through collaboration'. Such collaboration involves trust and shared responsibility for students' learning, the use of evidence based on sound pedagogic principles, shared leadership and structures that create collective action and that are respectful of diversity. As critically, collaboration must be regularly examined to ensure these conditions are maintained and in order to reap high-quality educational and social benefits. Peer-assisted learning with differentiated curriculum enhancements also has much evidence support. Mastropieri and Scruggs describe three peer methods that have been investigated including class-wide peer tutoring with content sheets, embedded mnemonic elaboration and differentiated activities. Peers include not only students learning together but also teachers working and learning together. They do note that although differentiated curriculum enhancements delivered by peers have promising results, few teachers presently implement the practices. So the question remains: how to upscale successful evidence-based interventions?

Concluding comment

This is a book of new agendas. It asks readers to understand where we have come from, and what now are the agendas for moving forward. There is no suggestion of rediscovering special schools or classrooms, or settling for anything but optimal inclusion. While we create new classifications, then the need for inclusion increases, not diminishes. What seems needed are better indicators of the impact of inclusion to help teachers celebrate when they are successful, and moving beyond the tensions of better classification diagnosis and the misuse of labelling. There is a clear message in this book that we already know a lot but it is now as much about getting this evidence into our systems and schools. The theme is more than 'What works' but is moving more to 'What works best'.

The major messages are primarily about mindsets. These mindsets can relate to the barriers, lack of resources, time and expertise; or these mindsets can use the evidence base to truly implement the underlying philosophies and intent of inclusion. Those who make inclusion work, and there are many examples in this book, often have the same time, resources and heterogeneity among their students as those who do not make it work. This book shows we can move past the negative and embrace the positive mindsets. The evidence is there: if the mind is willing, the system supportive and the quality of teaching high, inclusion has the chance of being successfully implemented.

Professor John Hattie, University of Melbourne

Reference

Tran, L., Sanchez, T., Arellano, B. and Lee Swanson, H. (2011) A meta-analysis of the RTI literature for children at risk for reading disabilities, *Journal of Learning Disabilities*, 44(3): 283–95.

Acknowledgements

The editors would like to acknowledge support and assistance from various colleagues and friends.

Working with so many excellent and dedicated teaching staff and students makes us realize how much quality is needed to be successful in the teaching profession. A debt of gratitude is owed to all the students we have had the pleasure of working with at the Universities of Dundee and Strathclyde in Scotland as well as Charles Sturt (Wagga Wagga, NSW) and Monash Universities in Australia – you inspire us constantly. A debt of gratitude is owed to many colleagues in educational psychology and teaching for sharing ideas for this book: Anita Smiley, Heather Rendall, Mark Smith, Gillian Wilson, Michael Wilson, Dr John Pugh, Jacquie Bradley, Elaine Morrison, Lee Dunnachie, Richard Walsh, Dr Hilary Farquarson, John Toland, Frank Waters and Moira Craig. Special thanks goes to Wayne Parkins, Gerald Wurf and Christina Davidson who keep the engine running at Charles Sturt University in Wagga Wagga. A very special thank you goes to South Lanarkshire Council's Principal Educational Psychologist, Elizabeth King, a wonderful person, only matched by her skills as a psychologist. Thanks also to special friends such as Kate A. Parkins, Cesare Togneri, Richard Smith, Anna Bakewell, Quincy M.E., Pepe Siekierska-Boyle, The Gorbal's Pychiatrist in Residence, Dr Tom Henderson and Moira Elita Togneri – we thank you for your continuing encouragement to complete the project.

The editors appreciate the help of Jake Kraska, Shane Costello, Kristina Haebich, Ange Jaman and Linda Varcoe of Monash University for their dedicated work in ensuring consistency in style and referencing across this book, as well as for their assistance in producing an index.

A debt of gratitude is owed to Fiona Richman, Commissioning Editor at McGraw-Hill, for her encouragement and assistance.

CHRISTOPHER BOYLE AND KEITH TOPPING
Introduction: Setting a scene for positive inclusion

Here is a book that is different to most others in this field. It provides clear insight from vastly experienced 'experts' on inclusion. There is no rival publication that has brought together such a wealth of knowledge and insight between the covers of one book. We, as editors, believe that whether you read chapters in any order you fancy (as this book is designed to accommodate) or read these pages in a more sequential fashion, you will be satisfied.

It is difficult for practitioners to find outstanding examples of inclusion in terms that they understand. The aim of this book is to highlight such successes. There is a focus on the practising of inclusive education in reality. Teachers reading the book are helped to be clear about what variables are likely to make a difference in practice. This is a book that concentrates on how to make inclusion work – from the view of internationally established practitioners.

The idea of theory, 'how to', and the barriers to inclusive education

This book provides the reader with three distinct sections, which address important international perspectives as to:

- what inclusion is;
- how it should be implemented; and finally
- how perceived barriers can be overcome.

Part I attempts to encapsulate *what inclusion* is *exactly*, with chapters which focus on the theoretical concepts of inclusive education. This part discusses contemporary theories of inclusion from the perspective of each author. Each chapter contains aspects of the following: the context, describing critical features of the relevant educational, cultural and social context; the author's personal perspective of the inclusion debate, and both personal and professional experiences as well as considering influence from both central and local government. This section begins with Topping's '**Conceptions of inclusion: widening ideas**', which focuses on various agendas that affect inclusive education such as socio-economic status, race and gender. Topping discusses the financial impact of the inclusion agenda, whereby the educational and social opportunities of many students are second to the fiscal aspect of inclusion planning, and concludes with directions for methods to widen ideas in inclusive education.

In Chapter 2, '**Inclusion in the United States: theory and practice**', Michaud and Scruggs provide a comprehensive analysis of the main arguments and discussion points with regards to inclusive education in the US. The main thrust of the chapter is the consideration of 100 per cent inclusion and whether advocates of this goal have the best interests of the students in mind – and, indeed, whether this is actually achievable or necessary.

Consideration of the inclusion debate from an Italian perspective is the contribution of Chapter 3, entitled '**The "Italian" model of full inclusion: origins and current directions**', where Lauchlan and Fadda describe the historical development and contemporary application of inclusion in Italy. The authors also provide access to Italian language studies (e.g. Ianes and Canevaro 2008; Demo and Zambotti 2009) that have hitherto not been described in the English-language literature. Italy is usually held up as an excellent model of inclusive practice, and the effectiveness of their approach is discussed in relation to various Italian stakeholders.

Roger Slee completes Part I with Chapter 4, entitled '**Inclusion in schools: what is the task?**', producing an insightful and (some may suggest) polemical account of his experiences of inclusion, which considers the evolution of inclusion through various international perspectives. Slee puts forward various analytical tools which practitioners and theorists should be aware of in order to enhance the measurement of success in inclusion practice. As Slee himself states, 'My premise is that reductive understandings have produced a form of inclusive education that sustains old exclusions and creates new ones'.

Part II is the largest, and arguably the most important section of this book. The reader is provided with a wide array of models of inclusive practice that *are* successful. This section will act as a guide for education professionals, postgraduates and undergraduates, to help implement evidence-based practices to promote inclusion successfully. There are seven chapters (compared to four each in Parts I and III), each one providing specific details about 'how to' implement inclusion policies in various contexts. Each chapter will provide a context and description of the model, which will enable readers to adopt the model into their own particular education context. Through the explanations you will understand and be able to replicate what makes a programme successful in your own environment.

In Chapter 5, Norwich considers '**How inclusion policy works in the UK (England): successes and issues**' and provides a historical and contemporary context. He offers the notion of the different types of inclusion being on a continuum and draws on the work of Cigman (2007), who suggests there are two types of inclusionists – the 'moderates' and the 'universalists'. In the context of this polarized debate, Norwich delves into detail in his analysis and puts forward ways to embrace inclusive education.

Salend and Whittaker highlight '**Inclusive education: best practices in the United States**' in Chapter 6, with a detailed review of what current research is indicating are the best methods to implement inclusion programmes. The authors discuss Response to Intervention (RtI) systems, which provide a systematic method and a structured way of ensuring that students' inclusive needs are addressed and provided for. Salend and Whittaker also highlight many other best practice approaches, and optimistically conclude by stating that there are signs that the US federal government '. . . is promoting initiatives that could promote sustainable educational change . . .'.

In Chapter 7, Ashman considers the importance of '**Facilitating inclusion through responsive teaching**' and emphasizes the need to move away from the focus on inclusion *per se* and more towards the importance of strong pedagogical approaches, which naturally provide successful teaching environments for all students. Ashman puts forward a convincing and evidenced argument, thus suggesting that responsive teaching is the key aspect to inclusive interventions that removes the need to focus on 'special education'.

The suggestion that interaction among teaching staff is essential to inclusive education is put forward by Boyle in Chapter 8, entitled '**Teachers make inclusion successful: positive perspectives on inclusion**'. This follows other studies (e.g. Goodman and Burton 2010; Boyle *et al.* 2012) that emphasize the importance of peer support in successfully achieving an inclusive environment. Boyle uses data from interviews with teaching staff to suggest that linking with other teachers provides more valuable support than that of the school management team.

Villa and Thousand discuss the need for '**Creating and sustaining inclusive schools**' in Chapter 9. They do this through reflecting on 30 years of research and experience in the sphere of education, and focus on what they call the 'critical variables' in order to make this happen. The authors strongly argue for more emphasis on collaboration with students in order to achieve an optimal inclusive environment and the reader is provided with various resources and suggestions to achieve this.

In Chapter 10, '**Developing inclusive practices: innovation through collaboration**', Deppeler continues the theme of the importance of working alongside other stakeholders and emphasizes the usefulness of *Collaborative Inquiry* (CI) in order to redress the issue of schools not being set up to accommodate active participants in processes. The author puts forward strategies for encouraging collaboration, including the reported success of coaching in teaching as suggested in Yopp *et al.* (2011). This indicates how teachers can operate effectively irrespective of the support from the school management team and the commensurate deployment of resources.

Rose writes in Chapter 11, '**Beyond the school gates: promoting inclusion through community partnerships**', that 'inclusive practices that are focused solely upon action in schools are unlikely to succeed'. This emphasizes Rose's exploration of the understanding that schools do not exist separately to the community of which they are geographically part. Therefore, inclusive practices must take cognisance of the available community resources. Rose uses an exemplar of good practice in this regard, thereby demonstrating a collective approach to robust inclusive practices.

Part III considers the nature of the events that have prevented successful inclusion in the past and continue to be barriers that have to be overcome. Whether students with special needs have received more equitable education is a moot point and this is developed in Lloyd (2008) in more detail. However, the four chapter authors in this section all suggest solutions in order to prevent readers from experiencing many barriers to inclusion in their practice.

In Chapter 12, '**How can teacher attitudes, co-teaching and differentiated instruction facilitate inclusion?**', Mastropieri and Scruggs highlight some of the persistent challenges that have affected inclusive education implementation. The authors suggest that teacher attitudes, peer relationships, student outcomes and co-teaching are the four areas where barriers are most likely to occur. These areas are described in some detail, with a discussion of why barriers exist. There are commensurate suggestions for methods to promote inclusion despite these barriers.

In Chapter 13, '**Understanding and addressing barriers to the implementation of inclusive education**', Garrick Duhaney examines the philosophical and socio-cultural barriers that can prevent the implementation of inclusion. A discerning discussion on fatalism and karma highlights the complex nature of the different cultural belief systems that can act as a barrier to successful inclusion, which many readers would have been unaware of. Garrick Duhaney, as with the other authors in this section, provides robust methods for overcoming these barriers, thus making inclusive education more attainable.

In Richler's Chapter 14, '**Systemic barriers to inclusion**', the reader is taken into international legislation from various bodies such as the United Nations, World Bank, World Health Organization and the United Nations Educational, Scientific and Cultural Organization. This provides a unique worldwide insight into various policies that are supposed to transcend international boundaries and offer a model for nation states to aim for regarding equity in education. Richler provides the reader with an in-depth understanding of the relevant legislation, but also, and more importantly, informs as to the reasons for its existence. Suggestions to overcome barriers are offered.

The final contribution in this section is Chapter 15, '**Inclusive schools in Australia: rhetoric and practice**'. Conway outlines barriers that exist in relation to including students in mainstream schools, e.g. the increase in autistic spectrum disorder and the negative reaction of teachers to this trend. Conway considers the issues from an Australian perspective and puts forward methods for schools to disregard rhetoric and move towards positive practices of inclusive education.

Conclusion

So what do the editors and contributors hope for, from this book? If you are a researcher, we hope that you come away with a clearer concept of inclusion set within a wider theoretical model of inclusive practice. You should also have a clearer idea about how inclusion might be measured, and in this way be able to contribute to the onward debate regarding the evaluation of inclusion. The book should also give you a much sharper notion of the issue of cost-effectiveness, so that you can be alert to the need to accurately price interventions in real-cost terms.

If you are a policy maker at local or central government level, we hope you are clear that policies in themselves, however beautifully written, rarely directly affect what goes on at grassroots level. We hope you are convinced of the need to truly involve students and staff at classroom level in collaborations to debate unfolding policies, since the policy needs to be *their* policy. Policies can indeed lead to practice, but generally they do not do so strongly, so the gathering of best practice to inform policy development is crucial. Policies also need to be written in terms that can be implemented, not in sweeping generalizations that might mean anything.

If you are a professional practitioner whose task is to train and consult with teachers, we hope you have a strong view of the necessity of an evidence base in the area of inclusion, and are determined to take that forward in your advice and recommendations.

Finally, if you are a teacher, we hope you have a much clearer idea of what inclusion is and what are proven methods to enable you to get there, with the methods outlined in sufficient detail (in this book or in sources referred to in it) to enable you to implement them with a high degree of fidelity. You should also be aware of what problems or barriers might present themselves, and how you can circumnavigate these. Indeed, you should be a more competent and professional practitioner.

Of course, this book is only a snapshot in time. Education will move on (although sometimes it moves backwards rather than forwards), and there will be future developments, which we cannot conceive of at the moment. We hope this book has prepared you for this onward journey, and helped sharpen your enquiring mind as you seek to promote ever more inclusive environments.

References

Boyle, C., Jindal-Snape, D., Topping, K. and Norwich, B. (2011) The importance of peer-support for teaching staff when including children with special educational needs, *School Psychology International*, 32(3): 167–184, DOI: 10.1177/0143034311415783.

Boyle, C., Scriven, B., Durning, S. and Downes, C. (2011) Facilitating the learning of all students: 'the professional positive' of inclusive practice in Australian primary schools, *Support for Learning*, 26(2): 72–8. DOI: 10.1111/j.1467-9604.2011.01480.

Cigman, R. (ed.) (2007) *Included or Excluded? The Challenge of the Mainstream for Some Special Educational Needs Children*. London: Routledge.

Demo, H. and Zambotti, F. (2009) Alcune relazioni tra percorsi di integrazione scolastica e percezione di integrazione sociale in contesti normali, *L'integrazione scolastica e sociale*, 8(5): 459–73.

Goodman, R. L. and Burton, D. M. (2010) The inclusion of students with BESD in mainstream schools: teachers' experiences of and recommendations for creating a successful inclusive environment, *Emotional and Behavioural Difficulties*, 15(3): 223–37. DOI: 10.1080/13632752.2010.497662.

Ianes, D. and Canevaro, A. (2008) *Facciamo il punto su . . . l'integrazione scolastica*. Trento: Centro Studi Erickson.

Lloyd, C. (2008) Removing barriers to achievement: a strategy for inclusion or exclusion, *International Journal of Inclusive Education*, 12(2): 221–36.

Yopp, D., Burroughs, E. A., Luebeck, J., Heidema, C., Mitchell, A. and Sutton, J. (2011) How to be a wise consumer of coaching: strategies teachers can use to maximize coaching, *Journal of Staff Development*, 32: 50–3.

Part I

Theories of inclusion: what exactly is 'inclusion'?

1

KEITH TOPPING
Conceptions of inclusion: widening ideas

Introduction

'Inclusion' – a word much more used in this century than in the last. It has something to do with people and society valuing diversity and overcoming barriers. But what exactly does it mean? Do different people mean different things by it? Where would you find it? How do you create it? How do you know when you have created it? This chapter hopes to illuminate the way to some of the answers to some of these questions. You will not find all the answers here, but the hope is that you will emerge asking more intelligent and challenging questions. Like learning, inclusion is a dynamic process, not a static condition – a journey, not a destination. This chapter takes a European perspective, as Chapter 2 deals with developments in the United States.

This chapter addresses that sub-set of the social inclusion agenda that is within educational contexts, including early years provision, primary elementary and secondary high education. It addresses inclusion issues arising from special educational needs and disability, but goes far beyond that to consider those arising from social class, socio-economic disadvantage, race, gender, and other factors. One practical reason for this wide scope is that these factors often interact, and consideration of only one factor in isolation can lead to faulty conclusions.

The definition of social inclusion has steadily widened over the years, and is now assumed to involve every student in every school, as well as all the adults in each school (Thomas *et al.* 2004). Conceptual change led to legislative change – but unfortunately development was all too slow and legislative change often had unintended consequences. Changes in policy and practice were often more driven by questions of finance than by professional idealism. Now we have a very wide concept of inclusion but in many cases a very narrow spectrum of measures intended to actually achieve it – and not all of these are effective. However, there are some examples of good practice, where the question 'does inclusion work?' actually makes sense. For some onlookers, whether inclusion 'works' is like asking whether God exists – it is a question of faith, not evidence. However, some evidence of cost-effectiveness is likely to be more than useful when arguing the case with non-believers.

Definitions and historical changes

Exploring some of the main concepts and boundaries of the territory of inclusion can prove a tricky business.

Special education and disability

It all started with 'special educational needs' (SEN) (as we now call them – in the past much more offensive terms were used). In the previous century, concern about pupils with serious learning difficulties led to the development of whole industries providing 'special education' in 'special schools'. This development of provision was paralleled by feeder industries categorizing children into 'special' or otherwise. Much of this segregation into 'special schools' proceeded without reference to any evidence as to whether such pupils learned more effectively in such settings. However, once the 'special education' industries were well established, professional vested interest in the status quo tended to resist any changes. And once a child was in a special school, few ever returned to the mainstream.

In fact, it is difficult to find convincing evidence that pupils do better in special schools (e.g. Peetsma *et al.* 2001). However, much of the subsequent movement in political and public opinion toward the 'integration' or 'reintegration' of pupils with learning difficulties into 'mainstream' schools stemmed more from ethical arguments than from any functional rationale. Even before 'integration' became widespread in practice, the rhetoric moved on and 'inclusion' became the new buzzword (Nind *et al.* 2003).

Social inclusion and political agendas

The concept of educational inclusion was now set in the much wider context of 'social inclusion', implying concern about all those of all ages who were marginalized, unproductive and non-participative in society. Social exclusion is associated with a combination of problems such as poor skills, unemployment, low incomes, poor housing, high crime environments, bad health and family breakdowns. It should not be assumed that these are purely urban phenomena (Shucksmith 2000).

Margaret Thatcher (erstwhile UK right-wing Prime Minister) famously stated that there was no such thing as society, and therefore presumably no such thing as social inclusion. Such concerns had been previously debated in the context of 'equal opportunities' – which of course did not mean simply treating everyone equally, since that would merely reinforce pre-existing differences – rather, it implied treating different people differently so that they would have equal opportunities to maximize their potential.

Human rights

Human rights are grand ethical ideas which can prove difficult to translate into effective practice on the ground. The rights and entitlements of children (in particular) have received increasing attention in recent years (e.g. Alaimo and Klug 2002), being strongly endorsed by the UN Convention on the Rights of the Child, by UNESCO in the Salamanca Statement, and reflected in the United Nations' call for 'Education for All'. This has been coupled with developments in practical methods to promote pupil involvement and participation in their own schooling (e.g. Beresford 2003). Richler's Chapter 14 provides an extensive discussion of international legislation and its impact on various signatories to these agreements.

Conceptual and legislative change – and unintended consequences

As these changes unfolded, previous ways of understanding educational needs were challenged. Within special education, the old system of categorization of children located the problem within the child, conceptualizing it as a deficit or defect in the individual, and applying a medical, diagnostic model – as if special difficulties were some kind of disease. Pseudo-diagnostic labels such as 'educationally subnormal' were used in the UK even into the 1970s.

From 1980 onwards, such categorization of children (which implied a permanent condition and that they were labelled for life) was made illegal in the UK (although in the US such categorization carried on). Political pressure from disability groups and parental advocacy had begun to change societal values, with consequent effects on legislation. Instead, the emphasis in assessment was to be on specifying the needs of the child – what kind of teaching and resources were most likely to affect educational progress.

Unfortunately, this apparently positive development degenerated all too rapidly into a welter of bureaucracy, with statutory assessments conducted by highly qualified professionals used by various stakeholders as a tool to unlock resources. However, the pool of resources did not grow rapidly enough to meet the increased demand, so these expensive levers often yielded rather small movement. Also, a postcode lottery operated, some local authorities maintaining statements or records of special educational needs on over twice as many children as other authorities with very similar demographic characteristics. Additionally, the articulate and assertive middle classes who could play the system tended to do disproportionately well out of it, diverting resources from more needy children from socio-economically disadvantaged families.

Nonetheless, the emphasis on needs did result in a movement away from medical models of disability, and towards social and educational models of understanding, which acknowledged that educational difficulties are dependent upon the educational context in which the child is situated, and the type and quality of the teaching they receive – in other words, factors outside the child as well as inside (Mittler 2000). Subsequently, assessment of children became even broader. There was more emphasis on dynamic assessment (how the child could perform given some assistance with the task) rather than static assessment (no help given with the task). There was also increasing emphasis on a range of contexts or ecologies in which the child operated in different ways at different systemic levels – ecosystemic assessment. It followed that if the micro-ecology changed, the child's performance and behaviour was likely to change.

Government thinking was also becoming more ecosystemic, acknowledging the interaction of a multiplicity of variables. Traditionally various central and local government services for children and families had been delivered by separate agencies, sometimes characterized not only by a lack of co-ordination but at times by active enmity and obstruction. Central government increasingly called for 'joined-up' or integrated services. Some local government authorities introduced developments such as 'community' or 'full-service' schools as vehicles for this (at times while remaining patently un-joined-up themselves) (Dyson and Todd 2010). Others combined education and social services for children into a notionally integrated 'Children's Services' department (Daniels 2010).

However, other government policies had unintended consequences which hampered inclusion. In England, for example, the emphasis on reaching attainment targets, free parental choice of school and the publication of league tables of raw scores on high-stakes tests of questionable reliability and validity created powerful disincentives for head teachers (school principals) to open their doors to pupils whose performance might in any way damage the reputation and consequently the viability of the school. At the same time, these factors created a pressure on existing school populations to achieve the new targets, doubling the barriers to inclusion.

Beyond this, there was developing thinking that the term SEN had become redundant, and might actually be unhelpful (given its overtones of bipolar categorization rather than continuous dimension). The notion that there is an obligation on the school to create a suitable learning environment for all children has not been accepted quickly. As it becomes accepted that every child has a right to learn differently and teaching has to take account of these differences, then inclusion should truly become a school improvement issue, with quality assurance at its core.

Conceptual confusion and behavioural divergence

However, this plethora of conceptions has led to considerable semantic confusion. The different implicit definitions of 'inclusion' espoused by different workers might not be immediately evident in their discussion of the topic. Catlett and Osher (1994) undertook a content analysis of various policy and position statements from national organizations in the US on the inclusion of students with disabilities. Less than half of these actually offered a definition of inclusion, and no two definitions were alike. Small wonder that teachers and parents become confused.

Rhetoric also often departs from reality. Croll and Moses (2003) tracked a number of local authorities (all of whom had policy statements committing them to the fullest possible 'inclusion') over a period of years, during which time some of these authorities actually increased the number of pupils in segregated special provision. Indeed, the move towards actual inclusion of pupils with special educational needs had been characterized as 'painfully slow' (Gold 2003). Based on statistics analysed by Norwich (2003), the Centre for Studies on Inclusive Education (www.csie.org) calculated that at current rates of change it would take the average local education authority 55 years to reach the inclusion levels already achieved by the London Borough of Newham – and the worst performing local authority well over 100 years.

Expanding concepts of inclusion

All commentators now agree that inclusion should mean much more than the mere physical presence of pupils with special educational needs in mainstream schools (e.g.

Nind *et al.* 2003). Such pupils should also be able to access the mainstream curriculum successfully, which may need supporting, individualizing or differentiating in some way. Indeed, in the UK there is now a legal obligation on schools to provide curricular and physical access for *all* pupils. Apart from issues of learning, they should feel, behave as, and be treated as full members or citizens of the school community. Farrell and Ainscow (2002) have described this as the Presence – Acceptance – Participation – Achievement cycle. Beyond this, inclusion implies celebrating the diversity and supporting the achievement and participation of *all* pupils who face learning and/or behaviour challenges of any kind, in terms of socio-economic circumstances, ethnic origin, cultural heritage, religion, linguistic heritage, gender, sexual preference, and so on. However, ideally inclusion should go even further, and schools should engage *all* families and the community as well as *all* children, seeking effective intergenerational learning across the lifespan, which might occur inside schools or outside or through a combination of these. These expanding notions of inclusion are illustrated in the four levels of Figure 1.1.

However, the area of social and educational inclusion remains chronically under-theorized, limiting attempts to bring consistency and cohesiveness to the field (despite the courageous efforts of such as Clough and Corbett 2000, Dyson and Millward 2000 and Norwich 2000). Brendtro *et al.* (1990) asserted that inclusion was not a new concept, but rather something that operated very effectively before cultures were economically and culturally driven by 'things material' and social mobility led to the decline of family and community life. If it 'takes a whole village to raise a child', it is

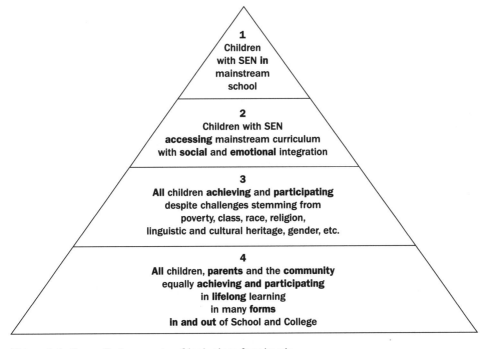

Figure 1.1 Expanding concepts of inclusion: four levels

likely to take a bundle of resources to raise a child with special challenges if the community and family have disintegrated.

Perceptions of inclusion

Epidemiological surveys in the UK suggest that 20 per cent of the child population have some degree of special educational need. Of these, 2 per cent have such substantial special needs as to merit detailed assessment and special provision enshrined in statutory documentation (Croll and Moses 2003). Of course, divisions are arbitrary and lines could be drawn anywhere. Over the last 20 years in the UK, teachers have perceived an increase in the number of children with special needs in mainstream classes. However, this perception does not quite match with other data, since the decline in the special school population has actually been quite small (Croll and Moses 2003). The biggest increase in mainstreaming has occurred for children with learning difficulties. However, teachers tend to express greatest concern about pupils with emotional and behaviour difficulties – perhaps because such children are perceived as most likely to damage the education of their classmates as well as being most stressful for the teacher (Scruggs and Mastropieri 1996; Hastings and Oakford 2003; Cole 2004).

Some children who are seen as having special educational needs in one classroom are not seen as having them in another (Van der Veen *et al.* 2010). In the predominantly female teacher environment of the primary school, many more boys than girls are perceived as having special needs (Guarino *et al.* 2010). Also, teachers tend to perceive learning difficulties more readily in children with language difficulties, and behaviour difficulties more readily in male children of African and Caribbean origin, although both tendencies have become less strong in recent years (Agbenyega and Peers 2010). Children with physical and/or sensory impairments tend to be perceived as less of a problem in mainstream environments, although presumably their presence occasions considerable problems of access to buildings and to specialist ancillary services (Gray 2009; van der Veen *et al.* 2010). Teacher belief systems are likely to have a significant effect on 'inclusion'. Teachers with and without experience and training with pupils with various levels and types of special educational need might have very different perceptions and expectations, self-confidence and self-efficacy, resulting in very different effectiveness in teaching and learning (Boyle *et al.* 2012a). Additionally, special educational needs legislation has typically ignored interaction with socio-economic disadvantage. The correlation between poverty and attainment at the age of 11 is –0.7 (Croll 2002), suggesting that half of the variance in attainment between schools (and children) could be accounted for by poverty.

Does inclusion work?

Much of the discourse of inclusion takes it for granted that inclusion is a 'good thing', like motherhood and apple pie. Some of this comes from the human rights agenda. Of course, human rights can be viewed from another angle – if a parent or child prefers a segregated special school (as some do), should they have a human right to have it? Others might take a more pragmatic view, and wish to look at the evidence for the relative effectiveness of inclusive and segregated educational placements.

There is some research concerning the effectiveness of different kinds of provision for pupils with special educational needs at Inclusion Levels 1 and 2 (in Figure 1.1). The evidence suggests that any differences in outcomes for children with special needs between special and mainstream schools are small, but tend to favour mainstream school, in terms of both educational attainments and social integration. Socially, children with special needs in mainstream school tend not to be as well accepted as 'normal' children, but they nevertheless enjoy a fair degree of social integration, while learning to cope in a situation more akin to the outside post-school world than the protective environment of a special school.

In a seminal review, Madden and Slavin (1983) concluded that there was no evidence that segregated placements enhanced either academic or social progress compared to mainstream placements. Staub and Peck (1994) reviewed many studies of mainstreaming, and found no evidence of deleterious effects for pupils with special needs or their classmates. Salend and Garrick Duhaney (1999) found little difference in outcomes between mainstream and special placements overall. Peetsma et al. (2001) conducted a four-year longitudinal study of matched pairs of pupils, one in special and one in mainstream placement. The mainstream pupils academically outperformed the special school pupils. Manset and Semmel (1997) reviewed learning outcomes for mainstreamed and segregated pupils, finding no difference in mathematics but a small advantage for mainstreamed pupils in literacy.

Special educational provision is hardly likely to be effective on a one-size-fits-all basis, so presumably it is important to place pupils in learning environments specifically designed and resourced to meet their own specific individual needs (Westwood 2004). But there is more to it than this. In a large meta-analysis, Wang et al. (1993) found that classroom practices had more influence on student learning than curriculum design and policy, and much more than school-wide practices and policies or state and district policies. Salend and Garrick Duhaney (1999) asserted that the quality of the programme was the critical variable, rather than its nature or location. This implies that there should be more emphasis on quality assurance.

Perhaps surprisingly, few studies address issues of cost-effectiveness. If special and mainstream placements are equally effective, it would seem to make sense to place children in the environment which costs less. Such a placement would release resources to help other children. Crowther et al. (1998) conducted one of the few studies in this area, finding that special schools for pupils with learning difficulties in the UK were consistently higher in cost than mainstream placements.

The process of change

Adoption of ideas in theory is a start, but adoption of those ideas in practice can take much longer. The speed of adoption in theory depends partially upon clarity of conceptualization and exemplification and the absence of overt conflict with ruling cultural value judgements, leading to gradual initial acceptance of the idea, which then begins to permeate prevailing public opinion and eventually becomes enshrined in regulation or legislation (statutory legitimation). These developments might be more or less influenced by empirical research. Rationally, the evidence on the positive effects and unintended consequences of any policy or practice shift should be explored in pilot research projects before any widespread implementation. However, this happens relatively rarely in education, and policy and practice often change because of shifts in opinion rather than the evidence base, sometimes because of political decisions taken thoughtlessly on the run or evangelistic campaigns operated by those with a drum to beat, a career to make or a product to sell.

Adoption in practice is likely to be much slower, and will depend upon the quantity and quality of content and delivery of continuing professional development made available to practitioners. Of course, big national initiatives create a need to find many expert trainers all at the same time – by definition almost impossible. Adoption in practice will also depend upon prioritization among competing pressures for time and resources, both at the level of the individual practitioner and at larger systemic levels. New initiatives tend to be seen as additional burdens, for which by definition no time is available since all the available time is already being used. Practitioners are rarely told what to leave out in order to make space for a new initiative.

Also, practitioners may be more comfortable doing what they have always done rather than exploring more challenging and difficult areas in which they are likely to make mistakes. If senior management is punitive and blaming rather than encouraging and supportive, practitioners have very little incentive to change. Belief and motivation play a large part. Practical professionals might never believe something is possible until they have seen someone else do it. Concrete exemplars of good practice – positive models of possibility – tend to be more effective than evangelistic exhortation. However, resistant practitioners might still argue that the positive model is insufficiently proximate to their own context to be credible: 'Well, it might work with that class, but it could never work with mine . . .'.

Eventually, however, islands of good practice become more numerous, sooner or later every practitioner has contact with at least one, and the small islands begin to join up into larger islands. Unfortunately, another cycle can then begin to operate. As Sindelar *et al.* (2006) showed, the initial examples of good practice might have emanated from especially innovative, energetic and well-organized teachers, who made them work by virtue of their general capability as much as by the intrinsic benefits of the initiative. Such teachers tend to gain promotion and move on to other schools. Later replications might suffer from dilution of the initiative in content as well as in quality of delivery. If there have been early empirical studies of effectiveness, these might overestimate later effectiveness when the initiative is delivered by more ordinary professionals in less favoured contexts.

There are a number of barriers to change at a systems level. Teacher training in the UK remains highly focused on curricular subjects, rather than generic pedagogical skills, especially at secondary level. The teacher's role is still often seen as that of inter-generational transmitter of received wisdom and cultural heritage – the 'sage on the stage'. Such a role is not readily adaptable to pupil diversity. The information technology revolution has yielded a world in which knowledge is both vast and transient, and accessible from anywhere in a host of ways. Given this, transferable skills such as the capacity for critical thinking and creativity seem likely to prove more useful in an accelerating future. Additionally, social and communication skills seem likely to be increasingly important.

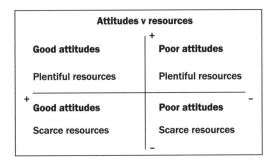

Figure 1.2 Attitudes v resources
Source: Boyle *et al.* 2012b

Teachers often cite a 'lack of resources' as a barrier to mainstreaming pupils with special needs. Adequate appropriately expert practitioner time, adequate appropriate physical space, adequate appropriate learning and teaching materials and adequate high-quality Continuing Professional Development (CPD) are certainly essential. 'Main-dumping' (placing pupils with special needs in mainstream environments without consideration of and/or meeting their specific additional support needs) is not to be condoned (Thomas *et al.* 1998). However, 'lack of resources' is often cited as a barrier without any clarity about exactly what resources are needed and why. Correspondingly, pumping the wrong type of resources into a mainstream environment without a specific action plan may worsen the situation rather than improve it (see Figure 1.2).

Conclusion

The definition of social inclusion has widened, and is now taken to mean at least all children achieving and participating despite challenges stemming from disability, poverty, social class, race, religion, linguistic and cultural heritage, gender, and so on. However, the definition is still unclear and it remains under-theorized. Mainstream special needs pupils tend to outperform segregated special needs pupils. Other mainstream pupils are not disadvantaged by the presence of special needs pupils.

The quality of classroom practice is the critical variable in successful inclusion. However, at classroom level, intense and time-consuming continuing professional development is key to progress, but is sometimes lacking or not well delivered. Concern about children with behavioural difficulties outweighs concern about other pupils. At school level, leadership is key, but the senior management team might not be successful. At the level of supportive professionals, the system for ascertaining special need is variously implemented, bureaucratic and wasteful. Co-ordination between professionals is often uncertain. Government policies may be largely rhetoric, accompanied by little idea of how to make inclusion work, or intent and ability to deliver targeted resources to make this happen.

Even when high inclusion is achieved, it may be difficult to sustain. There have been few studies of cost-effectiveness of interventions to promote inclusion.

Nonetheless, gains have been made. For example, the UK has long since moved away from diagnostic labelling. Learning needs assessment specific to the current context – this has long been the order of the day. Teachers and professionals must look harder for evidence-based and cost-effective ways of enhancing inclusive practice which definitely work – at least in some environments. The rest of this book will develop this theme. Meanwhile, it is worth remembering the bible: 'We, being many, are one body – and every one, members one of another – having gifts differing according to the grace that is given to us. . . .' (Romans 12: 5–6).

References

Agbenyega, J. and Peers, C. (2010) Early childhood inclusion: a silver lining in the dark clouds for African immigrant children?, *International Journal of Whole Schooling*, 6(2): 46–58.

Alaimo, K. and Klug, B. (eds) (2002) *Children as Equals: Exploring the Rights of the Child.* Lanham, MD: Rowman & Littlefield.

Beresford, J. (2003) *Creating the Conditions to Involve Pupils In Their Learning.* London: Falmer.

Boyle, C., Topping, K. J. and Jindal-Snape, D. (2012a) Teachers' attitudes towards inclusion in high schools. Paper submitted for publication.

Boyle, C., Topping, K., Jindal-Snape, D. and Norwich, B. (2012b) The importance of peer-support for teaching staff when including children with special educational needs, *School Psychology International*, 32(3): 167–84. DOI: 10.1177/0143034311415783.

Brendtro, L. K., Brokenleg, M. and Van Bockern, S. (1990) The circle of courage, in *Reclaiming Youth At Risk: Our Hope for the Future.* Bloomington, IN: National Educational Service.

Catlett, S. M. and Osher, T. W. (1994) What is inclusion, anyway? An analysis of organizational position statements. Eric Document Reproduction Service No. ED369234.

Clough, P. and Corbett, J. (2000) *Theories of Inclusive Education.* London: Chapman.

Cole, T. (2004) Policies for positive behaviour management, in K. J. Topping and S. Maloney (eds) *Inclusive Education.* London and New York: Routledge Falmer.

Croll, P. (2002) Social deprivation, school-level achievement and special educational needs, *Educational Research*, 44: 43–53.

Croll, P. and Moses, D. (2003) Special educational needs across two decades: survey evidence from English primary schools, *British Educational Research Journal*, 29(5): 731–47.

Crowther, D., Dyson, A. and Millward, A. (1998) *Costs and Outcomes for Pupils with Moderate Learning Difficulties in Special and Mainstream Schools* (Research Report RR89). London: Department for Education and Employment.

Daniels, H. (2010) The mutual shaping of human action and institutional settings: a study of the transformation of children's services and professional work, *British Journal of Sociology of Education*, 31(4): 377–93.

Dyson, A. and Millward, A. (2000) *Schools and Special Needs: Issues of Innovation and Inclusion.* London: Chapman.

Dyson, A. and Todd, L. (2010) Dealing with complexity: theory of change evaluation and the full service extended schools initiative, *International Journal of Research and Method in Education*, 33(2): 119–34.

Farrell, P. and Ainscow, M. (2002) Making special education inclusive: mapping the issues, in P. Farrell and M. Ainscow (eds) *Making Special Education Inclusive.* London: Fulton.

Gold, K. (2003) Give us inclusion. . . but not yet, *Times Educational Supplement*, May 23: 19.

Gray, C. (2009) A qualitatively different experience: mainstreaming pupils with a visual impairment in Northern Ireland, *European Journal of Special Needs Education*, 24(2): 169–82.

Guarino, C. M., Buddin, R., Pham, C. and Cho, M. (2010) Demographic factors associated with the early identification of children with special needs, *Topics in Early Childhood Special Education*, 30(3): 162–75.

Hastings, R. P. and Oakford, S. (2003) Student teachers' attitudes towards the inclusion of children with special needs, *Educational Psychology*, 23(1): 87–94.

Madden, N. A. and Slavin, R. E. (1983) Mainstreaming students with mild handicaps: academic and social outcomes, *Review of Educational Research*, 52(4): 519–69.

Manset, G. and Semmel, M. I. (1997) Are inclusive programs for students with mild disabilities effective?, *Journal of Special Education*, 31(2): 155–80.

Mittler, P. (2000) *Working Towards Inclusive Education: Social Contexts*. London: Fulton.

Nind, M., Sheehy, K., Simmons, K. and Rix, J. (eds) (2003) *Inclusive Education: Diverse Perspectives*. London: Fulton.

Norwich, B. (2000) Inclusion in education: from concepts, values and critique to practice, in H. Daniels (ed.) *Special Education Reformed: Beyond Rhetoric?* London: Falmer.

Norwich, B. (2003) *LEA Inclusion Trends in England 1997–2001*. Bristol: Centre for Studies in Inclusive Education.

Peetsma, T., Vergeer, M., Roeleveld, J. and Karsten, S. (2001) Inclusion in education: comparing pupils' development in special and regular education, *Educational Review*, 53(2): 125–35.

Salend, S. J. and Garrick Duhaney, L. M. (1999) The impact of inclusion on students with or without disabilities and their educators, *Remedial and Special Education*, 20(2): 114–26.

Scruggs, T. E. and Mastropieri, M. A. (1996) Teacher perceptions of mainstreaming/inclusion, 1958–1995. A research synthesis, *Exceptional Children*, 63: 59–74.

Shucksmith, M. (2000) *Exclusive Countryside? Social Inclusion and Regeneration in Rural Britain*. York: Joseph Rowntree Trust.

Sindelar, P. T., Shearer, D. K., Yendol-Hoppey, D. and Liebert, T. W. (2006) The sustainability of inclusive school reform, *Exceptional Children*, 72(3): 317–26.

Staub, D. and Peck, C. A. (1994) What are the outcomes for non-disabled students?, *Educational Leadership*, 52(4): 36–40.

Thomas, G., Walker, D. and Webb, J. (1998) *The Making of the Inclusive School*. London: Routledge.

Thomas, G., Walker, D. and Webb, J. (2004) Inclusive education: the ideals and the practice, in K. J. Topping and S. Maloney (eds) *Inclusive Education*. London and New York: Routledge Falmer.

Van der Veen, I., Smeets, E. and Derriks, M. (2010) Children with special educational needs in the Netherlands: number, characteristics and school career, *Educational Research*, 52(1): 15–43.

Wang, M. C., Haertel, G. D. and Walberg, H. J. (1993) Toward a knowledge base for school learning, *Review of Educational Research*, 63(3): 249–94.

Westwood, P. (2004) Adapting curriculum and instruction, in K. J. Topping and S. Maloney (eds) *Inclusive Education*. London and New York: Routledge Falmer.

2

KIM MICHAUD AND THOMAS E. SCRUGGS

Inclusion in the United States: theory and practice

In the United States at the present time, few if any question the essential right of individuals with disabilities to a free, appropriate public education. However, the optimal place for this education has been the subject of some debate. Zigmond and Kloo (2011) made a clear distinction between the definitions and corresponding purposes of *general* versus *special education*. While the term *general education* describes the free, public schooling that is 'mandated for and offered to *all* children' (Zigmond and Kloo 2011: 160), *special education* is specifically tailored for *individual* students, 'who have physical, cognitive, language, learning, sensory and/or emotional abilities/disabilities that deviate from those of the general population and whose abilities/disabilities require special education services...making an appropriate education available...' (Zigmond and Kloo 2011: 160). In the United States, *general* and *special* education programmes took various forms since colonial times, but remained totally separate until the end of the twentieth century. Until that time, students with physical or cognitive disabilities were legally excluded from public *general education* classes (Mastropieri and Scruggs 2010a).

History

General education

Public *general education* began in the United States long before it actually became a sovereign nation. In 1642, the Massachusetts General Court required heads of households to provide occupational training, and further to ensure that children could read to appreciate and understand the laws of the state (Urban and Wagoner 2008). Shortly after America gained her sovereignty, *general education*, public or private, state mandated or not, was conducted in one-room schoolhouses in order to produce a 'body of moral, loyal and productive citizens' (Urban and Wagoner 2008: 8). By the 1830s, under the leadership of Horace Mann and in response to the Industrial Revolution, *general education* underwent another reform. Schooling became conducted in large buildings, classes were segregated according to age, it was paid for by the state, mandated, and its primary function was to help children learn how to lead moral lives and develop into trained, qualified workers.

The 1960s and the years that followed brought yet more changes, including limits on racial segregation, educational rights for individuals with disabilities, restrictions on prayer in public schools and, more recently, relatively less emphasis on vocational education in favour of college preparation (Gerber 2011). In response to concerns about failing schools, laws such as 'No Child Left Behind' were enacted to promote higher achievement. These policies have not only affected general education, but special education as well, for it is within this time period that special and general education intersected officially and legally (Urban and Wagoner 2008; Gerber 2011).

Special education

As was stated previously, *special* education paralleled but did not intersect *general* education until recently. From colonial times until the early nineteenth century no education was provided for those with disabilities, for they either resided in poor-houses or charitable centres, or remained at home with no education (Kirk and Gallagher 1979; Zigmond and Kloo 2011). Education was irregularly provided during the nineteenth century for individuals with visual or hearing impairments, mild to severe retardation, and severe emotional disabilities in residential programmes such as the Perkins School for the Blind in Boston (Osgood 2008). When *general* education became mandatory at the state level, individuals with disabilities were sent to the general education classrooms, since it was mandated, although when they caused what was considered an 'undue burden' upon the teachers they were either expelled or excluded in separate classrooms (Zigmond and Kloo 2011). By the 1950s, students with disabilities could receive education through services or programmes which we now define as the *continuum of services*: consultant assistance, separate classes, specialized day schools, residential and hospital programmes were available to educate those with a variety of disabilities. However, at this juncture, public schools were not yet required to provide education for all students, including those with disabilities (Gerber 2011). For example, as late as 1973 in the state of Virginia, schools were allowed to exclude children thought to be physically or mentally incapable from school tasks (Code of Virginia 1973).

This all changed with the passage of Section 504 of the Rehabilitation Act of 1973, a federal 'civil rights law that prevents discrimination against individuals with disabilities by any institution that receives federal funds and provides for a free, appropriate public education (FAPE)' (Mastropieri and Scruggs 2010a: 11). It applies to all students with disabilities, guarantees against discrimination, and focuses on accessibility and equivalence (Zigmond and Kloo 2011). Two years later, in 1975, the first special education law was passed. Public law 94–142 (1975), later called the Individuals with Disabilities Education Act (IDEA), was enacted to ensure that states, in return for federal funds, would provide all students with disabilities a free and appropriate education in the least restrictive environment (LRE). What is fundamental about this law is that it promised *unequal* education opportunities for students with disabilities, not just *equal* access to education (Zigmond and Kloo 2011).

There are several important provisions that are central to this federal legislation. In order to ensure that all students with disabilities, regardless of severity, can receive a free and appropriate public education, an Individual Education Plan

(IEP) must be written. This is a written agreement between the school and the parents detailing the unique curricula that will be provided to that individual student so that he/she can access an appropriate education. When the IEP is written, it must delineate the goals of instruction(s), what individual(s) will provide the various instructions, the setting(s) of those instructions, and the means of assessing goal attainment. An important provision must be taken into consideration when determining how these services are to be delivered to the student, for 'critical to IDEA legislation is the concept of *least restrictive environment* . . . students with disabilities must be educated in the setting least removed from the general education classroom' (Mastropieri and Scruggs 2010a: 7). It is required that each school district provides a continuum of alternative placements (IDEA Regulations, 34 C.F.R. 300.551; see also Rozalski *et al.* 2011). However, since the placement in the general education classroom is seen as a presumptive right, reasons for alternative placements must be clearly documented (Yell 1995).

No Child Left Behind (NCLB)

The No Child Left Behind Act (2001) was the latest reauthorization of the Elementary and Secondary Education Act of 1965 (ESEA). Its underlying focus, therefore, was to ensure that all students, in particular those low-achieving students in high-poverty schools, be challenged to reach proficiency in language, arts and maths by 2014 (Education Trust 2004; Forte 2010; Schraw 2010). This federal mandate is to be worked out individually by the states by requiring them to implement a system of standards, assessments and accountability. States are also required to put aside a portion of their federal Title I funds (funds received to provide quality education to low-income children) to provide additional assistance to schools showing difficulty in meeting their progressively increasing standards (Education Trust 2004). These funds are to be used for expenditures such as transporting students to a better performing school, supplying technical assistance, implementing different curricula, hiring a private management contractor, or converting to a charter school (Council for Exceptional Children 2002; Education Trust 2004).

Each year a school must determine if it is meeting the achievement goals that its state had set.

> If the school as a whole and each individual group *within* the school has met or exceeded the statewide goal in math and language arts, 95 per cent of all students and groups of students have taken the test, and the school has met the statewide goal for the additional academic indicator, then the school has met AYP.
>
> (Education Trust 2004: 3)

If a school does not reach the Adequate Yearly Progress (AYP) in the same subject for two consecutive years, then parents, teachers and outside experts must work together to develop a two-year plan for improvement. Subsequent years of lack of adequate student progress leads to using state funds for additional tutoring, restructuring, transportation to other schools, or alternative governance. Conversely, if a school is shown to make AYP two years in a row, it is no longer seen to be in need of improvement (Education Trust 2004).

Students with disabilities who can access grade-level standards with accommodations participate in the state assessment with the accommodations that are indicated in their IEPs. For students whose IEP team determines that it is not appropriate to participate in the state assessment they are given alternative assessments. State districts can provide up to 1 per cent of all students with alternative assessments, a cap which was put in place to eliminate systems that had had inappropriate lowered expectations for students with disabilities. A district or even a state can apply for a waiver of this cap if it is determined that more than 1 per cent of its students are severely cognitively disabled. Because there are schools who serve this particular population, the 1 per cent cap does not apply at the school level (Education Trust 2004).

It is certainly desirable that all students be educated so that they can achieve levels of proficiency; however, it has been argued that NCLB does not fully take into consideration the individualization necessary to provide education to students with disabilities (Crockett 2002). NCLB state guidelines base the goals and their assessments upon what is deemed proficient only for the non-disabled population. Although this is certainly suitable for some, it does not take into consideration the full range of disabilities. In fact, there is a resultant increased practical and philosophical tension that exists in the United States school system which continues to erode the evidence-based unique individualization that special education could provide to the full range of disabled students (Zigmond *et al.* 2009), regardless of setting.

It is for this reason that the Council of Administrators of Special Education (2007) included recommendations to Congress which would incorporate the individual protections of IDEA into NCLB by having IEP teams individualize both assessments and goals that are personally appropriate for each student with a disability. Likewise, the recommendations for inclusion of functional life skill assessment and recognition of high school diplomas earned in more than four years are important special education leadership policy adjustments (Zigmond *et al.* 2009).

The history of education in the United States has demonstrated a continuing development toward greater equity and inclusivity. Presently, debate focuses upon not whether all students with disabilities are entitled to a free and appropriate education, but rather what settings best meet these entitlements. These perspectives are now described.

Full educational inclusion as a basic civil right

Shortly after the implementation of PL 94–142 (IDEA), and in the spirit of least restrictive environment, special education underwent incremental changes toward greater inclusion of students with disabilities in the general education class, from special class and special school, to resource room with 'mainstreaming', toward advocacy for full inclusion in general education class activities for students with mild disabilities (Will 1986) and severe disabilities (Taylor 2004; see also Fuchs and Fuchs 1994; Kavale 2002). By the 1990s, arguments for 'full inclusion' of all students with disabilities entirely in the general education classroom were commonly heard (Stainback and Stainback 1990; Lipsky and Gartner 1996; Taylor 2004).

Advocates for full inclusion have argued that a full-time general education placement is a basic civil right for all students, including those with disabilities (Lipsky and Gartner 1996); conversely, removal to special classes or resource rooms is viewed as a form of segregation similar to racial segregation (Wang and Walberg 1994). These advocates refer to the Supreme Court verdict on *Brown v Board of Education* (1954) regarding 'separate but equal' schools, and subsequent civil rights legislation as support for their position. In further support, it is observed that many minority students are overrepresented in special class placement (Gartner and Lipsky 1989). It is argued, then, that inclusion is to be viewed as an inherent right not to be denied, rather than a privilege to be earned (Sapon-Shevin 2007).

It has been further argued that full inclusion reduces stigma, where students are no longer required to leave the general education classroom for special services (Kliewer and Biklen 1996); that full inclusion is more efficient, by preventing fragmenting of the school day, lost time in multiple transitions, and lack of generalization from special class learning (Raynes *et al.* 1991); and that full inclusion promotes equality:

> The most important reason to include all students in the mainstream is that it is the fair, ethical, and equitable thing to do … It is discriminatory that some students, such as those 'labeled' disabled, must earn the right to be in the regular education mainstream or have to wait for educational researchers to prove that they can profit from the mainstream, while other students are allowed unrestricted access simply because they have no label.
>
> (Stainback and Stainback 1990: 6–7)

Taylor (2004) listed a number of objections to the widely accepted concept of least restrictive environment (LRE). For example, that it legitimizes restrictive environments, therefore rendering them inevitable for many students. It also confuses intensity of services with segregation, assuming different settings are necessary for different services. LRE infringes on the rights of individuals, by assuming some degree of restriction is necessary, and looking to 'professionals' to make this determination. Further, LRE equates development and change with moving through various educational environments, rather than altering the environment to accommodate student development (see also Heward 2009 for a discussion). In sum, many full inclusion advocates, while appreciating the principle of IDEA legislation, find little to admire in any separate placement for instructional purposes, and prefer to see all students in their regularly assigned, general education classroom (Gartner and Lipsky 1989).

These arguments generally have taken a moral or rational perspective, and indeed some characterize empirical evidence as unnecessary (e.g. Stainback and Stainback 1990). However, empirical evidence, when examined, reveals mixed outcomes for fully inclusive education. While some research has indicated superior outcomes for students with disabilities in fully inclusive classrooms, others have found results favouring the use of special resource classes as a supplement to general education

(Carlberg and Kavale 1980; Epps and Tindal 1988; Manset and Semmel 1997; Salend and Duhaney 1999; see McLeskey and Waldron 2011 for a discussion). It seems likely that it is the unevenness of instruction within different settings that produces these mixed results. Several of these researchers (e.g. Epps and Tindal 1988; McLeskey and Waldron 2011) have concluded that it is the quality of instruction that leads to higher achievement in any setting, and that many important instructional variables can be implemented in most settings.

Individualized education delivered through the continuum of services: what really is 'inclusive'?

Many advocates of special services, however, think differently about the real meaning of inclusion. Speaking with reference to the continuum of services, Kauffman and Hallahan (1995: 172) argued:

> Exceptional children by definition require extraordinary education – that which is different from the standard education that serves most students well . . . Failure to create and maintain explicit structures accommodating exceptional individuals inevitably results in the neglect of those for whom the core services are inadequate.

Proponents of the LRE model argue that many services, specialized equipment or resources and specialized curricula are not available in general education classrooms, and general education teachers have not yet been uniquely trained to apply the pedagogical skills and strategies required by exceptional students (Kauffman and Hung 2009; McLeskey and Waldron 2011; Zigmond and Kloo 2011).

McLeskey and Waldron (2011) reviewed the characteristics of high-quality instruction of both reading and maths for elementary school-aged students with learning disabilities (LD). Their table, which delineates the components of this high-quality instruction, indicates that this instruction should be, 'intensive, explicit, should be delivered to small groups, and should be closely monitored' (McLeskey and Waldron 2011: 50). Such specialized instruction has been shown to result in the ability of a substantial percentage of this population of students to catch up with their peers (McLeskey and Waldron 2011). Unfortunately, a number of research investigations indicate this type of instruction is not consistently being delivered by general education teachers (Zigmond and Baker 1995; McLeskey and Waldron 2002), nor by general education or special education co-teachers in general education classrooms (Weiss and Brigham 2000; Murawski and Swanson 2001; Scruggs et al. 2007). In addition, some research has suggested that even special educators in resource rooms were found to be unable to provide the instruction that they had specialized in because they were overwhelmed with large class sizes of heterogeneous students from across several grade levels (Moody et al. 2000).

Similar to students with LD, students with an intellectual disability (ID) typically require direct, systematic instruction in maths, reading and daily living skills which often can be effectively delivered by special educators trained to use interventions for supporting cognitive deficits (Kauffman and Hung 2009; see also Scruggs and

Michaud 2009). Kauffman and Hung, therefore, also recommended that the continuum of services must be available for students with intellectual disabilities.

> Special education for children with intellectual disabilities should occur in the general education classroom whenever possible, but the first concern of special education should be improving children's learning, not the place or with whom they learn.
>
> (Kauffman and Hung 2009: 455)

As was stated at the beginning of this chapter, education for blind and deaf students began in the early nineteenth century in residential institutions. It was within these residences that the special instructional tools and strategies were perfected that these students needed to overcome their physical limitations in order to receive an education which would allow them to reach their potential and live full lives. Speaking about educating blind students, Bina (1995) indicated that 'without [the] solid foundation like Braille and mobility skills, positive integration into schools now or later in life becomes extremely difficult' (Bina 1995: 272). Similarly, deaf students who do not grow up learning American Sign Language taught by parents who are also deaf, and who are mainstreamed into general education classrooms with only the aid of an interpreter, may not only struggle academically but also may face a diminished ability to communicate with others (Lane 1995).

LRE advocates have argued that the continuum of services can provide the individualized, *special* instruction that students with disabilities need academically, socially and practically in order to maximize their unique potential. They have also maintained that it is the civil right of students with disabilities to receive an appropriately different education when needed (e.g. Kauffman 2011).

It must be emphasized, however, that the debate today focuses no longer on whether students with disabilities should be allowed access to the general education classroom, but rather whether 100 per cent inclusion in all cases is always in the child's best interests. Such arguments focus rather on the degree to which students with disabilities can best benefit from different settings. In fact, the great majority of students with disabilities in the United States today receive most of their education in general education classrooms (Mastropieri and Scruggs 2010a).

Another potential concern with continuum of services arguments is that they may lead to assumptions about the appropriateness of general education classes that may be overly pessimistic. For example, the second author once observed in an elementary grade classroom that was undertaking the study of 'small things' with microscopes. The well-meaning teachers suggested that a totally blind girl included in the class be excused from this unit. The girl's parents correctly insisted the girl be included in the unit, the consequence of which was a greater understanding on the part of teachers and students of the most important objectives of the unit, and the best ways of meeting them for all students (Mastropieri and Scruggs 2010b). In another example, Mastropieri *et al.* (1998) worked in a 'hands-on' inclusive science classroom that included students with learning disabilities, intellectual disabilities, emotional and physical disabilities, all working collaboratively on science activities in co-operative groups. Students in this class greatly outperformed students in non-inclusive classes studying the same content from textbooks. Further, students with 'disabilities' scored at the class average on end-of-unit tests, and far ahead of the students in the non-inclusive, textbook-based classrooms. Such results (see also, for example, Mastropieri *et al.* 2006; McDuffie *et al.* 2009, Marshak *et al.* 2011) reveal that students with disabilities often outperform expectations when placed in appropriately structured inclusive classes, with supports such as adapted materials, special learning strategies, peer mediation, and effective co-teaching.

Conclusion

The history of the United States reveals a clear trend toward more inclusive schooling environments for all students that continues to the present day. Today in the United States, nearly half of all students with disabilities receive instruction in the general education classroom at least 80 per cent of the school day, and over three quarters receive instruction in the general education classroom at least 40 per cent of the school day (US Department of Education 2007). Further, ideas of the complex nature of the concept of inclusion, although not entirely resolved, have been considerably refined over the years. Full inclusion advocates, while not entirely successful in eliminating separate special services, have nevertheless greatly influenced the movement of students with disabilities into general education settings. Advocates for the continuum of services also have provided arguments favouring their position; in both cases, rhetoric has frequently replaced empirical evidence, which to date is equivocal. The observed variability of findings from empirical research results suggests schools and researchers should continue to pursue the means by which the best education for all can be achieved in the general education classroom. In the future, it is hoped that optimal instructional techniques for students with various disabilities will continue to be explored, as well as the optimal means for delivering this instruction in the least restrictive environment.

References

Bina, M. (1995) Mainstreaming, schools for the blind, and full inclusion: what shall the future of education for blind children be? in J. Kauffman and D. Hallahan (eds) *The Illusion of Full Inclusion: A Comprehensive Critique of a Current Special Education Bandwagon*. Austin, TX: PRO-ED.

Brown v Board of Education, 347 U.S. 483 (1954).

Carlberg, C. and Kavale, K. (1980) The efficacy of special versus regular class placement for exceptional children: a meta-analysis, *Journal of Special Education*, 14(3): 295–305.

Code of Virginia (1973) Section 22.275.3.

Council of Administrators of Special Education (2007) *Recommendations to Congress for the Improvement of the No Child Left Behind Act (NCLB)*. Available at: http://casecec.org/archives/position.asp [Accessed 2 April 2012].

Council for Exceptional Children (2002) No Child Left Behind has major implications for special education, *CEC Today*, 9(4): 4.

Crockett, J.B. (2002) Special education's role in preparing responsive leaders for inclusive schools, *Remedial and Special Education*, 23(3): 157–68.

Education Trust (2004) *The ABCS of 'AYP': Raising Achievement for All Students*. Available at: http://www.edtrust.org/sites/edtrust.org/files/publications/files/ABCAYP.PDF [Accessed 17 March 2012].

Epps, S. and Tindal, G. (1988) The effectiveness of differential programming in serving students with mild handicaps: placement options and instructional programming, in M.C. Wang, M.C. Reynolds and H.J. Walberg (eds) *Handbook of Special Education: Research and Practice. Volume I*. New York: Pergamon Press.

Forte, E. (2010) Examining the assumptions underlying the NCLB federal accountability policy on school improvement, *Educational Psychologist*, 45(2): 76–88.

Fuchs, D. and Fuchs, L.S. (1994) Inclusive schools movement and the radicalization of special education reform, *Exceptional Children*, 60(4): 294–309.

Gartner, A. and Lipsky, D. (1989) *The Yoke of Special Education: How to Break It*. ERIC Document Reproduction Service No. ED307792. Buffalo, NY: National Center on Education and the Economy.

Gerber, M.M. (2011) A history of special education, in J. Kauffman and D. Hallahan (eds) *Handbook of Special Education*. New York: Routledge.

Heward, W.L. (2009) *Exceptional Children: An Introduction to Special Education*, 9th edn. Columbus, OH: Merrill.

Individuals with Disabilities Education Act of 1990 Regulations, 34 C.F.R. 300.551.

Kauffman, J.M. (2011) *Toward a Science of Education*. Port Tobacco, MD: Full Court Press.

Kauffman, J.M. and Hallahan, D.P. (1995) Toward a comprehensive delivery system for special education, in J. Kauffman and D. Hallahan (eds) *The Illusion of Full Inclusion: A Comprehensive Critique of a Current Special Education Bandwagon*. Austin, TX: PRO-ED.

Kauffman, J.M. and Hung, L. (2009) Special education for intellectual disability: current trends and perspectives, *Current Opinion in Psychiatry*, 22(5): 452–6.

Kavale, K. (2002) Mainstreaming to full-inclusion: from orthogenesis to pathogenesis of an idea, *International Journal of Disability, Development and Education*, 49(2): 201–14.

Kelley, W. (2003) *Common Sense: A New Conversation for Public Education*. Stanford, CA: Creative Commons. http://www.commonsenseforpubliceducation.org/common-sense-book.pdf [Accessed 5 July 2011].

Kirk, S. and Gallagher, J. (1979) *Educating Exceptional Children*, 3rd edn. Boston, MA: Houghton Mifflin.

Kliewer, C. and Biklen, D. (1996) Labeling: who wants to be called retarded?, in W. Stainback and S. Stainback (eds) *Controversial Issues Confronting Special Education: Divergent Perspectives*, 2nd edn. Boston, MA: Allyn & Bacon.

Lane, H. (1995) The education of deaf children: drowning in the mainstream and the side-stream, in J. Kauffman and D. Hallahan (eds) *The Illusion of Full Inclusion: A Comprehensive Critique of a Current Special Education Bandwagon*. Austin, TX: PRO-ED.

Lipsky, D.K. and Gartner, A. (1996) Inclusion, school restructuring, and the remaking of American society, *Harvard Educational Review*, 66(4): 762–97.

McDuffie, K.A., Mastropieri, M.A. and Scruggs, T.E. (2009) Differential effects of co-teaching and peer-mediated instruction: results for content learning and student–teacher interactions, *Exceptional Children*, 75(4): 493–510.

McLeskey, J. and Waldron, N. (2002) Inclusion and school change: teacher perceptions of curricular and instructional adaptations, *Teacher Education and Special Education*, 25(1): 41–54.

McLeskey, J. and Waldron, N.L. (2011) Educational programs for elementary students with learning disabilities: can they be both effective and inclusive?, *Learning Disabilities Practice*, 26(1): 48–57.

Manset, G. and Semmel, M.I. (1997) Are inclusive programs for students with mild disabilities effective? A comparative review of model programs, *Journal of Special Education*, 31(2): 155–80.

Marshak, L., Mastropieri, M.A. and Scruggs, T.E. (2011) Curriculum enhancements for inclusive secondary social studies classes, *Exceptionality*, 19(1): 61–74.

Mastropieri, M.A. and Scruggs, T.E. (2010a) *The Inclusive Classroom: Strategies for Effective Differentiated Instruction*, 4th edn. Upper Saddle River, NJ: Pearson Education.

Mastropieri, M.A. and Scruggs, T.E. (2010b) The study of human exceptionality: how it informs our knowledge of learning and cognition, in T.E. Scruggs and M.A. Mastropieri (eds) *Literacy and Learning: Advances in Learning and Behavioral Disabilities* (Vol. 23). Bingley: Emerald.

Mastropieri, M.A., Scruggs, T.E., Mantzicopoulos, P.Y., Sturgeon, A., Goodwin, L. and Chung, S. (1998) 'A place where living things affect and depend on each other': qualitative and quantitative outcomes associated with inclusive science teaching, *Science Education*, 82(2): 163–79.

Mastropieri, M.A., Scruggs, T.E., Norland, J., Berkeley, S., McDuffie, K., Tornquist, E.H. *et al.* (2006) Differentiated curriculum enhancement in inclusive middle school science: effects on classroom and high-stakes tests, *Journal of Special Education*, 40(3): 130–7.

Mastropieri, M.A., Scruggs, T.E. and Mills, S. (2011) Special education teacher preparation, in J. Kaufmann and D. Hallahan (eds) *Handbook of Special Education*. New York: Routledge.

Moody, S., Vaughn, S., Hughes, M. and Fischer, M. (2000) Reading instruction in the resource room: set up for failure, *Exceptional Children*, 66(3): 305–16.

Murawski, W. and Swanson, L. (2001) A meta-analysis of co-teaching research: where are the data?, *Remedial and Special Education*, 22(5): 258–67.

O'Connor, R. and Sanchez, V. (2011) Responsiveness to intervention models for reducing reading difficulties and identifying learning disability, in J. Kaufmann and D. Hallahan (eds) *Handbook of Special Education*. New York: Routledge.

Osgood, R.L. (2008) *The History of Special Education: A Struggle for Equality in American Public Schools*. Greenwich, CT: Greenwood.

Raynes, M., Snell, M. and Sailor, W. (1991) A fresh look at categorical programs for children with special needs, *Phi Delta Kappan*, 73(4): 326–31.

Rozalski, M., Miller, J. and Stewart, A. (2011) Least restrictive environment, in J. Kauffman and D. Hallahan (eds) *Handbook of Special Education*. New York: Routledge.

Salend, S. and Duhaney, L. (1999) The impact of inclusion on students with and without disabilities and their educators, *Remedial and Special Education*, 20(2): 114–26.

Sapon-Shevin, M. (2007) *Widening the Circle: The Power of Inclusive Classrooms*. Boston, MA: Beacon Press.

Schraw, G. (2010) No school left behind, *Educational Psychologist*, 45(2): 71–5.

Scruggs, T., Mastropieri, M. and McDuffie, K. (2007) Co-teaching in inclusive classrooms: a metasynthesis of qualitative research, *Exceptional Children*, 73(4): 392–417.

Scruggs, T.E. and Michaud, K. (2009) The 'surplus effect' in developmental disabilities: a function of setting or training (or both)?, *Life Span and Disability*, 12(2): 141–9.

Stainback, W. and Stainback, S. (1990) Inclusive schooling, in W. Stainback and S. Stainback (eds) *Support Networks for Inclusive Schooling: Independent Integrated Education*. Baltimore, MD: Brooks.

Taylor, S.J. (2004) Caught in the continuum: a critical analysis of the principle of least restrictive environment, *Journal of the Association of Persons with Severe Handicaps*, 29(4): 218–30.

Urban, W.J. and Wagoner, E.L. (2008) *American Education: A History*, 4th edn. New York: Routledge.

US Department of Education (2007) *Twenty-seventh Annual Report to Congress on the Implementation of Individuals with Disabilities Act.* Washington, DC: Author.

Vellutino, F., Scanlon, D., Small, S. and Fanuele, D. (2006) Response to intervention as a vehicle for distinguishing between children with and without reading disabilities, *Journal of Learning Disabilities*, 39(2): 157–69.

Volonino, V. and Zigmond, N. (2007) Promoting research-based practices through inclusion?, *Theory into Practice*, 46(4): 291–300.

Wang, B. and Walberg, H. (1994) Four fallacies of segregationism, *Exceptional Children*, 55(2): 128–37.

Weiss, M.P. and Brigham, E.J. (2000) Co-teaching and the model of shared responsibility: what does the research support?, in T.E Scruggs and M.A. Mastropieri (eds) *Advances in Learning and Behavioral Disabilities* (Vol. 14). Oxford: Elsevier.

Will, M. (1986) Educating children with learning problems: a shared responsibility, *Exceptional Children*, 52(5): 411–15.

Yell, M.L. (1995) Least restrictive environment, inclusion, and students with disabilities: analysis and commentary, *Journal of Special Education*, 28(4): 389–404.

Zigmond, N. and Baker, J. (1995) Concluding comments: current and future practices in inclusive schooling, *Journal of Special Education*, 29(2): 245–50.

Zigmond, N.P. and Kloo, A. (2011) General and special education are (and should be) different, in J. Kauffman and D. Hallahan (eds) *Handbook of Special Education*. New York: Routledge.

Zigmond, N., Kloo, A. and Volonino, V. (2009) What, where, and how? Special education in the climate of full inclusion, *Exceptionality*, 17(4): 189–204.

3

FRASER LAUCHLAN AND ROBERTA FADDA
The 'Italian model' of full inclusion: origins and current directions

Introduction

Italy has an established history of inclusion and it has long been considered one of the leading nations with respect to including children with disabilities in mainstream schools (Daniels and Hogg 1991). Italy's model of inclusion has in the past been described as 'truly revolutionary' (Vitello 1991: 220), and educators in other countries have often looked to Italy to determine whether the full inclusion model works in practice (Begeny and Martens 2007). Italy is unique in that it has introduced several layers of legislation to support the inclusion of all 'disabled' children, stretching back over 40 years.

In the 1960s and 1970s, there was firm opposition from the Italian Communist Party against the segregation of children with disabilities, and also from a spontaneous and growing movement of teachers and parents of students with special needs. The social and cultural pressure from this movement eventually led to legislation, introduced in 1971 (National Law 118). This gave all disabled children (except for those affected by extremely severe physical and/or mental disabilities) the right not only to an education, but also to attend regular mainstream schools and to be included in regular classrooms. As one might imagine, at first there were many difficulties in the implementation of this colossal change in education policy (such disabled children did not attend mainstream schools up to this point) (Cecchini and McCleary 1985). Indeed, the period from 1971 to 1977 (i.e. before more specific legislation was introduced on how inclusion should be implemented) was known as the time of 'integrazione selvaggia' (wild integration) (Vitello 1994: 62), in which the policy of full inclusion rarely resulted in children being included appropriately in all school activities. It was widely acknowledged that more specific guidelines, as well as more concrete financial and structural supports, were required (Zelioli 1987).

In 1977, further legislation (National Law 517) was introduced to outline further the rights of 'disabled' children[1] to be included in ordinary schools, and no exceptions were made with regard to the severity of the child's disability. In addition, specific measures were established to ensure that their inclusion was given the best possible chance to work. These measures were as follows:

1   No more than two 'disabled' children could be placed into one regular class.

2   Classes with 'disabled' children could not exceed 20 pupils including the two 'disabled' children.

3   Support teachers (i.e. special needs teachers who have received additional training to that usually required to become a regular teacher) would be allocated to each school to support the inclusion of 'disabled' children. The recommended allocation of support was one support teacher for each group of four 'disabled' children.

4   All extracurricular activities must include all children.

5   Diagnosis and therapeutic services should be provided to children with 'disabilities' and their families by the local health agency.

In 1982, legislation was introduced that extended the model of full inclusion to pre-school and secondary school settings. By this time, special education teachers had become an integral part of the teaching staff at the different school levels. In the same year, special exam arrangements were introduced: students with special needs were permitted to use special communication strategies and flexible timing during the final evaluation in secondary school, and all architectonic barriers (i.e. relating to the architectural structure of schools) were removed. In 1992, further legislation (Italian Law 104) ensured that there was a consistent and comprehensive framework of assistance, which had the specific intention of promoting social inclusion and rights of 'handicapped persons'. For the first time it was guaranteed that all children with special needs would be included at school at every level, throughout their school careers, from day nurseries to university. Moreover, a comprehensive programme of intervention involving the school, the national health system, the families and all the community was defined. The educational programme was meant to be highly individualized, with the possibility of a variety of alternative activities in order not only to meet the special needs of the pupils, but also to fulfil their potential and foster their natural aptitudes. This was strengthened by further legislation in 1997 (Italian Law 59) and again in 2006 (Italian Law Nota 6258/A4), which established that schools should be completely autonomous in creating their own individual programmes for special needs children, based on their strengths and areas of need. The local health authorities, upon request of the parents, must produce an accurate evaluation not only of the difficulties of the pupil in different fields but also of his or her potentialities. On the basis of this evaluation, an Individualized Educational Programme (Piano Educativo Individualizzato – PEI) is developed jointly by the teachers, the parents and the clinicians of the local health services. This plan includes a detailed description of the interventions to be implemented within a given period of time, as well as the procedure of evaluation of the effects of the intervention. The amount of time spent on formulating the PEI can vary depending on the individual case; however, it would not be substantially different from the time spent drawing up similar programmes in other countries, for example, the Individualized Education Plan (IEP) in the UK.

In summary, the Italian model of full inclusion, first introduced in the 1970s, has been systematically implemented during the last 40 years, with the objective of promoting the well-being of 'disabled' children at school and in the community. The school is considered a powerful medium in which to teach disabled children not only academic knowledge but also the adaptive and social abilities which are necessary for full inclusion in society. However, while many admire Italy for taking such a decisive role in managing the inclusion of children with special needs, reservations about the lack of research demonstrating the positive outcomes of full inclusion have been expressed (Donfrancesco 1996; Manetti *et al.* 2001). More specifically, Meazzini (1987) claimed that the legislation introducing full inclusion resulted in the abandonment of academic goals, and instead led to the focus on poorly defined social objectives. We will examine the benefits and the criticisms of the Italian model of inclusion, considering recent studies, mostly published in Italian, that provide current perspectives on the effectiveness of the policy of full inclusion in Italian schools.

Attitudes among teachers, parents and school administrators

It has been widely argued that for full inclusion to be effective there needs to be a positive attitude towards inclusion by teachers, administrators and parents, as well as full investment in necessary adaptations and accommodations (Burstein *et al.* 2004). In Italy, there has been much research reporting the positive attitudes of teachers, parents and educators towards the full inclusion of children with disabilities in mainstream schools.

Reversi *et al.* (2007) surveyed the opinions of 173 primary and secondary school teachers via questionnaire. They were divided into two groups: a group of 85 mainstream teachers and a group of 88 specialist teachers (i.e. teachers that worked in mainstream schools to support the children with disabilities). They found that both groups of teachers demonstrated a positive evaluation of the disabled children regarding whether they had met their teaching and social objectives as set out at the beginning of the school year, and also with regard to whether their cognitive and social skills had been developed. There were no significant differences in the ratings provided by the two groups of teachers.

The children involved in the same study (102 disabled, 102 non-disabled) were asked to complete a questionnaire, which provided an evaluation of their social inclusion and level of loneliness at the schools (the participating children were taken from 36 different schools located in three different regions of Italy). Both disabled and non-disabled children rated themselves as having a low sense of loneliness, indicating that they felt socially included; however, it should be added that the loneliness ratings provided by the disabled children were higher than the non-disabled children. Reversi *et al.* (2007) concluded that their research demonstrated the high quality of inclusion (educationally and socially) experienced by the disabled children involved in the study.

Cornoldi *et al.*'s (1998) research surveyed the attitudes of 523 Italian teachers (91.8 per cent female – it is common in primary schools in Italy for women to be over-represented among staff) towards inclusion. Support for full inclusion among Italian teachers was found to be very strong: over 70 per cent of respondents agreed or strongly agreed with those items surveying their general attitude towards inclusion (e.g. 'I support the concept', 'I am willing to teach students with learning problems' and 'Students with learning problems benefit from inclusion'). However, teachers were less positive about the level of resources that were in place to support full inclusion. Only a small minority (approximately 15 per cent of respondents) agreed or strongly agreed with those items that surveyed their opinion regarding the following resource issues:

1   the availability of training to deal with special needs pupils;

2   the amount of personnel assistance, i.e. the availability of support teachers in the classroom;

3   whether they had enough time to adequately teach special needs pupils, and attend to their individual needs; and

4   whether they had suitably adapted resources and materials.

It was this last issue (the adequacy of classroom materials) that received the lowest level of agreement in the whole survey: only 8.1 per cent of Italian staff agreed that they had suitable materials, clearly indicating a concern about this aspect of classroom practice in supporting children with special needs.

Mega *et al.* (1998), in another survey of Italian teachers' attitudes towards inclusion, found that a majority had a positive attitude, and the respondents generally agreed that full inclusion promotes the development of social skills, learning skills and the tolerance and understanding of children with disabilities, and also helps develop the self-sufficiency of 'disabled' children. It was also found that such positive attitudes were more prevalent in primary school teachers than in teachers in secondary school.

Differences were also found in Cornoldi *et al.*'s research between primary and secondary school teachers' attitudes towards inclusion (i.e. more positive attitudes among primary teachers). Research by Balboni and Pedrabissi (2000) has attempted to provide an explanation for this difference in attitudes. Specifically discussing children with 'mental retardation', they argued that the higher up the school, the more complex inclusion becomes. The gap between special needs children and 'regular' children becomes ever wider in terms of social and cognitive development, which makes whole-class teaching significantly more difficult and complex. However, an interesting aspect to the Cornoldi *et al.* (1998) research was that, despite their differences in attitudes, the primary and secondary teachers did agree on the lack of material resources (i.e. special books, multimedia devices like computers or interactive boards) they received to implement inclusionary practices. Nevertheless, one may legitimately ask the question: when is it ever considered that there are enough resources being invested in inclusion?

Balboni and Pedrabissi (2000) reported on a major survey of the views of 1325 teachers and parents, regarding the specific issue of including children with 'mental retardation' in mainstream classes. Both regular classroom teachers (560) and special needs teachers (118) were included in the sample (678 teachers in total). In addition, 647 parents were involved in the study. The parents were parents of children who did *not* have special needs, divided into those who had experience of their child being in a classroom with a 'disabled' child (260 parents), and those who did not (387 parents). All teachers, when taken as a whole group, were more positive than parents about inclusion; however, among parents, it was those parents whose children had special needs pupils in their child's class who were more favourable about inclusion than those parents whose children did not have special needs children in their class. The success of full inclusion of children with disabilities may depend significantly on the attitudes of parents of those children in the same class who do not have special needs. The authors conclude that it is the experience of seeing their children attend the same class as children with disabilities that improves the attitudes of parents towards inclusion, such that 'parents with experience have acquired more realistic and direct information and thus believe that the inevitable difficulties created by inclusion do not compromise their children's learning, but rather represent an opportunity for humane and cultural growth' (Balboni and Pedrabissi 2000: 153). In a similar study by Vitello (1994), parents of those students with a disability discussed how inclusion helped their children become reliable and responsible, while parents of those without a disability cited the benefits of inclusion as developing their children's capacity to become better listeners and to develop their level of patience. In general, the parents emphasized the need for the enhancement of social skills and relationships of all children and felt that a full inclusion policy could support this for all children in the class.

Benefits and criticisms of Italian inclusion

Arguably the most significant review in English of the literature examining the success, or otherwise, of full inclusion in Italy was carried out by Begeny and Martens (2007). The authors reviewed the relevant literature (studies examining Italian inclusion, using both survey and experimental methods) over a 30-year period that had been published in English language journals. They found that support for the practice was generally mixed: some studies reported findings that demonstrated the benefits of inclusion, a similar number were unsupportive of the practice and slightly more studies reported mixed results. The studies that involved surveys of different stakeholder opinions (e.g. teachers, parents, administrators) generally reported results that were supportive of full inclusion. Instead, the studies that used experimental methods (e.g. examining the effects of inclusion over time on various measures of academic and social performance) reported results that were generally found to be less supportive of inclusion.

A significant finding reported by Begeny and Martens's literature review was that the majority of studies were conducted in primary schools and only four were carried out in middle or secondary school settings. The lack of inclusion research in secondary school settings in Italy has been highlighted elsewhere, and concerns have been noted about the need to improve inclusion practice in these settings, especially with regard to the training of support teachers and the social inclusion of the 'disabled' students (see Vitello 1994; Balboni and Pedrabissi 2000). Indeed, the problems of promoting inclusion in secondary schools are not unique to Italy. In a review of the issues involved in inclusion in secondary schools, Mastropieri and Scruggs (2001: 265) cite problems such as 'academic complexity, pace of instruction, teacher attitudes, and the potential consequences of high-stakes testing'.

In general, Begeny and Martens (2007) reported that survey studies were the most common method of evaluation of Italian inclusion, and very few studies used experimental methodology. Furthermore, as stated above, they found that, while most survey studies generally reported positive attitudes towards inclusion, the few experimental studies conducted questioned whether it is beneficial to have full inclusion. Begeny and Martens (2007: 89) concluded that there was 'relatively little information available regarding strategies and interventions that teachers can use successfully with students with disabilities in the general education classroom'. Moreover, they argued that, despite Italy demonstrating that it is possible to include all children with disabilities in mainstream schools, there was still a dearth of research evidence demonstrating that there are positive outcomes and benefits from such a policy. They highlighted the need for more experimental research outlining the positive outcomes of full inclusion of children with disabilities. The authors acknowledge the weakness of their review in not including all research that has been conducted and published in Italian, and that there is the possibility that there exists published research that provides 'sufficient empirical support' (Begeny and Martens, 2007: 90) for the policy of full inclusion. However, they argue that this research, if it does exist, should be made available to English-speaking and other non-Italian-speaking audiences.

The remaining part of this chapter aims to fill this gap, making available to the English-speaking reader some of the most significant studies on the benefits and criticisms of the Italian model of inclusion. While the first twenty years of inclusion in Italy have been documented mainly by descriptive studies, in which the main focus was to define the pedagogical grounds of full inclusion, from the 1990s until the present day there has been an explosion of empirical studies published in Italian only, which have attempted to evaluate the effects of the distinctive features of the Italian model of inclusion.

The quality of thirty years of the Italian model of full inclusion was evaluated in a recent study by Demo and Zambotti (2009), who surveyed 1844 children, adolescents and adults with special needs (977 males, 867 females) about their experience at school and its effect on their social life. The participants were divided into seven 'cohorts' depending on when they attended school, from the 1970s until 2001. The results of this study showed how the participants from the 1990s and 2000s were more positive about their inclusive experience than those attending in the 1970s and 1980s. These results have been interpreted by Demo and Zambotti (2009) as the effect of the legislation introduced in Italy over the years, alongside the increasing level of satisfaction among students, teachers and parents about how inclusion works in practice. The most impressive result of this study was the beneficial effect of schooling in the social life of the students: they felt that the more they stayed at school the more they were likely to be included into the life of their community. However, some criticisms were highlighted, for example the lack of specific training for teachers in the secondary school and the weak link with possible job opportunities after school.

The most comprehensive reviews of Italian literature on inclusion have been conducted by Ianes (1999) and Ianes and Canevaro (2008), who analysed more than one hundred studies published in Italian journals. According to these reviews, a significant number of studies have investigated the effects of class organization, demonstrating the success of co-operative learning (Comoglio 1998; Chiari 1999), peer tutoring (Ianes 1999), and similar strategies in which prosocial behaviours were enhanced (De Beni 1998; Canevaro 1999). These research studies were particularly effective in demonstrating the benefits gained by the special needs children in terms of the promotion of their learning and social abilities.

Other studies have documented how specific practices can help to promote a successful school day for children with special needs in mainstream classes, like the simplification and adaptation of ordinary textbooks to the individual needs of the pupils (Scataglini and Giustini 1998) and the use of highly personalized software (Celi and Romani 1997; Celi 1999). Moreover, research has found that the Individualized Educational Programme (Piano Educativo Individualizzato – PEI) tends to be more effective if developed in relation to the most important teaching goals of the whole class, even if they are addressed at a lower level of complexity (Ferraboschi and Meini 1995).

A significant number of studies have been published on specialized interventions for specific disabilities. For example, several studies document the positive effects of teaching metacognitive strategies to children with learning difficulties (Cornoldi 1995; Cornoldi et al. 1997). Moreover, the efficacy of personalized and highly structured teaching material has been demonstrated (De Beni and Pazzaglia 1991; Cornoldi et al. 1993).

In the last ten years, a growing interest in the inclusion of students with Pervasive Developmental Disorders led to a considerable number of studies that documented the effectiveness of structured teaching strategies, based on behavioural principles, the use of visual support and an individualized organization of the school environment (for example, desks placed in a circle, learning materials organized in numbered boxes and located in a bookshelf close to the child) in promoting social and academic skills (Micheli 1999; Cottini 2002; Farci 2005). Other studies have been conducted in Italy on samples of children and young people with genetic syndromes, like Down's Syndrome (Moniga et al. 2008), Fragile-X (Vianello and Lanfranchi 2009), Cornelia de Lange (Fiori et al. 2008) and Prader-Willi (Vianello 2008). These studies have documented how individuals with these specific syndromes can perform in academic (especially reading skills) and social domains at a level well above expectations that are made on the basis of intellectual assessment. It was argued that these results were an effect, at least in part, of the children being included in mainstream classes, alongside their peers without disabilities, rather than attending segregated special education classes.

The Italian model of inclusion also seems to promote the well-being of special education teachers. In a recent study, support teachers showed the same level of teaching efficacy as the other 'regular' teachers, indicating the benefits of sharing the responsibility of special education with the other teachers in the school system (Fadda and Lai 2011). These results were not necessarily expected, since special education teachers are known to be particularly at risk of burnout, due to the sometimes overwhelming expectations they experience in trying to make inclusive practice work effectively, including the need for highly specialized teaching methods (Brownell et al. 1997). Still, major criticisms persist in the Italian model of full inclusion, for example the problems that arise when the responsibility of inclusion lies solely with the support teachers of special needs (rather than being shared among all teaching staff), and the need for more teachers that are specialized in working with specific disabilities (Ianes and Canevaro 2008).

In summary, the growing number of empirical studies, mainly published in Italian journals, provide a more comprehensive account of the strengths and limitations of the Italian model of full inclusion than that provided by merely reviewing the literature in English language publications. It seems that the efficacy of intervention is better when it is highly specialized and highly individualized. However, it should be highlighted that the research studies reported above are not guided by formal national programmes, but derived from spontaneous actions, different from school to school, and therefore it is still difficult to draw conclusive results on a national scale. Certainly, more systematic collaboration between schools and universities might help to enhance the process of empirical evaluation of the best practice of inclusion in schools in Italy, at different levels (Mangiaracina and Fadda 2010).

Conclusion

Research has shown that, in Italy, the majority of teachers, parents and administrators hold positive views about the virtues of a full inclusion model of practice. However, it is clear that teachers, in particular, feel that further investment is required in suitable resources and materials to help the successful inclusion of children with a range of learning problems. There are other issues, such as the provision of additional support in the classroom, sufficient training and suitably adapted materials for special needs children, which are also of concern to teachers in Italy. In other words, while the positive attitudes of Italian teachers are encouraging, and should not be dismissed, they should not overshadow the need for true, successful inclusionary programmes that make a positive difference to children with special needs with respect to their social, cognitive and academic progress, as well as their acceptance from their peers (Cornoldi *et al.* 1998).

It has been argued in the past that there has been a lack of research in Italy that provides empirical evidence of, first, the beneficial outcomes of inclusion, both socially and academically, for the 'disabled' as well as the 'non-disabled' children and secondly, the nature of effective strategies and interventions that teachers can use with students with disabilities in mainstream classes (Donfrancesco 1996; Manetti *et al.* 2001; Begeny and Martens 2007). It is argued here that this perception has most likely been exaggerated by the gap that exists between the number of research studies on inclusion published in English when compared to those that are published in Italian. In this chapter we have described some of the most relevant empirical findings in the field published in Italian journals. Besides the specific results reported, these studies demonstrate the growing interest that exists in Italy in evaluating the benefits and the limitations of full inclusion, through observable and measurable means. Still, more research is needed, in particular longitudinal studies, in order to define the best evidence-based practice that will enhance the academic and social abilities of all children, and also the specific role the school plays in fostering these abilities to ensure the progress and development of all individuals, regardless of their disability (Canevaro and de Anna 2010).

Note

1   Please note that while the term 'disabled' may be considered outdated in many countries, it is used in this chapter as a translation of the Italian term 'disabili'. The term may be understood as referring to children who have additional support needs.

References

Balboni, G. and Pedrabissi, L. (2000) Attitudes of Italian teachers and parents towards school inclusion of students with mental retardation: the role of experience, *Education and Training in Mental Retardation and Developmental Disabilities*, 35(2): 148–59.

Begeny, J. C. and Martens, B. K. (2007) Inclusionary education in Italy: a literature review and call for more empirical research, *Remedial and Special Education*, 28(2): 80–94.

Brownell, M. T., Smith, S. W., McNellis, J. R. and Miller, M. D. (1997) Attrition in special education: why teachers leave the classroom and where they go, *Exceptionality*, 7(3): 143–55.

Burstein, N., Sears, S., Wilcoxen, A., Cabello, B. and Spagna, M. (2004) Moving toward inclusive practices, *Remedial and Special Education*, 25: 104–16.

Canevaro, A. (1999) Cosa ricordano e cosa imparano i compagni diclasse dall'integrazione, in D. Iares and M. Tortello, *Handicap e risorseper l'integrazione*. Trento: Centro Studi Erickson.

Canevaro, A. and de Anna, L. (2010) The historical evolution of school integration in Italy: some witnesses and considerations, *European Journal of Disability Research*, 4: 203–16.

Cecchini, M. and McCleary, I. D. (1985) Preschool handicapped in Italy: a research-based developmental model, *Journal of the Division for Early Childhood*, 9: 254–71.

Celi, F. (1999) Software didattico per l'apprendimento e l'integrazione, in D. Ianes and M. Tortello, *Handicap e risorse per l'integrazione*. Trento: Centro Studi Erickson.

Celi, F. and Romani, F. (1997) *Macchine per imparare*. Trento: Centro Studi Erickson.

Chiari, G. (1999) Apprendimento cooperativo: il metodo della ricerca di gruppo, in D. Ianes and M. Tortello, *Handicap e risorse per l'integrazione*. Trento: Centro Studi Erickson.

Comoglio, M. (1998) *Educare insegnando. Applicare il cooperative learning*. Roma: LAS.

Cornoldi, C. (1995) *Metacognizione e apprendimento*. Bologna: Il Mulino.

Cornoldi, C., De Beni, R. and Gruppo, M.T. (1993) *Imparare a studiare*. Trento: Centro Studi Erickson.

Cornoldi, C., Friso, G., Giordano, L., Molin, A., Poli, S., Rigoni, F. et al. (1997) *Abilità visuo-spaziali. Intervento sulle difficoltà non verbali di apprendimento*. Trento: Ed. Erickson.

Cornoldi, C., Terreni, A., Scruggs, T. E. and Mastropieri, M. A. (1998) Teacher attitudes in Italy after twenty years of inclusion, *Remedial and Special Education*, 19(6): 350–6.

Cottini L. (2002) *L'integrazione scolastica del bambino autistico*. Roma: Carocci.

Daniels, H. and Hogg, B. (1991) An intercultural comparison of the quality of life of children and youth with handicaps in Denmark, Italy, the United Kingdom and Germany, *Educational and Child Psychology*, 8: 74–83.

De Beni, M. (1998) *Prosocialità e altruismo*. Trento: Centro Studi Erickson.

De Beni, R. and Pazzaglia, F. (1991) *Lettura e metacognizione*. Trento: Centro Studi Erickson.

Demo, H. and Zambotti, F. (2009) Alcune relazioni tra percorsi di integrazione scolastica e percezione di integrazione sociale in contesti normali, *L'integrazione scolastica e sociale*, 8(5): 459–73.

Donfrancesco, R. (1996) Disabled children's integration in school: from social representation to subjectivity, *Giornale di Neuropsichiatria dell'Eta Evolutiva*, 16: 283–95.

Fadda, R. and Lai, P. (2011) Teaching efficacy negli insegnanti della scuola primaria, in R. Fadda and E. Mangiaracina (a cura di) *Dispersione scolastica e disagio sociale: Criticità del contesto educativo e buone prassi preventive*. Roma: Carocci Editore.

Farci, G. (2005) Per un'educazione speciale dell'alunno con disturbi pervasivi dello sviluppo. Riflessioni relative al contesto scolastico italiano, *Autismo e disturbi dello sviluppo*, 3(1): 9–22.

Ferraboschi, L. and Meini, N. (1995) *Recupero in ortografia*. Trento: Centro Studi Erickson.

Fiori, G., Lanfranchi, S., Moalli, E. and Vianello, R. (2008) Profili cognitivi e adattivi in minori con sindrome di Cornelia De Lange, in R. Vianello, M. Mariotti and M. Serra, *Esperienze e ricerche sull'integrazione scolastica e sociale*. Volume primo. Rassegne e ricerche (pp. 27–37). Bergamo: Junior.

Ianes, D. (1999) Strategie prioritarie per dare qualità all'integrazione scolastica, in D. Ianes and M. Tortello, *Handicap e risorse per l'integrazione*. Trento: Centro Studi Erickson.

Ianes, D. and Canevaro, A. (2008) *Facciamo il punto su ... l'integrazione scolastica*. Trento: Centro Studi Erickson.

Manetti, M., Schneider, B. H. and Siperstein, G. (2001) Social acceptance of children with mental retardation: testing the contact hypothesis with an Italian sample, *International Journal of Behavioural Development*, 25: 279–86.

Mangiaracina, E. and Fadda, R. (2010) *Giudizio morale e comportamento sociale – sfide e obiettivi per la scuola*. Roma: Armando.

Mastropieri, M. A. and Scruggs, T. E. (2001) Promoting inclusion in secondary classrooms, *Learning Disability Quarterly*, 24(4): 265–74.

Meazzini, P. (1987) Special education in Italy, in C. R Reynolds and L. Mann (eds) *Encyclopaedia of Special Education*, 2nd edn. New York: Wiley.

Mega, C., Castellini, K. and Vianello, R. (1998) Gli atteggiamenti degli insegnanti verso gli allevi con handicap: dalla scuola materna a quella superiore, in R. Vianello and C. Cornoldi (eds) *Learning, Metacognition and Personality*. Bergamo: Edizioni Junior.

Micheli, E. (1999) *Autismo, verso una migliore qualità della vita*. Reggio Calabria: Laruffa.

Moniga, S., Beschi, F. and Maeran, M. (2008) Formazione alla vita indipendente: progetto rivolto a ragazzi e giovani adulti con sindrome di Down, in R. Vianello, M. Mariotti and M. Serra (eds) *Esperienze e ricerche sull'integrazione scolastica e sociale*. Bergamo: Junior.

Reversi, S., Langher, V., Crisafulli, V. and Ferri, R. (2007) The quality of disabled students' school integration: a research experience in the Italian state school system, *School Psychology International*, 28(4): 403–18.

Scataglini, C. and Giustini, A. (1998) *Adattamento dei libri di testo*. Trento: Centro Studi Erickson.

Vianello, R. (2008) *Disabilità intellettive*. Bergamo: Junior.

Vianello, R. and Lanfranchi, S. (2009) Genetic syndromes causing mental retardation: deficit and surplus in school performance and social adaptability compared to cognitive functioning, *Life Span and Disability*, XII (1): 41–52.

Vitello, S. J. (1991) Integration of handicapped students in the United States and Italy: a comparison, *International Journal of Special Education*, 6: 213–22.

Vitello, S. J. (1994) Special education integration: the Arezzo approach, *International Journal of Disability, Development and Education*, 41(1): 61–70.

Zelioli, A. (1987) *Undici anni di integrazione scholastica degli alumni handicappati: l'esperienza, i problemi e le prospettive*. Lucca: Maria Pacini Fassi Editore.

4

ROGER SLEE
Inclusion in schools: what is the task?

Introduction – the aims of this chapter

Last century I worked in what was euphemistically called a teaching unit. In truth this was a place where children who troubled schools were sent to give them a second chance and, of course, to ease the tension in the school. Indeed, many of these children were troubled and troubling and I am not making light of this fact. Working with them was often difficult and the source of high anxiety. I have no doubt that this was a reciprocal feeling as far as the children themselves saw it.

The task for the teaching unit was to take these children away from the pressures they experienced in the regular school, build their usually lagging academic skills, assist them to manage their own behaviour and launch them back into a successful completion of their schooling. It was clear that our assignment at the teaching unit was to fix the problem children so that they would no longer compromise the smooth running of the classroom. Of course the task was described differently at the time. Then we applied the term integration, with all its overtones of assimilation, rather than the now respectable description of inclusion.

As I look back now on my time at the teaching unit in the Melbourne suburb of Fitzroy, it is hardly surprising that I struggled with the job. There seemed to be a widening gap between the original statement of task, what we did and what the schools expected. The rate of successful reintegration of children back into their regular classroom was, though not precisely reported at the time, very low. It was no secret that once schools had found an alternative place for their troubling student, they were unexcited by the prospect of the child's return. In fact teachers were agitating for the opening of more teaching units to place the growing tide of children who needed alternatives to the regular classroom.

Had we, the teachers in the unit or education policy makers in the Australian state of Victoria, undertaken some very rudimentary literature searches at the time we would have found that evaluations of this kind of education provision, and I offer the term education loosely, had been undertaken in England (Her Majesty's Inspectorate 1978; Basini 1981) and in Western Australia (Colliver 1983). These reports provide cause for concern. To summarize, they suggested that while it was procedurally easy to refer students to behaviour units, their transition back into school was less successful. Daines (1981) reported that children returning to school from off-site centres were likely to be suspended within six months of their return. Off-site units beget their own need. The demand for more places increases exponentially and more children find themselves being shifted outside the mainframe of schooling (Mongon 1988). Concern was also registered that the children's learning was attenuated as the reduced number of teachers and resources in the behaviour unit meant that not all aspects of the curriculum could be covered.

A particularly distressing finding was the disproportionate number of Caribbean boys referred to the units in England. Sally Tomlinson tracked this form of racial segregation through behaviour units in more detail (1979). Sadly David Gillborn (2008) at the Institute of Education in London reveals the continuity of this practice through what are now called Pupil Referral Units (PRU). The existence of off-site units was justified as an aide to assist disruptive students to return to school and to expand the educational and social opportunities. Mongon (1988: 194) asserts a different purpose:

> Since units appear to be, on the whole, of little benefit to those young people who attend them it is difficult to conclude anything other than that, in a reversal of practice, they are established for the benefit of people who do not attend them rather than for those who do.

You may be asking why I am reaching back into the last century to commence an essay for twenty-first-century teachers? After all, I have to confess that, in all likelihood, I was teaching in the behaviour unit before many of the readers of this chapter commenced school, or (gulp) were born. I am drawing on this experience to illustrate the question I have set myself to ask, if not to answer, in this chapter: *what work is inclusive education doing*? Is the form of inclusion we are observing or participating in what we intend or require? The rapid expansion of off-site units made more work in student support services. However, this was no guarantee of the delivery of the stated objective of all this effort and enterprise.

While I am trance-fixed in the past let me tell you about an academic conference where such questions also arose and heightened my anxiety about my complicity in the well-intentioned exclusion of disruptive children. The conference was about behaviour and fixing disruptive children so that they could be successful at school. One speaker silenced the auditorium as he spoke about his son's suicide following repeated suspensions from school. To assist other parents and young people, the father established a programme of camps where 'at risk' children were taken away and he tried to show them that they mattered and that people cared for them. Subscriptions to his programme were high and children were ushered onto the stage to tell of their individual journeys back from the precipice of catastrophe because of their camp experience. I am moved by the father's initiative and commitment. However, I worry that unless the structure and culture of schooling changes, such out of school experiences have a real struggle on their hands. One is mindful of Sisyphus condemned by the Gods to push the boulder up the steep hill as far as he could until it rolled back to the bottom, whereupon his task would recommence.

Let me hasten to say that I am not suggesting that the children who attended the teaching unit were not problematic for schools to handle, or that some might not have been unwell. Cooper (2008) suggests that I am one of a number of academics who deny physiological explanations for childhood difficulty in schooling. This is not the case (Slee 1995). I do, however, say that we need to subject science to critique, as we know of its long history of both benefits and deleterious effects.

In days gone by, children who troubled schools were typically referred to as disruptive, difficult, and less often as maladjusted and disturbed. It seems to me that the language we use to describe these children has changed profoundly and, along with it, so has the way we know or understand children who are difficult for schools to handle. Increasingly children are referred to as disordered. They are understood to be and confirmed through diagnosis as biologically defective. This shift in language reflects what Thomas Kuhn (1962) referred to as a paradigm shift or a revolution in understanding. In this chapter I want to encourage you to engage critically with the field of inclusive education to ask whether our new knowledge about behaviour, difference and disability is assisting schools to become more inclusive or if the language we use to calibrate and categorize the population has become a new dividing technology (Foucault 1973 and 1979) to assist with the difficult task of managing diverse populations in the outmoded institutional arrangement of schooling.

Divided into two main parts, this chapter will advance the proposition that making inclusion work is a far more complex task than is often suggested and that much of the inclusive education enterprise is inherently flawed. This is because of an incomplete analysis of exclusion and an insipid political will. The second part will suggest a revised agenda for making inclusion work. In this way we may avoid the constancy of what are too frequently and easily accepted as the *unintended consequences* of inclusive education.

Deploying a habit of exclusion

Enlisting the work of Daniel Levitin (2008), I suggested that, like music, exclusion has become a constant presence in our lives. According to Levitin (2008), the insinuation of music into our everyday worlds has been achieved through its antiquity and ubiquity. Borrowing this proposition, I transposed it to an analysis of exclusion (Slee 2010). Exclusion is also everywhere and it has been there for a very long time. As Zygmunt Bauman (1997) proclaims, all societies create their own strangers in their own inimitable ways. I don't intend to exhaustively reconstruct the landscapes and dynamics of exclusion in this brief essay. Rather, I will simply describe why I suggested that exclusion has become more pervasive and pernicious because we live in a condition of *collective indifference* (Slee 2010). Although the ink has hardly dried on the page, I now believe that the concept of collective indifference may infer that exclusion is benign and incidental. This is not the case. There is something very deliberate about excluding others to maintain our membership of networks of privilege.

In his book *Wasted Lives*, Zygmunt Bauman (2004) depicts the collateral casualties of economic progress through the creation of flawed consumers who become an *irksome surplus population*. Richard Sennett (2006) suggests that *the spectre of uselessness* in the culture of new capitalism casts a long shadow formed by the search for global sweatshops, the rapid advances of technology and a combination of ageism and skills exhaustion. Within this social dynamic more people are displaced and pushed to the margins while others intensify their attempts to maintain social respectability and material affluence. The hallmark of the neoliberalism that drives modern economies is an ethic of competitive individualism. We accept that we are absolved from responsibility for our production of the growing number of outcasts because so-called impersonalized forces are at work in this human drama:

> . . . the production of human waste has all the markings of an impersonal, purely technical issue. The principal actors in the drama are 'terms of trade', 'market demands', 'competitive pressures', 'productivity' or 'efficiency requirements', all covering up or explicitly denying any connection with the intentions, will, decisions and actions of real humans with names and addresses.
>
> (Bauman 2004: 40)

We fortify ourselves behind gated communities or we proliferate surveillance cameras and security forces to regulate those who are cast out. David Harvey (1996) produced a social cartography to reveal the geographies of injustice that separate the developing and developed worlds or the countries of the north and south, and more importantly etch boundaries across and within our own neighbourhoods in affluent nations. The map has been updated by Daniel Dorling (2010) to show the growing ravages of inequality and injustice. Wilkinson and Pickett (2009) draw on empirical data to demonstrate how the gap between wealth and poverty is widening in many affluent countries and that the social and economic impacts of this advancing inequality has deleterious and far-reaching effects.

We have erected a shield that allows us to look away from the tragedy of exclusion. This is achieved through a number of self-serving explanations that often attach blame to those who suffer most. We reserve pity and charity as compensation but do not seriously attempt to intervene to alter the architecture of privilege and disadvantage. Worse still, there is an enveloping public discourse of social inclusion. We trade in liberal sentiment that *values difference and diversity, celebrates multiculturalism* and seeks *reconciliation* with our indigenous peoples. The truth, says Bauman (2004), is that we live in a state of *ambient fear* characterized by *mixaphobia*. Dorling (2010: 1) frames the task ahead of us:

> Although few say they agree with injustice, nevertheless we live in an unjust world. In the world's richest countries injustice is caused less and less by having too few resources to share around fairly and it is increasingly maintained by widespread adherence to the beliefs that actually propagate it. These beliefs are often presented as natural and long-standing, but in fact they are mostly modern creations. What appeared fair and normal yesterday will often be seen as unjust tomorrow. Changing what is injustice today means telling some people, usually those in positions of power, that what they consider to be fair is in fact in many ways unjust.

Social institutions such as school not only mirror the larger problems, they continue to manufacture them (Connell 1994). Schools have become incubators of exclusion.

Exclusion in and from schools cannot be detached from the context within which they operate. The policies of education authorities across the globe demonstrate considerable convergence as expressions of the values of neoliberalism (Rizvi and Lingard 2009). The growing influence of transnational organizations and agencies such as the World Bank, the OECD, UNESCO and UNICEF has secured global educational discourses and programmes. The ethic of competition is marked by international league tables that publish the results of international testing programmes such as the Programme of International Student Assessment (PISA) and the Trends in International Maths and Science Study (TIMSS). This is replicated in national education jurisdictions where the drive has been for each to establish a national curriculum anchored to national testing programmes and policed through greater surveillance or inspection of teachers (Stobart 2008). The more schools are compared against the performance of each other and in some cases penalized for the poorer performance of students on standardized tests, the more selective they are likely to become about their student cohorts.

A student whose academic performance threatens a school's standing on the league table represents a risk. Schools are increasingly risk-averse. Various strategies are deployed to avoid compromising school, state or national success. One strategy is to train the students to do well on tests. As Lingard (1998) argues, equity programmes in education were replaced by an overriding obsession with literacy as a means for dealing with disadvantage. Other strategies include the unacknowledged practice of persuading some students to absent themselves on testing days and the reassignment of students to categories of special educational needs so that their performance will not jeopardize the school. This is our educational surplus population, the collateral damage of schooling.

The risk of exclusion is also undergirded by the structure of school funding in a country like Australia. The gap between the available resources for state schools in low socio-economic status schools compared with state schools in affluent communities is widening. This picture becomes more complex when we add the expanding private schools and religious school sectors to a very unbalanced financial statement. If we accept that poverty is an indicator of academic failure and thereby limits wider vocational and social opportunities, it would seem that making inclusion work would press us towards a redistribution of resources. I return to my earlier statement about there being an insipid political will for making inclusion work.

Let us strike out on a different path to conclude this interrogation of educational exclusion. Nikolas Rose's (2007) book entitled *The Politics of Life Itself* ought to be required reading for the student of inclusive education. He commences with an excerpt from *The Birth of the Clinic* (Foucault 1973, cited in Rose 2007: 9):

> ... the epistemological, ontological, and technical reshaping of modern medical perception at the start of the nineteenth century came about through the interconnections of changes along a series of dimensions, some of which seem, at first sight, rather distant from medicine.

Taking up this advice to adopt a range of analytic tools that straddle traditional knowledge disciplines to understand complex phenomena, Rose uses five lines of inquiry into bio-politics and contemporary knowledge of life. A rather limited summary follows:

- *Molecularization*: this refers to the way in which we have moved from the dissection table where we visualized the body at the molar level as an intricate interconnection of tissues, limbs, joints, organs, bones, cartilages, blood flows and other fluids. Technological transformations from the x-ray to informatics and computational modelling developed across the disciplines of biology, engineering, physics, mathematics renders life as DNA sequences. New ways of visualizing the body at the molecular level allows for new interventions and, of course, for political fracture around the nature and effects of interventions. What characteristics will we successively eradicate from the species as the knowledge and technology enables us to make these determinations?

- *Technologies of optimization*: new technologies for visualizing the body at the molecular level both reflect and propagate new ways of thinking about life and about intervening in what once was seen as its natural course. New knowledge of the molecular structure of the brain has given rise to very persuasive but contestable brain sciences (Rose 2005). Political fractures form around the nature and effects of new interventions. What characteristics will we successively eradicate from the species as the knowledge and technology enables us to make these determinations?

- *Subjectification*: within this line of inquiry Rose examines the new politics of health and medicine is to represent the way in which people come to see themselves according to their medical identity. Rabinow (1996) deployed the term *biosociality* to describe a new set of relations around medicine. Individuals and group identities are formed around genetic identities. People mobilize around genetic research projects to shape or reshape their genetic future.

- *Experts of life itself*: doctors enjoyed a privileged position as the custodians of medical knowledge, but this has changed, as have the social relations of medicine. People invest in themselves and their kin as an ongoing medical project. Experts exert pastoral power over a population seeking speech therapy, occupational therapy, art therapy, music therapy, physiotherapy, aromatherapy and psychotherapy. We enlist dieticians, nutritionists, personal trainers, marriage counsellors, mental health counsellors, educational counsellors, genetic counsellors, and fertility and reproduction counsellors to augment the services of traditional medicine.

- *Bioeconomics*: biocapital shapes relationships, sets political priorities, traverses national borders, builds a discourse of urgency, need and benevolence, and defines the parameters of important knowledge and the next big question (Slee 2010: 132). Governments, corporations and university research labs fall into step with each other in defining new medical priorities.

> Where funds are required to generate truth in biomedicine, and where the allocation of such funds depends inescapably upon a calculation of financial return, commercial investment shapes the very direction, organisation,

problem space, and solution effects of biomedicine and the basic biology that supports it.

(Rose 2007: 31–2)

What does this mean for making inclusion in schools work? This is not an argument to say that medical knowledge is simply self-serving or flawed. To suggest so would be nonsensical. Understanding medical knowledge itself and the phenomena it seeks to describe and explain does, however, require transdisciplinary augmentation. Rose's analysis of bio-politics presses me to suggest that not only have we not sufficiently understood the nuances of exclusion in and from education, but inclusive education has in some ways become an accomplice to exclusion.

More children are being diagnosed with an expanding range of disabilities, disorders and syndromes. Nikolas Rose's brother Steven has tracked this in relation to behaviour and attention disorders as an example of the deployment of the evolving science of the brain (Rose 2005). Diagnosis assists schools to claim more resources to assign to the child and also assists parents to argue for the educational entitlement of their children. In the area of behaviour disorders *DSM IV: Diagnostic and Statistical Manual of Mental Disorders* (American Psychiatric Association 2000) provides a catalogue of diagnostic options. The publication of the next edition of *DSM V* will no doubt increase the range of options for calibrating the student population.

While Kutchins and Kirk (1997) have traced the politics and interests of adding and deleting syndromes, illnesses and disorders to the *DSM* since its inception as a guide for the diagnosis of mental illness, I am not going to detail that. Let us simply contend that this has proven a contestable science. The withdrawal of homosexuality from the diagnostic manual as a mental illness is illustrative of the point. Neither will I rehearse the compelling critiques of the trajectory of attention disorders and of peak organizations such as CHADD that form around the disorder in the work of Rose (2005), Laurence and McCallum (2009), Tait (2010) or Graham (2010). Rather I return to Nikolas Rose (2007: 29–30) as a reflection on what is happening around categories of disorders and children in schools.

> . . . new specialists of the soma have emerged, each with their own apparatus of associations, meetings, journals, esoteric languages, star performers and myths. Each of these is surrounded by, a flock of popularisers, science writers and journalists. While often disowned by researchers themselves, they play a key translational and meditational role in forming the associations – made up of politicians, lay people, patient groups, research councils and venture capitalists and investors – on which such expertise depends.

Has all of this activity made teachers and schools more inclusive? I am not convinced that we have progressed towards authentic forms of inclusion. Inclusive education policies and practices, with their emphasis on diagnosis and the individuated allocation of resources to students, has not built the capacity of schools and teachers to develop inclusive curriculum and pedagogy across a broad range of differences. The generalist teacher has in effect been granted permission to withdraw while specialists or hired aides get on with the task of inclusion. One may possibly argue that while more children are being seized in the gaze of inclusive education, their experience of education may not yet be inclusive.

Special educational needs has in many respects become a means for managing those children who trouble schools and introduce risk to test performance of the school and thus affect compliance to state governments' measures of standards for the quality of the education provision. For some this may indeed mean that inclusive education is working. We are seeing the movement of more children into the mainstream. It is giving schools procedures and resources to manage different and difficult children. The traffic is not unidirectional. More special classes are being formed for the growing number of children diagnosed with behaviour disorders. Is this the task of inclusion?

Resetting the task

There are of course many teachers and schools that are providing authentic inclusive educational experiences for their children. This is no small achievement in the current social and educational climate. An important step towards making inclusive education work is building a catalogue of the stories of schools that have struggled to provide inclusive educational environments and experiences for all of their students (Part III of this book considers how to overcome the barriers to successful inclusion). It is also important to learn more about exclusion as a precursor to effectively finding better options. This suggests that we need to look beyond inclusive education policy and programmes to the architecture of schooling (organizational and built environment; workforce structure; fiscal arrangements; curriculum; pedagogy and assessment) to identify those factors that erect obstacles for disadvantaged and diverse student populations.

Previously I have attempted to map out an agenda for making inclusive education work. I did this by identifying five interrelated streams of tasks (Slee 2010). Put simply, inclusive education is not a project wherein we update and rehouse special education. Nor is it about inviting different groups to participate in an unreconstructed regular education. Inclusion requires far more thought and effort.

I will simply list the tasks and suggest key elements and questions of the tasks. It must be stated at the outset that approaching it this way risks us not recognizing the overlapping nature of the tasks and it is somewhat reductive. Nevertheless I offer this as an alternative to the advancement of special education-based inclusive education scenarios, which tend to reassert old privileges and exclusions.

The first task I call the *restorative task*. There is an urgent requirement to build trust between those seeking inclusive education as the template for schooling. Trust is achieved when we respect rights and privilege the voices of those who have been excluded through ensuring authentic participation in planning and community development. This will not happen spontaneously; it requires brokers and negotiation.

The second task is the *analytic task*. As has been argued throughout this chapter, exclusion has a complex architecture and culture. Reforming this must be advanced through a more careful research programme that asks awkward questions and brings multidisciplinary teams to the table. The research must observe extrinsic and intrinsic properties of exclusion. In particular the analytic gaze should include education structures, practices and cultures as part of the diagnostic process.

Following and overlapping this task is the *policy task*. It is futile to talk about inclusive education while reinforcing a culture of schooling that produces winners and losers. Education systems speak a language of inclusion while pursuing practices that create deep educational divisions. Inclusive education programmes are identified in prospectuses and on websites, while residual forms of schooling are provided for those who will lower standards. Expectations for success are not extended equally and this can be seen in contradictory elements of education policy. Moreover, if inclusion and justice are the prize, the funding of education must be radically altered to create opportunity for disadvantaged and underrepresented student populations.

The *education task* invites us to treat schools as a site for educating all students and to pursue changes to:

- the expectations and organization of schooling;
- curriculum so that it recognizes and represents all student identities;
- pedagogy and assessment so that it is a force for development of each student's potential;
- the culture of schools to embed them in community as a neighbourhood hub dedicated to building more holistic well-being.

Finally, and of course it precedes all else, is the *values task*. First is the necessity of instating value to those who hitherto have not been valued by and in schools. Second is the inscription of an inclusive set of guiding principles and values into the policies, practices and cultures of schools. This assumes a rejection of competitive individualism.

There is no doubt that this description of a revised inclusive education project is radically incomplete. As Stephen Ball (2008) remarks, the convention of a conclusion in a book is a modernist invention that undermines our sense of being engaged in an incomplete project. This chapter is offered as a beginning and it is offered for debate. For those who want to take Occam's razor to education policy and education research, this chapter will be an affront. My premise is that reductive understandings have produced a form of inclusive education that sustains old exclusions and creates new ones.

References

American Psychiatric Association (2000) *Diagnostic and Statistical Manual of Mental Disorders: DSM IV TR.* Washington DC: American Psychiatric Association.

Ball, S.J. (2008) *The Education Debate.* Bristol: The Policy Press.

Basini, A. (1981) Urban schools and disruptive pupils: a study of some ILEA support units, *Educational Review*, 33(3): 191–206.

Bauman, Z. (1997) *Postmodernity and its Discontents.* Cambridge: Polity.

Bauman, Z. (2004) *Wasted Lives. Modernity and its Outcasts.* Cambridge: Polity.

Colliver, R. (1983) *Severely Disruptive Behaviour in Western Australian Secondary Schools.* Perth: Education Department of Western Australia.

Connell, R. (1994) Education and poverty, *Harvard Educational Review*, 64(2): 125–49.

Cooper, P. (2008) Like alligators bobbing for poodles? A critical discussion of education, ADHD and the biopsychosocial perspective, *Journal of Philosophy in Education*, 42(3–4): 457–74.

Daines, R. (1981) Withdrawal units and the psychology of problem behaviour, in B. Gillham (ed.) *Problem Behaviour in the Secondary school*. London: Croom Helm.

Dorling, D. (2010) *Injustice: Why Inequality Persists*. Bristol: The Policy Press.

Foucault, M. (1973) *The Birth of the Clinic*. London: Tavistock Press.

Foucault, M. (1979) *Discipline and Punish. The Birth of the Prison*. Harmondsworth: Penguin Books.

Gillborn, D. (2008) *Racism and Education: Coincidence or Conspiracy?* Abingdon: Routledge.

Graham, L. (ed.) (2010) *(De) Constructing ADHD*. New York: Peter Lang.

Harvey, D. (1996) *Justice, Nature and the Geographies of Difference*. Oxford: Blackwell Publishers.

Her Majesty's Inspectorate (1978) *Behaviour Units: A Survey of Special Units for Pupils with Behaviour Problems*, Report for the Department of Education and Science (DES). London: HMI.

Kuhn, T. S. (1962) *The Structure of Scientific Revolutions*. Chicago, IL: University of Chicago Press.

Kutchins, H. and Kirk, S.A. (1997) *Making US Crazy. DSM IV: The Psychiatric Bible and the Creation of Mental Disorders*. New York: Free Press.

Laurence, J. and McCallum, D. (2009) *Inside the Child's Head. Histories of Childhood Behavioural Disorders*. Rotterdam: Sense Publishers.

Levitin, D. (2008) *The World in Six Songs*. New York: Dutton.

Lingard, B. (1998) The disadvantaged schools programme: caught between literacy and local management, *International Journal of Inclusive Education*, 2(1): 1–14.

Mongon, D. (1988) Behaviour units, maladjustment and student control, in R. Slee (ed.) *Discipline and Schools: A Curriculum Perspective*. South Melbourne: Macmillan.

Rabinow, P. (1996) *Essays on the Anthropology of Reason*. Princeton, NJ: Princeton University Press.

Rizvi, F. and Lingard, R. (2009) *Globalising Education Policy*. Abingdon: Routledge.

Rose, N. (2007) *The Politics of Life Itself. Biomedicine, Power and Subjectivity in the Twenty-first Century*. Princeton, NJ: Princeton University Press.

Rose, S. (2005) *The 21st Century Brain. Explaining, Mending and Manipulating the Mind*. London: Vintage.

Sennett, R. (2006) *The Culture of New Capitalism*. London: Yale University Press.

Slee, R. (1995) *Changing Theories and Practices of Discipline*. London: Falmer Press.

Slee, R. (2010) *The Irregular School*. Abingdon: Routledge.

Stobart, G. (2008) *Testing Times: The Uses and Abuses of Assessment*. Abingdon: Routledge.

Tait, G. (2010) *Philosophy, Behaviour Disorders and the School*. Rotterdam: Sense Publishers.

Tomlinson, S. (1979) *Educational Subnormality: A Study in Decision-making*. London: Routledge and Kegan Paul.

Wilkinson, R.G. and Pickett, K. (2009) *The Spirit Level: Why More Equal Societies Almost Always Do Better*. London: Allen Lane.

Part II

The 'how' of inclusion

5

BRAHM NORWICH
How inclusion policy works in the UK (England): successes and issues

Introduction

Inclusion in the UK has been an important issue in social and economic policy at least since the 1990s and especially since the Labour government came to power in 1997 and adopted explicit social inclusion policies. Inclusion came to be used in the UK in relation to educational policy and practice mostly after 1997 when the then new government made inclusion central to its SEN policy (DfES 1997). Given the current widespread use of the term inclusion in the UK and internationally, it might be thought that the term is old and established. Quite the contrary: its use is recent but what has been established are the values that the term inclusion represents, a mixture of equal opportunity, social respect and solidarity.[1] However, inclusive education represents a particular contemporary perspective on these social and political values which will be discussed in this chapter. As might be expected with such important and cherished values as these, there will be much contention about the meaning and importance of inclusion. The recent Conservative and Liberal Democrat coalition government's Green Paper[2] on special educational needs (DFE 2011) has questioned the 'bias to inclusion' in recent education policy and practice in England.[3] The contentious nature of the current inclusion debate is about whether inclusive developments for pupils with special educational needs over the last decade will be undermined by new government policies of more choice and diversity of schools: greater parental 'choice' of schools, the option for schools to be more independent of local authorities and the setting up of 'free' schools – government-funded but organized by parents and other voluntary groups. The government position is that it is for parents to decide on whether a child with special educational needs should be included in ordinary schools or not.

Origins and background to inclusive education policies

The term 'inclusion' came to be used in formulating the central vision of government after 1997 about 'raising of standards for all', including those with identified special educational needs in the SEN Green Paper (DfES 1997). There was a commitment to the 'inclusion of children with SEN within mainstream schooling wherever possible' (1997: 5), the first time that this term was used in an important policy document. Before then the language was about integration, which was promoted initially by the Warnock Report (DES 1978), the report of a government committee which introduced the system of 'special educational needs' and explicitly recommended the principle of provision in ordinary schools subject to some conditions.

In the UK the principle of inclusion or integration needs to be seen within the historical movement for comprehensive or common schools for all children and young people. Seen in this longer term context, some of the principles of inclusion have a longer history concerned with a political vision about schools, especially about secondary schools for all. Central to the debates about the organization of secondary schools in the UK has been the selection of children at age 11 for either a more academic education in grammar schools or in secondary modern schools where a less academic/vocationally oriented education was provided. Special schools had their place in this differentiated school system where 'ability' assessment played a large part in the selection process for these kinds of schools. The vision of schools for all, irrespective of gender, social class or ability, meant that more provision was to be made for children with special educational needs in ordinary schools. From this perspective special schools were seen as less favourable or totally unacceptable settings for children with special educational needs. However, within England there are still state-funded grammar schools (about 5 per cent of funded secondary schools). Though there was a historic move away from grammar to comprehensive schools from the 1960s, there was no national legislation to close state-funded grammar schools; it was left to local authorities to make this decision. This co-existence of grammar and comprehensive schools can be compared with the co-existence of special schools and ordinary or mainstream schools. The significance of the organization of secondary schooling for inclusion in England is also underlined by the disproportionate number of secondary aged pupils (compared to primary aged pupils) who are in special schools. About two-thirds of all special school pupils nationally are of secondary age. There are several reasons which have been suggested for this pattern of placement, including greater cognitive demand of the curriculum as well as inflexibility and size of secondary schools (Black 2009).

Assuming that the underlying values associated with inclusion (such as equal opportunity and solidarity) are not recent, how did inclusion come to be used when it did and what effect did these circumstances have on what inclusion has come to represent? Like integration, where the opposite is segregation, inclusion has often been defined by being the opposite of exclusion. Social inclusion has derived its meaning from being the opposite of social exclusion, which has been taken to refer to processes in which individuals and entire communities are blocked from rights, opportunities and resources, such as housing, employment, health care, civic engagement, democratic participation and due process (Power and Wilson 2000). What defines social exclusion in this formulation is that these rights, opportunities and resources are seen as those normally available to most members of society as they are central to social integration. It is interesting that social exclusion/inclusion is linked here to social integration, in which all people are said to participate fully in the life of the community.

A related perspective has framed social exclusion in terms of being deprived of social recognition, with social recognition dependent on a full citizenship that enables full participation in the life of a community (Honneth 1996). Honneth considers this citizenship to include economic, social and political participation. Social exclusion/inclusion can therefore be seen as primarily about various kinds of participation in a community.

This focus on social recognition also helps to make sense of another aspect of social exclusion/inclusion – its focus on whether the socially excluded are made to fit into the community and in the process lose some of their characteristics. This links to criticisms of ethnic and immigrant integration where the minority group is seen to assimilate in a way that denies recognition of their distinctive ethnic and cultural ways. Social inclusion therefore has been defined from one perspective to imply that the 'struggle for recognition' requires the 'mainstream' community to accommodate to the minority. A different perspective represents both assimilation (the minority fitting in) and accommodation (the 'mainstream' adapting systemically to the minority) as complementary social processes, with the one involving the other. There are therefore two distinct and inconsistent perspectives on accommodation: one which sees it as complementary to assimilation, and the other that sees accommodation as a binary opposite of assimilation. The latter is the one that has linked social inclusion to current ideas about inclusive education (Thomas and Vaughn 2004).

Inclusion in education

The terms 'inclusion' and 'inclusive education' came into use in England following the UNESCO Salamanca Statement (UNESCO 1994). This is shown by the entries in the British Education Index (BEI: one of the leading databases of academic and research publications in education). Though the database records publications with origins outside the UK, many are UK-based. From 1977 to 1984 there were only 13 publications that used the term inclusion in the title or abstract, and these were about Piaget's class inclusion task and the inclusion of a subject, e.g. art, in the school curriculum. There was nothing between 1984 and 1991, when the first entry to inclusion was recorded in an article that contrasted inclusion with integration in a further education context. But it was post the Salamanca Statement in 1994 that the growth of publications on social inclusion and inclusive education started. About 90 per cent of the publications recorded in the BEI with social inclusion or inclusive education in the title or abstract were published after 2000. Though the publications from 2000 until now have been steady, between a range of 47 to 89 per year, there has been an increasing proportion that are about inclusion beyond the field of disabilities and learning difficulties to refer to diversity of gender and ethnicity too.

With the introduction of the inclusion term, the main aim was to replace the then current term integration, which was represented as about placement of pupils in ordinary schools (Thomas and Vaughn 2004; Ainscow et al. 2006). Drawing on ideas from social inclusion thinking, discussed above, inclusion was framed as about participation in local schools with the emphasis on how ordinary schools would accommodate all pupils, not just those with SEN and disabilities. Integration came to be defined as about assimilation, where the pupil with SEN had to fit into the mainstream school and there may be no social or academic participation in the life and learning of that local school. Inclusion was about systems change to accommodate and provide for the diversity of all pupils in a school community, with no place for special schools or a continuum of placements. Connected to social participation was the importance of social belonging and acceptance (solidarity) in schools. This systemic focus of inclusion was underpinned by the social model of SEN/disability, which proponents brought in from the developing disability movement and disability studies (Oliver 1996). This was defined in terms of its supposed opposite, the medical model, which was represented as about individual deficits and needs that were identified by and under the control of professionals, who aimed to treat, remediate or ameliorate the impairment. By contrast, the social model located the causation of disability in the social conditions, the barriers to social participation rather than individual impairments, and used this analysis to instigate support to remove these barriers based on a human rights agenda.

Probably the best known initiative promoting inclusion in schools has been the Inclusion Index, a school self-auditing model which, though developed by academics and a voluntary advocacy group, was supported by government in its distribution to all schools (Booth *et al.* 2000). The model of inclusion in the Index has been 'the participation of all pupils in the cultures, curricula and communities of local schools' (Booth *et al.* 2000: 3). A related model of inclusive education has identified several dimensions of inclusive education – presence, social and academic participation and achievement (Ainscow 1999). This multidimensional model has been used to promote a wider concept of inclusion that goes beyond placement but, as will be discussed below, it is the breadth of its coverage which has exposed the inclusion movement to uncertainties and challenge.

The inclusion and disability rights 'movements' have been a powerful and positive force in practice for challenging negative attitudes to pupils with SEN and disabilities in education and improving access to facilities and teaching programmes in ordinary schools and classrooms (Shakespeare 2006). The Inclusion Index has also made it possible to identify gaps in the cultures, curricula and communities of schools with respect to the participation of all pupils, but has been silent about the mechanisms for initiating and sustaining radical systemic change within the competitive and meritocratic kind of society that exists in the UK. The vision of inclusion, how it has been expressed and its underlying assumptions have also generated debates and many questions. For some, inclusive education evokes tensions between idealism and realism as life orientations (Pirrie and Head 2007), in response to the image of inclusion as a continuing struggle and process that has no destination or end point (Naylor 2005). For others, representing inclusion as basically different from integration misrepresents the various dimensions of integration (locational, social and functional) and proposes an over-socialized model of SEN and disability that ignores how the personal and biological interact with the social in education (Norwich 2008).

There were risks in replacing integration by inclusion and not engaging with integration issues. Inclusion-as-participation has therefore tended to operate as an abstract and all-encompassing value commitment detached from other values and practical considerations. The debates about locational integration in the 1980s centred partly on the experiences of stigma and devaluation associated with going to special schools, and partly on the poor quality of provision available in these schools. The argument for integration was that without clear evidence of the learning advantages of special schools, and given the commitment to equality of opportunities, the presumption was towards ordinary schools (Galloway and Goodwin 1987). However, research reviews about learning outcomes over the last few decades have been interpreted as indicating no clear support for the positive academic or social effects of either supported mainstream or separate schooling (Lindsay 2007).

Policy developments and national statistics about placement

Following the Warnock Report (DES 1978) the then Conservative government adopted a policy of integration legislated in the 1981 Education Act. All children with special educational needs were to be educated in ordinary schools, subject to several key conditions:

1   that the child's special needs are met;

2   that others' education was not disrupted by integration arrangements;

3   that parents were supportive; and

4   that the arrangements were consistent with the 'efficient use of resources'.

This legislative formulation is central to the English system as it expresses, on one hand, that the priority is for all to be in the common school, but on the other qualifies this by setting up a balance of interests. This is a balance between the ordinary school priority and the interests of the key stakeholders, if these happen to be against an ordinary school placement: the child (getting the needed provision), their peers (not having their education disrupted), the child's parents (placement preference) and the local authority (which carries final responsibility for provision to use its resources efficiently). It is notable that the legislative system thirty years later still has the same form of priority and balancing. Back in the 1980s the framework made it possible to have a mixed model of provision, where special schools could still exist but there was also scope for increasing provision in ordinary schools without a commitment to closing all special schools. But the framework of balances is also open to change by altering the factors that are weighed in the balance. This is what the Labour government did in the 2001 Special Educational Needs and Disability Act by removing two of the four above factors in line with its increased commitment to inclusive education. The child must be educated in a mainstream school unless that is incompatible with:

1   the wishes of his or her parent; or

2   the provision of efficient education for other children.

Removing the two conditions (provision that meets individual special needs and efficient use of local authority resources) shows the higher priority given to the remaining ones about parental preferences or negative effects on other pupils (a position strongly endorsed by teacher professional associations and unions).

Providing for more children with special educational needs in ordinary schools has been underpinned by what has been internationally known as a continuum of provision (Pijl *et al.* 1997). This continuum has taken various forms, but has mainly concerned the range of placements, from the most separate to the most integrated into ordinary settings. Figure 5.1 is one way of representing this continuum.

> • **Full-time residential special school**
> • **Full-time day special school**
> • **Part-time special – part-time ordinary school**
> • **Full-time special unit or class in ordinary school**
> • **Part-time special unit/class – part-time ordinary class**
> • **Full-time in ordinary class with some withdrawal and some in-class support**
> • **Full-time in ordinary class with in-class support**
> • **Full-time in ordinary class**

Figure 5.1 Continuum of special education provision

From 1983 (when the 1981 SEN legislation came into operation) until 2001, there was a decrease in the percentage of children in English special schools, from 1.87 per cent to 1.30 per cent (Norwich 2002). The decrease was greater in the 1980s than the 1990s, with an overall percentage decrease of about 0.5 per cent. Those figures took account of state-funded special schools as well as non-state- and independent-funded special schools. More recent statistics do not include all of the non-state-funded schools, so the proportions reported from 2000 are slightly lower. Since 2000 the trend (using the more conservative count) has been for the proportion to be about 1.1 per cent and it has remained at that level until now (Ofsted 2010).

These figures suggest that despite the reduction of the special school population in the 1980s and 1990s, this trend has not continued even during a period from 1997–2010 when the Labour government made a strong commitment towards more inclusive education. Though the number of special schools has reduced by about 9 per cent from 1161 in 2002 to 1054 in 2010 (DFE 2011), the actual number of pupils in special schools has increased from 89,390 in 2006 to 90,760 in 2010 (DFE 2011). Put together these figures indicate a reduction of special schools, perhaps through reorganization into larger schools, but no notable decrease in the proportion of pupils in these schools.

In England, special educational needs is identified at three levels depending on who does the identification and broad severity. For the most severe needs this is done by local authorities who issue Statements, which ensure legally the provision set out in a record of needs and provision following a multidisciplinary assessment of the pupil. At the other two levels, needs are identified by ordinary schools, called School Action (by internal support staff such as the SEN co-ordinator) and School Action plus levels (when outside support services become involved too). Figure 5.2 shows the most recent statistics of the national incidence for these levels.

While the incidence in special schools has flattened out, there have been notable changes in the incidence of the SEN levels since the 1988 legislation that introduced the National Curriculum and the intensive national system of tests (Standard Assessment Tests). It is these tests which provided the attainment data that went into

	%
School Action	11.4
School Action plus	6.2
Statements	2.7
Statements and in special school	1.1

Figure 5.2 Incidence of SEN in relation to special school placement (as per cent of total English school population)
Source: DFE 2011

the school league tables. School funding also became based on pupil numbers, so completing the elements of a more market-oriented school system. As these systems came into operation, the proportion of pupils issued with Statements rose to about 3 per cent, as schools were less willing to provide for them without the resources made available from a Statement, and school exclusions for behavioural problems and misconduct increased notably.

England has been characterized as having a multi-tracked system of special education provision (Pijl *et al.* 1997), one with various degrees of separation of provision from the mainstream track, in line with the placement continuum outlined above. A multi-tracked system is contrasted with a dual track one, where the special system runs in parallel to the general or mainstream one and where there are few links between them. It is interesting, however, that the pattern of placement for pupils with Statements (the 2.7 per cent) shows a very low proportion of pupils in resourced units or provision in ordinary schools (6.8 per cent: see Figure 5.3) (Ofsted 2010).

Not only are mainstream units rare, but also the partnership between mainstream schools and special schools over curriculum and teaching has been the exception rather than the rule (Ofsted 2004, 2006). The latter report also drew conclusions based on inspection evidence about whether it mattered where pupils were taught. The conclusions were that the co-location of special schools on mainstream sites gave good opportunities for pupils with SEN to mix with their non-SEN peers, but no more than when there were resourced SEN units in mainstream schools. The report also concluded that the best outcomes for pupils with SEN depended not on the *type* of provision (placement) but on the *quality* of provision in the placement. This meant that effective provision was found in both special and mainstream schools. However, the inspectors also found more 'good' and 'outstanding' provision in resourced mainstream schools than elsewhere. The picture that emerges from these Ofsted reports

	%
• Government-funded mainstream schools	46.1
• SEN or resourced units in mainstream schools	6.8
• Government-funded special schools	37.2
• Independent special schools	5.6
• Pupil referral units (outside mainstream schools)	0.7
• Other	4.0

Figure 5.3 Percentage of pupils with Statements in different types of provision
Source: Ofsted 2010

was one that, though the English system is multi-tracked, it is an under-developed multi-tracked system, which resembles aspects of a dual track system.

Current inclusive practices

There is not space in this chapter to examine what research has contributed to our knowledge and understanding of inclusive provision in the UK (England), but it is relevant to the chapter to use the findings of a recent government-funded project (Dyson *et al.* 2004) to illustrate the recent pattern of schools that are assessed to be inclusive. As part of a wider analysis of inclusion and school attainment statistics, these authors conducted case studies of 16 primary and secondary schools which were identified nationally as being highly inclusive (some had additional resourced units for SEN and disability and some not). Of these 16 schools, 12 (six primary and six secondary) were also identified as high-attaining schools and four were lower attaining. The case studies examined how highly inclusive schools produced high levels of attainments, what strategies and forms of organization they used and how these schools differ from equally inclusive schools which do not generate such high attainments. The conclusions were that both higher and lower inclusive attaining schools operated similar models of provision. What is also of much interest is that case study research was used to identify a model of highly inclusive schools (see Figure 5.4).

What is notable about the model is that it involves the flexible use of mainstream and withdrawal settings for teaching and learning, that decisions were based on personal/individual assessment and that flexibility depends not only on additional funding for these pupils but the commitment of the school to using resources effectively. Also, these schools were committed to raising achievement and there was a sense of the practical challenges in educating a diversity of pupils. A final comment that is relevant to this model of inclusive provision is that the model is of schools that do not provide for the full range of pupils with SEN and disabilities in their communities, as some pupils would go to special schools and not these schools.

1 Provision for pupils with special educational needs tends to be characterised by flexibility.
2 This customisation of provision depends on careful assessment, planning and monitoring at an individual level.
3 Flexible provision is typically supported by the careful use of adult support.
4 Flexibility of provision is paralleled by flexibility of pedagogy in mainstream classes and by high-quality teaching in non-mainstream situations.
5 Schools typically have a commitment to the principle of inclusion which is shared by a large proportion of the staff.
6 Alongside strategies directed towards pupils with SEN, high-performing schools also have strategies directed towards raising achievement more generally.

Figure 5.4 Model of inclusive provision
Source: Dyson *et al.* 2004: 97

Debates about inclusion

The current debates about inclusion in education in England reflect differing policy orientations expressive of distinct ideological and political commitments. Though there was during the Labour period of government a consensus about using the term inclusion and inclusive education, the different and conflicting perspectives and conceptions were often obscured. Though the last Labour government defined inclusion as about 'the quality of a child's experience and providing access to the high quality education which enables them to progress with their learning and participate fully in the activities of their school and community' (DfES 2006, section 28), this was not the view in the Inclusion Index which the government had distributed to all schools. For the Inclusion Index, inclusive education was about: 'the participation in the cultures, curricula and communities of *local schools*' (Booth *et al.* 2000: 3; italics added).

For the government, inclusive education was not about all pupils being in local mainstream schools, but about access to quality education, progress in learning and participation in their school, whether it was an ordinary or special school. The problem is that this DfES definition was consistent with an emphasis on an *inclusive system*, which could involve special schools, rather than *fully inclusive ordinary schools*.

What has bedevilled the use of the inclusion concept in education has been its multidimensional nature and the inability to find common ground between interest groups over its dimensions. This can be brought out by reference to Ainscow's formulation of inclusion in terms of the dimensions of presence, participation and achievement (Ainscow 1999). The multidimensional aspects make it hard to know how to use the term, unless people qualify its use (for example, to say placement inclusion or participation inclusion), which has mostly not been the case. This affects both the everyday use by parents and teachers, as well as policy makers in schools, local authorities and central government. This problem was recognized in the House of Commons Education Select Committee Report on Special Educational Needs (House of Commons 2006). The Select Committee urged the government to work harder to define exactly what it means by inclusion (House of Commons 2006), but the government in its response only came up with the definition set out above (DfES 2006).

A further instance of this issue is that if inclusion is about academic and social participation in local ordinary schools, it is still unclear whether 'participation in local schools' implies and requires children with special educational needs and disabilities to be in ordinary classrooms for most or all of their learning. The Centre for the Study of Inclusive Education (CSIE), a pressure group associated with the Inclusion Index, accepted in its Charter that some children with special educational needs could spend *part of their time* outside the ordinary classroom:

> Time spent out of the ordinary classroom for appropriate individual or group work on a part-time basis is not segregation. Neither is removal for therapy or because of disruption, provided it is time-limited, for a specified purpose . . . Any time-out from the ordinary classroom should not affect a student's right to full membership of the mainstream.
>
> (Thomas and Vaughn 2004: 137)

This concession to part-time withdrawal raises a further question. Are part-time placements in off-site settings for appropriate and time-limited learning compatible with inclusive education, if the children are still members of ordinary schools and classes? This specific CSIE position could be seen as a step towards justifying separation, and shows an interconnection between included and separate provision.

The most significant recent challenge to contemporary ideas and practice associated with inclusive education came from Mary Warnock, chair of the 1978 government committee that endorsed integration. She rejected educational inclusion as being 'all children under the same roof', preferring a learning concept of inclusion, which is about 'including all children in the common educational enterprise of learning, wherever they learn best' (Warnock 2005). Her perspective on inclusion can be seen to prioritize engagement in learning over placement, a view which has also been recently proposed for the area of education of pupils with social, emotional and behaviour difficulties by Cooper and Jacobs (2011). Research also shows that some teachers working in separate settings see a degree of withdrawal to a separate setting as being inclusive in the sense of making it possible for certain children to engage in learning the same curriculum as other children (Norwich 2008).

The Labour government towards the end of its period of office focused resources on 'closing the gap in achievement between pupils with special educational needs and disability and those without'. This was the largest single funded initiative in this field in the UK, Achievement for All (involving about £30 million invested to promote developments in 10 local authority mainstream schools). This programme showed that the Labour government's inclusion priority was on achievement rather than other aspects of inclusion, reflecting the overriding Labour educational policy priority from 1997 to 2010. During the mid-2000s the Conservative Party was developing policy in favour of more special schools, as shown by a statement from its Policy Commission on Special Needs in Education:

> . . . closing special schools and sending large numbers of children with special education needs to mainstream schools has caused great distress. This is why we need to recreate many more special school places.
>
> (Conservative Party 2007: 4)

The recent coalition government SEN Green Paper (DFE 2011) has picked up this line of policy by proposing to 'remove the bias towards inclusion', which is portrayed as obstructing parents' choice and leading to the unnecessary closure of special schools. As some commentators have noted, the supposed bias to inclusion has been more in policy stance and the signing of international conventions than actual provision and placements (Lamb 2011: see figures above). Coalition policies also need to be seen within their general stance to public services, which is a move towards increasing consumer-led market models. This involves increasing parental choice for a diversity of competing providers (schools), including state-funded autonomous schools (so called independent 'free schools' and Academies).

Conclusion

How inclusion is done in England is similar in some key respects to how it is done in many other western countries, but different given its particular historical, political and cultural traditions (Norwich 2008). There have been changes at the practical level, where there is some consensus about or acceptance of social and political changes, while political and ideological debates and conflicts still persist. Cigman (2007) has characterized the differences over inclusion in education as the difference between universal and moderate inclusion. In Cigman's analysis, 'moderates' see inclusive education as compatible with, and indeed as requiring, the existence of 'special schools' for a small number of children. By contrast 'universalists' tend to be antagonistic to such schools, seeing them as threatening the project of universal inclusion. This is a useful distinction, but perhaps better framed as a continuum: between universal inclusion at one pole and optimal inclusion at the other pole. Positions can be taken up along this continuum; more towards universal or more towards optimal inclusion. I also find Cigman's analysis of the underlying issue in inclusion to be useful: that the debates are about what is possible. In education this is the possibility of fundamental transformation of schools to respond to all differences and that categories of difference (such as special educational needs or disability) can be abandoned, as they are socially constructed and therefore not 'real'. In this analysis 'universalists' tend to hold on to the promise of possibility, while 'moderates' do not.

It can be argued that 'optimal' inclusion is a preferable term to 'moderate' inclusion because it recognizes the need to balance some of the dimensions associated with inclusion (placement, participation, belonging and achievement). It is also compatible with recognizing that there are other values as well as tensions between values relevant to education and society generally that require some optimal resolution. These value tensions cannot be transformed away, from this perspective, but can be resolved through finding settlements that combine values optimally in variable social and economic circumstances. These involve basic tensions between:

- choice and equity (Clarke *et al.* 2010);
- stigma avoidance (respect) and equity (positive difference) (Minow 1990); and
- meritocracy and solidarity (Anderson 1999).

These are critical areas in wider social policy development which cannot be discussed further in this brief chapter. However, it is clear that the prospects for inclusion in education as regards special educational needs and disability depend crucially on these values and policy formulations. Though there are continuing points of contention, these debates and conflicts should not obscure where there is common ground in the political settlements that exist in England and no doubt in other countries too. It is likely that progress will depend on finding common ground as social and economic circumstances change. This is more likely if those involved engage constructively with others who hold different perspectives. Though constructive dialogue is in short supply currently in inclusion policy, there is still some longer term prospect that it can be achieved.

Notes

1   Solidarity is taken to mean the integration, and degree and type of integration, shown by a society or group with people and their neighbours. It refers to the ties in a society – social relations – that bind people to one another.
2   A Government policy paper setting out aims and ideas for future policy and legislation.
3   Education policy and practice is devolved in the UK, so that differences have emerged between the nations making up the UK. This chapter relates specifically to policy and practice in England.

References

Ainscow, M. (1999) *Understanding the Development of Inclusive Schools*. London: Falmer Press.

Ainscow, M., Booth, T. and Dyson, A. (2006) *Improving Schools, Developing Inclusion*. Abingdon: Routledge.

Anderson, J. (1999) Post-industrial solidarity or meritocracy, *Acta Sociologica*, 41 (4): 375–85.

Avramidis, E. and Norwich, B. (2011) *SEN: The State of Research – Compromise, Consensus or Disarray?* London: Open University Press.

Black, A. (2009) Pupils in secondary special schools in England. Masters dissertation, University of Exeter.

Booth, T., Ainscow, M., Black-Hawkins, K., Vaughn, M. and Shaw, L. (2000) *Index for Inclusion: Developing Learning and Participation in Schools*. Bristol: CSIE.

Cigman, R. (2007) *Included or Excluded? The Challenge of the Mainstream for Some Special Educational Needs Children*. London: Routledge.

Clarke, J., Newman, J. and McDermont, M. (2010) Delivering choice and administering justice: contested logics of public services, in M. Adler (ed.) *Administrative Justice in Context*. Oxford: Hart Publishing.

Conservative Party (2007) *Commission on Special Needs in Education*. Available at: http://www.conservatives.com/tile.do?def=news.story.page&obj_id=137766 [Accessed on 23 May 2011].

Cooper, P. and Jacobs, B. (2011) *From Inclusion to Engagement: Helping Students Engage with Schooling Through Policy and Practice*. London: Wiley.

DES (Department of Education and Science) (1978) *Special Educational Needs: Report of the Committee of Enquiry into the Education of Handicapped Children and Young People* (Warnock Report). London: HMSO.

DFE (Department for Education) (2011) *SEN Green Paper: Support and Aspiration – A New Approach to Special Educational Needs and Disability*. London: DFE.

DfES (Department for Education and Skills) (1997) *SEN Green Paper: Excellence for All*. London: DfES.

DfES (2006) *Government Response to Education and Skills Committee Report on Special Education Needs*. London: DfES.

Dyson, A., Farrell, P., Polat, F., Hutcheson, G. and Gallannaugh, F. (2004) *Inclusion and Pupil Achievement Research Report 578*. London: DfES.

Galloway, D. and Goodwin, C. (1987) *The Education of Disturbing Children: Pupils With Learning and Adjustment Difficulties*. London: Longman.

Honneth, A. (1996) *The Struggle for Recognition: Moral Grammar of Social Conflicts*. Bristol: The Policy Press.

House of Commons Education and Skills Committee (2006) *Special Educational Needs. Third Report of Session 2005–06*. London: The Stationery Office.

Lamb, B. (2011) Support and aspiration – cultural revolution or pragmatic evolution?, *Journal of Research in Special Educational Needs* (in press).

Lindsay, G. (2007) Educational psychology and the effectiveness of inclusion/mainstreaming, *British Journal of Educational Psychology*, 77: 1–29.

Minow, M. (1990) *Making All the Difference: Inclusion, Exclusion, and American Law*. Ithica, NY: Cornell University Press.

Naylor, C. (2005) *Inclusion in British Columbia's public schools: always a journey, never a destination?* Paper presented to Canadian Teachers' Federation Conference, Building Inclusive Schools: A Search for Solutions, 17–19 November, Ottawa.

Norwich, B. (2002) *Special School Placement and Statements for English LEAs 1997–2001*. Report for CSIE, University of Exeter.

Norwich, B. (2008) *Dilemmas of Difference, Inclusion and Disability: International Perspectives and Future Directions*. London: Routledge.

Ofsted (2004) *Special Educational Needs and Disability: Towards Inclusive Schools*. London: Ofsted.

Ofsted (2006) *Inclusion: Does It Matter Where Pupils Are Taught? Provision and Outcomes in Different Settings for Pupils with Learning Difficulties and Disabilities*. London: Ofsted.

Ofsted (2010) *SEN and Disability Review*. London: Ofsted.

Oliver, M. (1996) *Understanding Disability: From Theory to Practice*. Basingstoke: Macmillan.

Pijl, S.J., Meijer, C.J.W. and Hegarty, S. (eds) (1997) *Inclusive Education: A Global Agenda*. London: Routledge.

Pirrie, A. and Head, G. (2007) Martians in the playground: researching special educational needs, *Oxford Review of Education*, 33: 19–31.

Power, A. and Wilson, W.J. (2000) *Social Exclusion and the Future of Cities*, CASE Paper 35. London: Centre for Analysis of Social Exclusion.

Shakespeare, T. (2006) *Disability Rights and Wrongs*. London: Routledge.

Thomas, G. and Vaughn, M. (2004) *Inclusive Education: A Reader*. Maidenhead: Open University Press.

UNESCO (1994) *The Salamanca Statement and Framework for Action on Special Needs Education*. Paris: UNESCO.

Warnock, M. (2005) *Special Educational Needs: A New Look*. London: Philosophy of Education Society of Great Britain, Impact Series N11.

6

SPENCER SALEND AND CATHARINE WHITTAKER
Inclusive education: best practices in the United States

Introduction

A variety of historical, philosophical and socio-cultural factors including legislative mandates and legal decisions have contributed to the growth of inclusive education in the United States (Salend 2011). Although the definition and implementation of inclusive education varies across different regions and local educational agencies within the United States, this chapter presents best practices for creating inclusive education classrooms that can have a positive impact on students, educators and families. In identifying and discussing the best practices, research-based studies have been cited as well as current policies for implementing inclusive education in the United States. Although these best practices are supported by research, the studies are not longitudinal, often lack random selection and assignment of students, and have small sample sizes (Sindelar *et al.* 2006). Therefore, practice-based evidence related to the data collected and experiences reported by educators and students about what works in their inclusive education classrooms has also been cited (Maheady and Gard 2010).

Best practice: implement Response-to-Intervention (RtI) systems

In the United States, there has been an over-identification of students with socially constructed disabilities being served in special education which, coupled with the intersection of issues of class, gender, age, language, background and geography, has resulted in the persistent problem of disproportionate representation of students from culturally and linguistically diverse backgrounds (Artiles *et al.* 2010; Sullivan 2011). To address over-identification and disproportionate representation, schools have implemented Response-to-Intervention (RtI) systems, a multi-tiered identification and instructional model for determining the extent to which students respond to more intensive and individualized research-based interventions to succeed in inclusive educational classrooms (Fuchs and Fuchs 2007). The RtI model involves:

- universal screening of all students;
- identification of students needing more intensive instruction;
- tiered instruction based on a sequence of more intensive interventions;
- fidelity in the implementation of interventions;
- collaboration among educators;
- progress monitoring to assess students' response to interventions and to make adjustments in the instructional programme; and
- identification for special education of students who do not respond to effective interventions (Fuchs and Fuchs 2007).

Best practice: develop Individualised Education Programmes (IEPs) tailored to students' strengths and challenges

If students are identified as needing special education, an Individualized Education Programme (IEP) is developed listing the special education and related services they will receive to address their unique academic, social, behavioural, communication, functional and physical strengths and challenges. The IEP also contains several components designed to help students with disabilities access the general education curriculum and succeed in inclusive education classrooms (Gibbs and Dyches 2007). In addition to these components, the IEP should address factors related to students' behaviour, English language proficiency, and visual and hearing abilities.

Best practice: adopt a competency-oriented approach

Educators create an effective inclusive learning environment by engaging in teaching behaviours, language and interactions that focus on students' strengths and similarities rather than their challenges and differences (Smith 2009; Connor 2011). Such a competency-oriented approach is adopted by educators when they:

- view all students as multidimensional individuals with unique strengths, backgrounds, challenges and talents;
- refer to students in terms of what they can do and who they are rather than in relation to the things with which they have difficulty;
- use inclusive language and individuals' first language and refrain from using terms associated with pity, suffering and notions of normality (e.g. *handicapped, crippled, afflicted, suffering from, victim of, normal,* or *able-bodied*), or which focus on students' struggles (*dropouts* or *disadvantaged*) (Russell 2008);
- affirm important aspects of who students are, how they define themselves, and how they experience the world. For example, rather than ignoring a student's wheelchair use, recognize and accept it as an essential part of the student's life experience (Salend 2011);
- acknowledge students and their similarities and accomplishments; and

- support students' individuality, independence and self-determination. Offer assistance only when necessary, and avoid behaviours that embarrass students and hinder social interactions (Giangreco and Broer 2007; Smith 2009; Swedeen 2009; Connor 2011; Salend 2011).

Best practice: foster acceptance of individual differences, diversity, friendships and peer supports

Promoting the acceptance of individual differences, diversity and friendships among students are desired outcomes of effective inclusive education programmes (Meadan and Monda-Amaya 2008; Smith 2009). However, rather than assuming that students appreciate diversity and their classmates' individual differences, effective inclusive educators provide learning experiences that teach students to respect and learn from each other's similarities and differences and facilitate friendships and peer supports (Bacharach 2011; Salend 2011).

Promoting acceptance of individual differences and diversity

Effective inclusive educators use a variety of strategies to foster acceptance of individual differences and diversity and replace inappropriate stereotypes with meaningful information related to students and the supports that foster their inclusion (Smith 2009). These strategies include using guest speakers, videos, books and literature, and curriculum guides related to a range of individual differences (Salend 2011). In choosing strategies, educators need to consider the extent to which the strategy teaches meaningful and non-stereotypical information, and fosters follow-up learning experiences and actions that students can take to support their classmates (Meadan and Monda-Amaya 2008; Smith 2009).

Facilitating friendships and peer supports

Educators also need to use a variety of strategies that facilitate friendships and peer supports (Meadan and Monda-Amaya 2008; Smith 2009; Swedeen 2009). Toward this end, effective educators structure the learning environment so that all students have ongoing opportunities to collaborate, interact and establish equal-status relationships (Swedeen 2009). Equal-status relationships among students can also be encouraged by teaching about friendships and social networks, offering social skill instruction, using circles of friends and community-building activities (Zambo 2010; Salend 2011). Educators also foster peer supports by employing positive peer reporting, peer mentoring, buddy and partner systems, and peer support committees (Chadsey and Gun Han 2005; Fenty *et al.* 2008; Salend 2011).

Best practice: collaborate and communicate with professionals and family members

A key component of effective inclusive education programmes is good collaboration and communication among educators and family members (Dettmer *et al.* 2009). Ongoing collaboration and communication can foster a mutual commitment that supports student learning and strengthens the link between home and school (Swedeen 2009).

Teaching collaboratively

Many inclusive education classrooms are structured so that educators work in co-teaching arrangements, where educators teach together and share all instructional, assessment, grading, classroom management, family involvement and clerical roles (Friend and Cook 2010; Murawski and Lochner 2011). As presented in Table 6.1, co-teaching teams use a variety of teaching arrangements depending on their instructional goals, the expertise and roles of the teachers, and the characteristics of their students (Salend 2011).

Co-teaching teams report that the lack of planning time, administrative support, resources and professional preparation coupled with undefined roles and scheduling difficulties are barriers to successful co-teaching (Villa *et al.* 2008; Murawski and Lochner 2011). Achieving an equal status relationship so that both team members perform meaningful roles in the classroom also serves as a major challenge (Simmons and Magiera 2007). For instance, if one team member always functions in the role of instructional leader while the other team member typically provides support, the

Table 6.1 Co-teaching arrangements

Co-teaching arrangement	Co-teaching roles	Instructional purposes
One teaching/one helping	One educator teaches the whole class and the other educator moves around the classroom to monitor and assist students	To use the expertise of one educator to teach content and the services of the other educator to provide individual support
Parallel teaching	Both educators simultaneously teach similar content to equivalent groups	To teach new content or review and practise previously taught content in smaller groups
Station teaching	Both educators simultaneously teach different content to equivalent groups and then switch groups to teach the same content	To teach or review content that is difficult but not sequential, or different topics, information or terminology
Alternative teaching	One educator offers instruction to a smaller group or individual students while the other educator teaches a larger group	To individualize instruction, remediate skills, promote mastery/automaticity, or offer enrichment
Team teaching	Both educators plan and perform varied roles in teaching the whole class	To integrate the teaching skills and content expertise of both group members

Sources: Villa *et al.* (2008); Friend and Cook (2010); Salend (2011)

effectiveness of the team is limited. Therefore, effective co-teaching teams work toward establishing compatibility and parity by communicating regularly to identify and evaluate goals, address problems, plan instruction, share administrative and instructional responsibilities, learn new approaches, meet with families, and foster and assess student learning (Villa et al. 2008; Friend and Cook 2010; Murawski and Lochner 2011).

Collaborating and communicating with families

Collaborating and communicating with family members is an essential ingredient of successful inclusive education classrooms. To support this collaboration with families, it is important for educators to gain their trust, advocate for them and their children, protect and respect their legal rights and confidentiality, and provide them with educational programmes that enhance their active involvement in their children's education (Salend 2011). Additionally, effective educators use a variety of oral, written and technology-based strategies to maintain ongoing communication with families about aspects of inclusive education and the learning progress of their children.

In collaborating and communicating with families, it is important for educators to accommodate families' diverse strengths, challenges, beliefs, cultural, linguistic and experiential backgrounds, and resources (Harry 2008; Dettmer et al. 2009). For instance, effective inclusive educators adjust their styles and services to accommodate cross-cultural communication differences, and socio-economic factors (e.g. varied work schedules, transportation and childcare issues).

Best practice: implement a comprehensive and balanced classroom management plan that is consistent with the school's positive behavioural intervention and supports

For students to succeed in inclusive education classrooms, their behaviours should enhance their learning and social relationships, which can be fostered by educators implementing a comprehensive and balanced classroom management plan (Salend 2011). Such a plan recognizes the link between positive behaviours and effective instruction, and includes a range of strategies for fostering students' positive behaviours (see Table 6.2).

School-Wide Positive Behavioural Interventions and Supports (SWPBIS)

A teacher's classroom management plan should be consistent with the School-Wide Positive Behavioural Interventions and Supports (SWPBIS) (Sugai et al. 2008). SWPBIS systems alter the pedagogical practices and the characteristics of the learning environments to minimize problem behaviours and aid students in developing the behaviours that help them succeed in inclusive classrooms. Anti-bullying efforts to address all forms of bullying are also integral aspects of an SWPBIS. Like RtI systems, SWPBIS are implemented in tiers, which provide a continuum of academic, behavioural and social interventions and supports based on data related to students' responses to them.

Table 6.2 Interventions for fostering students' positive behaviours

Interventions	Description	Implementation in inclusive classrooms
Relationship-building strategies	Techniques for establishing meaningful and genuine caring relationships with and among your students	• Demonstrate a personal interest in students • Develop students' self-esteem • Acknowledge and praise students • Engage in appropriate verbal and non-verbal communication • Use affective education techniques • Employ conflict resolution and peer-mediated programmes
Social skills instruction	Techniques for explicitly teaching the behaviours that foster socialization among students	• Teach social skills via use of modelling, self-modelling, role playing, prompting, scripting, learning strategies, literature, social stories and power cards • Use social skills curricula
Antecedent-based strategies	Techniques for making changes in classroom events, environment and stimuli that precede behaviours	• Design the classroom to support teaching, learning, socialization and positive behaviours • Give clear and direct directions • Establish, teach and enforce rules • Use prompting and teacher proximity and movement • Follow routines • Help students make transitions
Self-management strategies	Techniques where students are actively involved in monitoring, evaluating and changing their behaviours	• Teach students to use self-recording, self-evaluation, self-reinforcement, self-managed free token systems, and self-instruction
Group-oriented management strategies	Techniques that employ group and peer influence to foster positive behaviour and decrease inappropriate behaviour	• Use interdependent group strategies where the contingency is applied to and based on the performance of the whole group (e.g. group free token systems, group randomized systems, good behaviour game, group evaluation) • Use independent group strategies where the contingency is applied to all students based on their own performance (e.g. token systems)

Sources: Austin and Sciarra (2010); Maheady and Jabot (2010); Rafferty (2010); Salend (2011)

Functional Behavioural Assessment (FBA) and Behavioural Intervention Plan (BIP)

Important aspects of SWPBIS systems also include a Functional Behavioural Assessment (FBA) and a Behavioural Intervention Plan (BIP). An FBA is a student-centred, multimethod, problem-solving process that involves gathering information to:

- define and assess student problem behaviours;
- determine why, where and when a student engages in these behaviours;
- identify the academic, instructional, social, affective, cultural, environmental and contextual factors that seem to trigger and maintain the behaviours; and
- plan appropriate interventions to change the behaviours and address the purposes they serve for students (Chandler and Dahlquist 2010).

Based on the functions of the behaviour identified via the FBA process, a BIP is developed to change student behaviour by implementing instructional and behavioural strategies and modifying the classroom environment (Austin and Sciarra 2010; Salend 2011).

Best practice: differentiate instruction and incorporate the principles of Universal Design for Learning (UDL)

Differentiated instruction

Effective inclusive educators use differentiated instruction to link curriculum, instruction and assessment to accommodate the learning strengths and challenges of their students (Tomlinson 2005; Van Garderen and Whittaker 2006). Differentiation occurs within one or more of the following five classroom elements: content, process, product, affect and learning environment. Table 6.3 provides definitions of these elements and examples of how effective educators can implement them in their inclusive classrooms.

Table 6.3 Definitions and examples of the elements of differentiated instruction

Elements of differentiated instruction	Inclusive education classroom examples
Content: what is taught and how access to the information is fostered	• Provide digital texts at a variety of reading levels • Give students guided notes • Employ varied examples, referents and illustrations related to student interest and backgrounds • Use multilingual materials • Bookmark a variety of internet sites

Process: how students understand and 'own' the knowledge and skills taught	• Use peer-mediated instruction • Highlight critical information in text • Use tiered assignments that present content at various levels of complexity • Teach students to use a wide variety of presentation formats
Product: how students demonstrate what they know, understand, can do, and need to learn	• Develop instructional rubrics and individualized learning challenges • Create assessments that have a real world goal, an active student role, audience, situation, product and criteria, and employ technology • Provide students with appropriate testing accommodations
Affect: how students link their thoughts and feelings in the classroom	• Adopt a competency-based approach • Help students examine multiple perspectives on topics • Ensure equitable participation of all students
Learning environment: how the classroom supports students' learning, behaviour and socialization	• Arrange classroom to allow for large-group, small-group and individual work • Make a variety of supplies available • Establish procedures for working on different tasks

Source: Adapted from Van Garderen and Whittaker (2006)

Universal Design for Learning

Educators who effectively differentiate their instruction incorporate the principles of Universal Design for Learning (UDL) to support and assess their students' learning (Salend 2011). UDL provides educators with a framework for fostering student learning by providing multiple means of:

- *representation*, which involves using a range of options for presenting information and materials so that all students can access and understand them (e.g. use combinations of graphic organizers, video-and audio-based instructional materials, models);

- *expression*, which involves providing all students with a range of response options for demonstrating their learning and mastery of content (e.g. use combinations of story webs, outlining tools and concept-mapping tools, technology-based projects, and co-operative learning); and

- *engagement*, which involves employing a range of teaching behaviours, devices and strategies to prompt and encourage all students to perform at their optimal levels and be actively involved throughout the learning process (e.g. use combinations of providing student choices, linking instruction to students' backgrounds and interests, prompting students to use learning strategies and self-management techniques, and employing peer-mediated and technology-based instruction) (Kurtts *et al.* 2009).

Best practice: employ instructional and assistive technologies

Technological advances have led to development of a range of instructional and assistive technologies that foster differentiated instruction, and facilitate the implementation of UDL (King-Sears 2009; Beard *et al.* 2011). In choosing appropriate technologies, educators need to consider the extent to which the technology aligns with their curriculum, instructional goals and educational philosophy as well as their students' strengths, challenges and preferences.

Instructional technologies

Recent and emerging instructional technologies provide teachers with a variety of ways to present content via multiple modalities (Beard *et al.* 2011). Digital multimedia, technology-based simulations and virtual learning experiences allow educators to create interactive, individualized and motivating universally designed experiences that link text, sound, animation, video and graphics (King-Sears 2009). Educators and students can also support the teaching and learning process by creating web pages and sites, blogs, podcasts, digital stories, WebQuests, and Tracks, and using Wikis (Salend 2009).

Assistive technologies

Many students with special needs can benefit from the use of high- and low-tech assistive devices that support their learning, socialization, behaviour, independence and communication in inclusive education classrooms (Beard *et al.* 2011; Salend 2011). For example, screen- and text-reading programmes, digitized books and materials, symbol-supported text and line guides can support students who struggle with reading. Similarly, word processing, spell checking, word cueing and prediction, symbol-supported writing and text organization programmes, and specialized writing tools can aid students who struggle with writing (Evmenova *et al.* 2010; Prest *et al.* 2010). Professionals should base the selection of assistive devices on an individualized technology assessment, which provides a process for choosing appropriate devices that students will use and not abandon.

Best practice: teach students to use a range of learning strategies

An integral aspect of differentiating instruction is teaching students to use a range of learning strategies, which are ways that 'a learner plans, executes, and evaluates his/her own performance on a learning task' (Schumaker and Deshler 2009: 83). Most learning strategies have relatively brief, sequenced steps that are organized around a mnemonic device designed to cue meta-cognitive functions that lead to positive educational outcomes. Research shows that learning strategies can improve students' reading (Gajria *et al.* 2007; Englert 2009), writing (Englert 2009; Graham and Harris 2009; Schumaker and Deshler 2009), mathematical performance (Montague and Dietz 2009), study skills (Strichart and Mangrum 2010), and social skills (Fenty *et al.* 2008). Since many students with special needs use inefficient and ineffective strategies, they can benefit from explicit learning strategy instruction (see Englert 2009; Graham and Harris 2009; Schumaker and Deshler 2009 for research-based models for teaching students to use learning strategies).

Best practice: use peer-mediated instruction

Effective inclusive educators differentiate instruction by using peer-mediated instruction, where students work collaboratively to accomplish a shared academic goal (Harper and Maheady 2007; Salend 2011). One form of peer-mediated instruction is co-operative learning, which has been shown to be effective in fostering friendships, self-esteem and the academic performance of students of varied academic abilities and different experiential, language and cultural backgrounds (Johnson and Johnson 2009). Co-operative learning activities have five components that distinguish them from group work: positive interdependence, individual accountability, face-to-face interactions, interpersonal skills, and group processing (Johnson and Johnson 2009).

A variety of peer-mediated instructional arrangements have been used effectively in inclusive education classrooms (see Table 6.4). In addition, the understanding of information presented during teacher-directed activities can be fostered by

Table 6.4 Peer-mediated instructional arrangements

Peer-mediated instructional arrangement	Description
Peer tutoring (Stenhoff and Lignugaris/Kraft 2007)	Students work in dyads and tutor and assist each other in learning new skills.
Class-wide peer tutoring (Harper and Maheady 2007)	Students work in teams with each teammate serving as a tutor and guiding the team in answering a teacher-prepared list of questions and awarding points to teammates. At the end of the week, teammates take individual tests and receive points based on their performance. Teams earn reinforcement based on the points they earned throughout the week.
Jigsaw (Ash *et al.* 2009)	Each group member is assigned a task that is essential to the group's project. Expert groups are formed by having a member of each group meet with peers from other groups who have been assigned the same subtask. The expert group members collaboratively complete their part of the assignment, which is then integrated into the original group's product.
Learning together (Johnson and Johnson 2009)	Students work in groups to complete one product, which is then evaluated and each group member receives the group grade.

having students work together via such collaborative discussion team strategies as Send a Problem, Numbered Heads Together and Think–Pair–Share (Harper and Maheady 2007).

Best practice: use culturally relevant and responsive instructional practices

Effective inclusive educators also differentiate their instruction by using instructional practices that are relevant and responsive to their students' experiences, cultural perspectives and language backgrounds (Klingner and Soltero-Gonzalez 2009). They use a multicultural curriculum as well as diverse instructional strategies and materials to establish meaningful connections between students' experiences and backgrounds and the content they are learning (Taylor and Whittaker 2009). For English language learners, inclusive educators use effective ESL and dual language practices such as total physical response, sheltered English, natural language approaches, and new vocabulary and concept instructional techniques (Klingner and Soltero-Gonzalez 2009; Echevarria *et al.* 2010; Salend 2011).

Best practice: use a range of assessment strategies to monitor student learning and inform teaching practices

Effective inclusive educators use a range of formative and summative assessment strategies (Salend 2009). They employ formative assessments to assess and support student learning, and examine and reflect on their teaching and the ways to improve it. They also employ summative assessments to document student learning and the outcomes associated with their inclusive classrooms. Using both forms of assessment, they evaluate the impact of their inclusive education classrooms on students, families and educators (Salend 2011). They also use these data to identify the strengths of their inclusive education classrooms as well as those aspects in need of revision.

A primary factor in assessing the impact of inclusive education classrooms is the extent to which the classroom fosters positive academic, affective, social, behavioural and attitudinal outcomes for their students (Goe *et al.* 2008). To examine the impact of their instruction on student learning, effective inclusive educators employ a range of classroom-based assessment techniques, which involve the use of learning products associated with daily classroom instruction. Thus, they use curriculum-based measurement, observations, performance assessment, active responding systems (i.e. clickers, dry erase boards, response cards), think-alouds, portfolio assessment and instructional rubrics to obtain a complete picture of their students' performance and learning progress (Salend 2009). Educators can supplement these data with other indicators of student progress such as graduation rates, attendance patterns, participation in extracurricular activities, behavioural referrals and course failures as well as student success in making the transition from school to adulthood (Salend 2011).

Changes in students' academic performance can also be documented via use of standardized and teacher-made tests. However, to assess students with special needs more accurately, effective inclusive educators provide many students with special needs with a range of appropriate testing accommodations including:

- *presentation mode testing accommodations*, which refer to changes in the way test questions and directions are presented to students;

- *response mode testing accommodations*, which refer to changes in the ways in which students respond to test questions or determine their answers;

- *timing, scheduling and setting testing accommodations*, which refer to adjustments with respect to where, when, with whom, and for how long and often students take tests; and

- *linguistically based testing accommodations*, which refer to ways to lessen the extent to which students' language proficiency hinder their test performance (Salend 2009).

The value of testing data and the test performance of students with special needs can also be enhanced by the creation of universally designed valid and accessible teacher-made tests, the teaching of effective study and test-taking skills to students, and the use of technology-based testing (Salend 2011).

Conclusion

Citing research-based studies and practice-based evidence, this chapter presented a summary of best practices supporting the successful implementation of inclusive education in the United States. While most schools in the United States have incorporated some of these practices, the degree of implementation varies, depending upon a variety of legal, economic and social factors. As a result, systemic reform that involves the co-ordination of governmental, district and school systems to support and sustain the use of these best practices remains an ongoing national challenge, especially in underfunded schools (Noguera 2006; Fullan 2009).

In order to address these barriers to successful inclusive education, school districts would benefit from a comprehensive self-assessment of the degree of implementation and efficacy of these best practices. Since the practices described in this chapter vary in scope (i.e. school-wide, programme, class, group, individual), focus (i.e. academic, socio-emotional, cultural, behavioural), and individuals involved (i.e. administrators, teachers, staff, students, family and community members), it also is critical that input amongst constituencies involved be solicited and acted upon. Furthermore, educators need to continuously monitor and reflect upon the impact of their instructional practices and tailor them to the unique characteristics of their students, classrooms, schools and communities (Maheady and Gard 2010).

Providing knowledge about best practices is one component of the complex process of educational change (Fullan 2006). The success of their implementation is dependent upon a variety of complex factors related to moral purpose, leadership, vertical and horizontal networking and capacity building, meaningful professional development, the local context, a commitment to short and long term, and cyclical re-energizing (Fullan 2006; Noguera 2006). There are some promising indications that the federal government in the United States is promoting initiatives that could promote sustainable educational change, but whether these initiatives will be supportive rather than punitive, systematic rather than localized, and inclusive of all populations, remains to be seen.

Note

Portions of this chapter were adapted from Salend, S. J. (2011) *Creating Inclusive Classrooms: Effective and Reflective Practices*. London: Pearson Education.

References

Artiles, A. J., Kozleski, E. B., Trent, S. C., Osher, D. and Ortiz, A. (2010) Justifying and explaining disproportionality, 1968–2008: a critique of underlying views of culture, *Exceptional Children*, 76: 279–99.

Ash, G. E., Kuhn, M. R. and Walpole, S. (2009) Analyzing 'inconsistencies' in practice: teachers' continued use of round robin reading, *Reading and Writing Quarterly*, 25(1): 87–103.

Austin, V. L. and Sciarra, D. T. (2010) *Children and Adolescents with Emotional and Behavioral Disorders*. Columbus, OH: Merrill/Prentice Hall.

Bacharach, L. (2011) Creating a classroom culture where diversity is the students' biggest asset, *School Talk*, 16(2): 4.

Beard, L. A., Bowden Carpenter, L. and Johnston, L. (2011) *Assistive Technology: Access for All Students*, 2nd edn. Columbus, OH: Merrill/Prentice Hall.

Chadsey, J. and Gun Han, K. (2005) Friendship-facilitation strategies: what do students in middle school tell us?, *TEACHING Exceptional Children*, 38(2): 52–7.

Chandler, L. K. and Dahlquist, C. M. (2010) *Functional Assessment: Strategies to Prevent and Remediate Challenging Behavior in School Settings*, 3rd edn. Columbus, OH: Merrill/Pearson Education.

Connor, D. J. (2011) Questioning 'normal': Seeing children first and labels second, *School Talk*, 16(2): 1–3.

Dettmer, P., Thurston, L. P., Knackendoffel, A. and Dyck, N. J. (2009) *Collaboration, Consultation, and Teamwork for Students with Special Needs*, 6th edn. Columbus, OH: Merrill/Pearson Education.

Echevarria, J. A., Vogt, M. J. and Short, D. J. (2010) *Making Content Comprehensible for Secondary English Learners: The SIOP Model*. Boston, MA: Allyn and Bacon.

Englert, C. S. (2009) Connecting the dots in a research program to develop, implement, and evaluate strategic literacy interventions for struggling readers and writers, *Learning Disabilities Research and Practice*, 24: 93–103.

Evmenova, A. S., Graff, H. J., Jerome, M. K. and Behrmann, M. M. (2010) Word prediction programs with phonetic spelling support: performance comparisons and impact on journal writing for students with writing difficulties, *Learning Disabilities Research and Practice*, 25: 170–82.

Fenty, N. S., Miller, M. A. and Lampi, A. (2008) Embed social skills instruction in inclusive settings, *Intervention in School and Clinic*, 43: 186–92.

Friend, M. and Cook, L. (2010) *Interactions: Collaborative Skills for School Professionals*, 6th edn. Upper Saddle River, NJ: Pearson Education.

Fuchs, L. S. and Fuchs, D. (2007) A model for implementing responsiveness to Intervention, *TEACHING Exceptional Children*, 39(5): 14–23.

Fullan, M. (2006) The future of educational change: system thinkers in action, *Journal of Educational Change*, 7(3): 113–22.

Fullan, M. (2009) Large-scale reform comes of age, *Journal of Educational Change*, 10(2/3): 101–13.

Gajria, M., Jitendra, A., Sood, S. and Sacks, G. (2007) Improving comprehension of expository text in students with LD: a research synthesis, *Journal of Learning Disabilities*, 40: 210–25.

Giangreco, M. F. and Broer, S. M. (2007) School based screening to determine overreliance on paraprofessionals, *Focus on Autism and Other Developmental Disabilities*, 22: 149–59.

Gibbs, G. S. and Dyches, T. (2007) *Guide to Writing Quality Individualized Education Programs*. Columbus, OH: Merrill/Pearson Education.

Goe, L., Bell, C. and Little, O. (2008) *Approaches to Evaluating Teacher Effectiveness: A Research Synthesis*. Washington, DC: National Comprehensive Center for Teacher Quality.

Graham, S. and Harris, K. R. (2009) Almost 30 years of writing research: making sense of it all with the wrath of Khan, *Learning Disabilities Research and Practice*, 24: 58–68.

Harper, G. F. and Maheady, L. (2007) Peer-mediated teaching and students with learning disabilities, *Intervention in School and Clinic*, 43: 101–7.

Harry, B. (2008) Collaboration with culturally and linguistically diverse families: ideal versus reality, *Exceptional Children*, 74: 372–88.

Johnson, D. R. and Johnson, F. P. (2009) *Joining Together: Group Theory and Group Skills*, 10th edn. Columbus, OH: Merrill/Pearson Education.

King-Sears, M. (2009) Universal design for learning: technology and pedagogy, *Learning Disability Quarterly*, 32: 199–201.

Klingner, J. and Soltero-Gonzalez, L. (2009) Culturally and linguistically responsive literacy instruction for English language learners with learning disabilities, *Multiple Voices for Ethnically Diverse Exceptional Learners*, 12(1): 4–20.

Kurtts, S. A., Matthews, C. E. and Smallwood, T. (2009) (Dis)solving the differences: a physical science lesson using universal design, *Intervention in School and Clinic*, 44: 151–9.

Maheady, L. and Gard, J. (2010) Classwide peer tutoring: practice, theory, research and personal narrative, *Intervention in School and Clinic*, 46: 71–8.

Maheady, L. and Jabot, M. (2010) Group-oriented contingencies: working effectively in inclusive settings, Paper presented to the Annual Conference of the New York State Council for Exceptional Children, Saratoga Springs, New York, 8–9 October.

Meadan, H. and Monda-Amaya (2008) Collaboration to promote social competence for students with mild disabilities in the general classroom: a structure for providing social support, *Intervention in School and Clinic*, 43: 158–67.

Montague, M. and Dietz, S. (2009) Evaluating the evidence base for cognitive strategy instruction and mathematical problem solving, *Exceptional Children*, 75: 285–302.

Murawski, W. W. and Lochner, W. W. (2011) Observing co-teaching: what to ask for, look for, and listen for, *Intervention in School and Clinic*, 46: 174–83.

Noguera, P. A. (2006) A critical response to Michael Fullan's 'The future of educational change: system thinkers in action', *Journal of Educational Change*, 7(3): 129–32.

Prest, J. M., Mirenda, P. and Mercier, D. (2010) Using symbol-supported writing software with students with Down Syndrome: an exploratory study, *Journal of Special Education Technology*, 25: 1–12.

Rafferty, L. A. (2010) Step-by-step: teaching students to self-monitor, *TEACHING Exceptional Children*, 4(2): 50–9.

Russell, C. L. (2008) How are your person first skills?: A self-assessment, *TEACHING Exceptional Children*, 40(5): 40–3.

Salend, S. J. (2009) *Classroom Testing and Assessment for All: Beyond Standardization*. Thousand Oaks, CA: Corwin Press.

Salend, S. J. (2011) *Creating Inclusive Classrooms: Effective and Reflective Practices*, 7th edn. Columbus, OH: Merrill/Pearson Education.

Schumaker, J. B. and Deshler, D. D. (2009) Adolescents with learning disabilities as writers: are we selling them short?, *Learning Disabilities Research and Practice*, 24: 81–92.

Simmons, R. J. and Magiera, K. (2007) Evaluation of co-teaching in three high schools within one school district: how do you know when you are *truly* co-teaching?, *TEACHING*

Exceptional Children Plus, 3(3): Article 4. Available at http://escholarship.bc.edu/education/tecplus/vol3/iss3/art4 [Accessed 3 June 2009].

Sindelar, P. T., Shearer, D. K., Yendol-Hoppey, D. and Liebert, T.W. (2006) The sustainability of inclusive school reform, *Exceptional Children*, 72: 317–31.

Smith, R. M. (2009) Front and center: contradicting isolation by supporting leadership, and service by students with disabilities, *TEACHING Exceptional Children Plus*, 5(5): Article 4. Available at http://escholarship.bc.edu/education/tecplus/vol5/iss5/art4 [Accessed 4 July 2009].

Stenhoff, D. M. and Lignugaris/Kraft, B. (2007) A review of the effects of peer tutoring on students with mild disabilities in secondary settings, *Exceptional Children*, 74: 8–30.

Strichart, S. S. and Mangrum, C. T. (2010) *Study Skills for Learning Disabled and Struggling Students*, 4th edn. Saddle River, NJ: Merrill/Pearson Education.

Sugai, S., Simonsen, B. and Horner, R. H. (2008) Schoolwide positive behavior supports: a continuum of positive behavior supports for all students, *TEACHING Exceptional Children*, 40(6): 5–6.

Sullivan, A. L. (2011) Disproportionality in special education identification and placement of English language learners, *Exceptional Children*, 22: 317–34.

Swedeen, B. L. (2009) Signs of an inclusive school: a parent's perspective on the meaning and value of authentic inclusion, *TEACHING Exceptional Children Plus*, 5(3): Article 1. Available at http://escholarship.bc.edu/education/tecplus/vol5/iss3/art1 [Accessed 1 June 2009].

Taylor, L. S. and Whittaker, C. R. (2009) *Bridging Multiple Worlds: Case Studies of Diverse Educational Communities*, 2nd edn. Boston, MA: Allyn and Bacon.

Tomlinson, C. A. (2005) *How to Differentiate Instruction in Mixed-ability Classrooms*, 2nd edn. Upper Saddle River, NJ: Merrill/Prentice Hall.

Van Garderen, D. and Whittaker, C. (2006) Planning differentiated, multicultural instruction for secondary inclusive classrooms, *Exceptional Children*, 38(3): 12–21.

Villa, R. A., Thousand, J. S. and Nevin, A. I. (2008) *A Guide to Co-teaching: Practical Tips for Facilitating Student Learning*, 2nd edn. Thousand Oaks, CA: Corwin Press.

Zambo, D. M. (2010) Strategies for enhancing the social identities and social networks of adolescent students with disabilities, *TEACHING Exceptional Children*, 43(2): 28–37.

7

ADRIAN F. ASHMAN
Facilitating inclusion through responsive teaching

Introduction

This chapter focuses on the use and application of teaching and learning principles, as a way of facilitating the inclusion of students with special learning needs in regular classrooms. The chapter is divided into three main sections. The first provides the context in which students with special learning needs have been accommodated in regular schools in Australia. In the second section, I argue for a reorientation in approach to classroom teaching that de-emphasizes the notion of inclusion and places emphasis on the delivery of the curriculum in ways that support efficient and effective learning for all students, not just those who experience learning problems. I refer to this approach as 'responsive teaching'. The third section provides some practical suggestions about the application of a responsive teaching approach in regular classrooms.

The Australian education context

Schooling in Australia has two unrelated histories: that of the Indigenous, traditional owners of the land we call Australia; and that of the Western world following British colonization that began in the closing years of the eighteenth century. It is questionable whether there has ever been a distinction between 'special' and 'regular' education in Indigenous communities.

There is scant information about schooling in the early years of the British settlement in Sydney Cove colony but it was likely available to the privileged few only. From the 1920s, the delivery of education in Australia followed similar approaches to those in other countries with the progressive development of two parallel systems: regular education that accommodated the overwhelming majority of students, and special education, where the remaining small percentage received their education and/or care in segregated classes, schools and residential facilities. By the 1960s, school system policies had changed to reflect 'mainstreaming' trends, then 'integration', and finally 'inclusion'. In 1992, the *Commonwealth Disability Discrimination Act* set conditions that were considered relevant to the application of inclusive education policies and practices, and more recently, the Commonwealth government moved to clarify expectations and legal obligations under disability discrimination legislation through the establishment of the *Disability Standards for Education 2005*. For an elaboration of Australian legislative provisions, see Poed and Elkins (2012).

Accountability and school practices

In Australia, inclusive education has emerged over the past thirty years in response to the recognition of the social injustices that kept students with special learning needs separated from peers who were progressing according to developmental norms. And while there have been significant developments in legislation and policy, the reality of fully inclusive school systems, schools and classrooms is still some distance off. One might be allured by policies and their associated rhetoric to believe that inclusive education is not only common but omnipresent in Australian schools. This is a false assumption.

There are certainly excellent examples of inclusive practices in many schools although reports of these in the professional literature (internationally and domestically) are scant (see Ashman 2007). The national imperative to achieve the highest academic standards in most, if not all, primary and secondary schools has drawn attention away from the need to provide educational opportunities that accommodate students with extraordinary learning needs. These students include those with cognitive or behavioural difficulties and those with high ability or talents. This tendency has become more apparent since the introduction of system-wide assessments, for example in Years 2, 5 and 7. More recently, there has been a national agreement between State and Australian Territory governments for the introduction of a common school curriculum across agreed Key Learning Areas of English, mathematics, science, health and physical education, the arts, languages other than English, studies of society and the environment, and technology. At the time of writing, this is resulting in curriculum revision and national standardization after the establishment of the Australian Curriculum, Assessment and Reporting Authority (ACARA 2010).

The National Curriculum Board (2009) set out a curriculum framework detailing what teachers are required to teach and what students are expected to learn for each school year. This might seem a sensible approach to ensure consistency across jurisdictions and uniform high student exit standards. However, it is likely that a significant number of students within the school population will be disadvantaged. It is expected that school administrators will strive to meet the system demands of accountability following the introduction of the National Assessment Program – Literacy And Numeracy (NAPLAN) tests in Years 3, 7 and 9, a test for which training kits are already available.

While ACARA acknowledges that children learn at different rates, it places responsibility on classroom teachers to provide instruction that ensures that all students achieve as close to their latent abilities as possible. Curiously, ACARA has indicated that teachers are to apply the standards to all learners. These new requirements sit against a background of an already existing tendency for school administrators to compete for students with known high abilities and the threat of public scrutiny of the academic achievements of individual schools published on government websites, such as *My School* (http://www.myschool.edu.au/). See Hardy and Boyle (2011) for a discussion about measurement of school performance in this way.

Responsive teaching

There is no simple way in which teachers can accommodate the inevitable pressures that will occur with the full rollout of a national curriculum, accountability for high student achievement in regular education classes, and the imperative of teaching students with heterogeneous educational backgrounds and capabilities in regular classrooms. One might begin by dealing with historical resistances and opposition to educational mainstreaming, integration, and now inclusion from parents and teachers. Along with this comes the need to improve the exposure of those in pre-service teacher education programmes and of existing teachers to realistic inclusive education practices. These have been discussed extensively in Forlin (2010).

In many places in the professional literature, writers have referred to the lack of teachers' responsiveness to students with diverse learning needs as a major obstacle to fully inclusive education. In other places, writers refer to responsive teaching (see e.g. Tomlinson 2003; Algozzine and Anderson 2007; Rock *et al.* 2008; Van Kraayenoord and Elkins 2012) when talking about inclusive education practices. This is the term I prefer because it places the emphasis on a positive reaction by teachers to individual student needs.

Continuing to refer to inclusive education highlights diversity and special learning needs, inadvertently emphasizing the difference in capability between included students and their peers. Truly inclusive classrooms exist because they do away with the concept of special learning needs; because *every* child has a special learning need. It is up to the teacher to respond to students' preferred learning styles and create environments that anticipate – rather than react to – these needs. By developing an approach to teaching that is responsive to the needs of all students, teachers can concentrate on communicating knowledge effectively rather than heeding disability or impairment labels that provide little information about how to maximize students' academic and social development.

In a very simplistic way, the key to achieving responsive teaching is planning, and this involves:

- knowing each student's learning characteristics and capabilities;
- focusing attention on the ecology of the teaching–learning environment that maximizes human and physical resources; and
- developing instructional styles and techniques that accommodate learner diversity.

I begin my discussion here with the second bullet point to draw attention to the complexity of teaching–learning settings, which are the foundation stones of responsive teaching.

Teaching–learning ecology

Learning does not occur in a void. Learners interact with their environments and with those with whom they share them. Ashman and Conway (1997) argued that all learners, regardless of personal or cultural characteristics, age and ability, are subject to the same set of influences that affect what, and how, they learn. They described these influences in terms of a teaching–learning ecology that includes the learner, the setting, the instructor and the curriculum. These components are described very briefly below.

The learner

Each learner has a unique learning history and profile comprising a knowledge base, mental and emotional dispositions toward learning, and an ever-expanding collection of learning and problem-solving strategies generated over the course of his or her life. Each learning activity has prerequisite knowledge that includes specific detail (e.g. arithmetic or historical facts) and how to perform tasks (e.g. to count or read). Learning also involves access to, and use of, a constellation of problem-solving strategies that enable us to adapt to new learning experiences. These strategies include setting priorities, making decisions and planning with a particular outcome in mind. Such organizational capabilities are vital to independent learning, problem solving and initiative taking.

Emotional dispositions to learning are also fundamental because they predispose the learner to become – or not become – involved. Motivation is one important element linked to past experiences and to a willingness to attempt new tasks or activities and to take learning risks. When learners experience success they are more likely to engage in similar or new learning activities than if they perceive a learning event to be boring or if they experience repeated failure. Hence, there is an intimate connection between knowledge, skills and affective variables. Responsive teaching requires the assessment of students' preferred learning styles to enable the teacher to make appropriate adjustments for each student.

The setting

The most basic ecological component is the setting in which teaching and learning occurs (Jamieson-Proctor and Burnett 2006). If this is not conducive to teaching and learning then it is difficult (although not necessarily impossible) for the other three components to compensate. The setting includes physical facilities and resources, space, time, equipment, the level of noise, light and ambient temperature. While teachers and learners can adapt to adverse conditions, one of the duties of a responsive teacher is to monitor and manage the setting so that suitable facilities and resources are available to meet students' needs.

The instructor

Learning is often mediated by an instructor or teacher who decides what will be learned, and how that learning will occur. The teacher might be a peer, a family member or a friend, and learning might occur in a formal school setting or via model-ling, imitation or independently alone in an informal learning situation (e.g. a skate-board park). Teachers operate according to the same intellectual and emotional dimensions as their students (i.e. knowledge, affective elements, organizational capabilities). Sometimes the facilitator of learning might be a website, computer software, or textbook in which the creator's effort has been devoted to structuring the knowledge to encourage engagement. A responsive teacher recognizes individual differences, is willing to accommodate students' needs, confident in their professional capabilities and enthusiastic about embracing new ideas and teaching challenges.

The curriculum

Finally, what is to be taught and learned and how the curriculum is conveyed deter-mine learning outcomes. The curriculum might refer to all learning regardless of the age or ability level of the students (i.e. everything students are to learn in school), to a systemic curriculum (e.g. as defined by the key learning areas), or to the content and processes that a teacher might develop for a specific student. The curriculum is not only a body of specific details but also a mosaic of skills and strategies, a management device that sets out the level of learning performance required, how the student's capabilities influence participation and progress, and measurable goals or outcomes.

Consolidating the ecology

The four components (learner, setting, instructor, curriculum) must operate within a balanced (or counterbalanced) environment for the achievement of successful learning outcomes. How can this be realized?

The professional education literature is replete with instructional theories, models, frameworks, designs, approaches, practices, processes, tips, hints and advice. There is considerable overlap with regard to what is thought will improve instruction and learning. Of course, not all of these theories, practices and tips lead to successful learning and problem solving, as Hattie (2009) has shown. What seems to make the greatest difference to learning outcomes is not the model or approach that one advo-cates but rather the teacher's enthusiasm, interest and passion about students and their achievements. At its most basic level, responsive teaching is about providing learning opportunities that make the curriculum accessible to all students. The key to achieving this is to eschew approaches that focus on characteristics that one cannot change or influence (see Howell and Nolet 2000) and concentrate on those components of the teaching–learning ecology that are most amenable to change. These alterable features include aspects of the environment (e.g. space, resources), the instructor's characteristics (e.g. beliefs, attitudes and practices), and the curriculum. Focusing on these enables teachers to respond to each student's needs to ensure successful learning outcomes.

Figure 7.1 is a graphic representation of responsive teaching. It is not a single approach but a model that encourages invention and innovation. In that figure, I have separated the learner from the other three components of the teaching–learning ecology because teachers cannot influence many learner characteristics, such as their

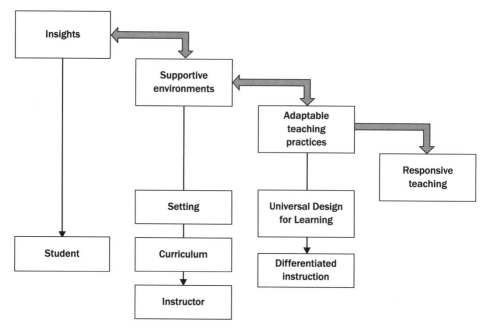

Figure 7.1 A graphic representation of responsive teaching

cognitive capabilities, family/cultural backgrounds and influences, and learning histories.

In the model, I refer to the learner component as 'insights'. My intention here is to minimize the emphasis on formal assessment and testing.

Insights

Policies about inclusion and the need to achieve the best outcomes for all students mean that assessment is not simply about identifying how much a student has learnt. It is about gaining an understanding of how each student learns, the difficulties being experienced, and how contextual issues such as teaching approaches, a student's history, and cultural and social factors have affected, and will affect, learning.

Insights can be gathered from the teacher's observations of, and dialogues with students, through formative and summative assessments that are part of classroom assessments including authentic learning tasks (e.g. portfolios and reflections), and from system or national assessment (e.g. NAPLAN). Comprehensive textbooks (e.g. Sattler and Hoge 2006) deal with a range of data gathering practices such as interviews, observations, and both formal (norm-referenced) and informal testing. Interviews with parents and other stakeholders (e.g. cultural leaders, education and related professionals) can augment personal observations about how a child approaches a range of learning tasks and discussions with teachers who have taught a child can supplement information collected from school counsellors and other education professionals.

Insights also relate to the student's learning preferences and interests, interpersonal and social skills, and social, emotional, academic and career goals and aspirations. All of this information can be recorded in a Student Log (I have capitalized this term simply to indicate that this could become a living record of a student's characteristics and achievements). The teacher could collect insights under a number of headings, such as Academic (e.g. 'Reads just below grade level, can answer most content questions; prefers to work alone; is a visual learner'), Social (e.g. 'Sometimes amuses classmates, although they often laugh "at" rather than "with" Tom'; 'sometimes enjoys showing/talking to teacher before class'), Emotional (e.g. 'Will team up with any willing partner'), and Family (e.g. 'Mother responsive when contacted by school counsellor; mother now regularly meets informally and formally with teacher').

Student Logs can be expanded like a diary over the course of a school year and shared with the student's teachers in following years. Such a written record ensures that important knowledge about students' progress and their learning characteristics and responses is not lost. It takes no more than 15 minutes to prepare a single Student Log. A class set can be completed over one or two weeks.

Supportive environments

Being aware of the importance of the setting, the instructor's characteristics and the curriculum is the starting point for classroom adaptations. Again, generating a written assessment of each component can help the teacher to identify where changes are needed. The following relate to the setting:

- *spaces*: flexible work areas, age-appropriate, ambient lighting, furniture, breakout capacity, storage, on-campus, community facilities and locations;
- *time*: 'ideal' learning times, home, vacation, private;
- *grouping*: whole-group, small-group, individual, library, family-managed, independent discovery;
- *equipment*: interactive whiteboards, computers and peripherals, web access; software, digital storage, curriculum-specific resources, digital cameras/phones, assistive technology;
- *human resources*: co-teacher, aides, volunteers, community visitors, mentors, technical/digital support, support professionals.

These relate to the curriculum:

- *lesson planning*: aims and key question(s), articulated curriculum goals, prerequisite knowledge, resources available and needed, levels of knowledge, student learning outcomes, and outcome products (project, sheet);
- *teaching and learning issues*: literacies, independent learning and problem solving, remediation and support, and extension activities (e.g. homework).

And these relate to the instructor:

- *self-appraisal*: beliefs and attitudes, content knowledge and experience, confidence dealing with diverse student needs, willingness to seek support and address challenges, and facility with information and communication technologies (ICT);
- *personal development*: identified personal needs, faculty/administrative support, management of support personnel, workload and extra-curricular responsibilities, and access to continuing professional development.

Figure 7.2 gives a short example of notations made by a Year 8 teacher using these points as guidelines.

My class (Year 8B)

My classroom

Traditional classroom layout, rows of desks
Teacher's desk to right front
Space for small class groups & small teaching spaces but congested then
6 working desktops, laptop, interactive whiteboard; limited software
Internet access although no school computer lab.
Some use of digital photography (teacher has camera), no central digital storage
Limited school financial resources to devote to ICT or digital resources
Classroom support (e.g. 1 aide 2/7, 2 parent volunteers 2/7)

The curriculum

Literacy and numeracy foci
Need for high level of individualization
Limited differentiation of curriculum, solid but conservative lesson plans
Lessons rarely involve ICT
Curriculum delivered via theme format
Consolidation of learning usually via worksheets
Assessment usually via written assignment or mini-test
School imperative for high achievement on national tests

Me

4-years experience, Years 8 and 9; English specialization; Geography minor
Limited in-service experiences and opportunities
Committed to students, supportive of all students, prefer whole-class teaching
Modest ICT experience and skills; Receptive to ICT
Heavy teaching and supervision load
Limited student-free lesson planning periods
Link to education uni lecturer friend
Good collegial support from colleagues

Figure 7.2 Notes made by a Year 8 teacher with regard to the alterable features of her classroom

The snapshot shown in Figure 7.2 can be amended and expanded as the teaching year progresses. A document like this is another work-in-progress and is a useful reference for a teacher's reflection on changes and innovations that have occurred over a teaching year.

Adaptable teaching practices

Responsive teaching is not an instructional system or single approach that is to be taught, accepted and adopted to the exclusion of a teacher's already established, tried-and-tested practices. Each of the components is fully under the teacher's control (i.e. gaining insights about the students; evaluating the setting, demands of the curriculum, and self-appraisal). Of course, responsive teaching does involve a willingness to embrace change where it is needed but always within the teacher's comfort zone and the existing resource environment.

Many regular education class teachers express concerns about their ability to accommodate the diversity of student characteristics and abilities in their instructional practices. How can they present the curriculum in a way that is appropriate for the student with a learning difficulty at one end of the capability continuum, while also providing relevant learning experiences for gifted or talented students at the other?

There are two sets of teaching principles (not approaches or systems) that can be employed to assist with this situation: Universal Design for Learning and curriculum differentiation. Each of these involves making adjustments within the teaching–learning context. Let me deal briefly with each of these in the context of responsive teaching.

Universal Design for Learning

Universal Design (UD) derives from architecture and built environment concepts and the belief that buildings and spaces must be designed so that they are accessible to everyone, including those with disability or impairment. Its origin is a result of initiatives taken during the 1981 International Year of Disabled Persons and was inspired by product development and design concepts of the American, Ron Mace (see Mace 1998). Accessibility is now a fundamental principle in merchandise design and architecture such that products, spaces and places must be accessible to everyone to the greatest extent possible without the need for adaptation or specialized construction.

A fundamental consideration of inclusion has been the need for appropriate curriculum planning to enable access and participation for all students so that their progress through the education system occurs at an appropriate pace. Universal Design was clearly a relevant concept. Those who worked in the application of UD to teaching and learning invented the term Universal Design for Learning (UDL).

UDL has been defined in many ways, although the emphasis is on creating a curriculum that does not involve adaptation or retrofitting, gives students control over the way in which they gain access to information and, thus, encourages their independence in learning and problem solving. It provides for equal access to all by removing the barriers to knowledge and learning without diminishing the challenges (see Bauer and Kroeger 2004).

UDL involves the application of three primary principles:

- *representation*, that is, using various ways of presenting essential concepts (e.g. making class notes available to students along with oral presentations, transcripts or video clips that can be downloaded from the web);
- *engagement*, that is, work that is designed so that it caters for students' skill levels, preferences and interests (e.g. different reading capabilities or experiences); and
- *expression*, that is, the inclusion of alternative means of expression that allow students to demonstrate mastery in various ways (e.g. via oral, written, or multimedia presentations). See http://www.udlcenter.org/aboutudl/udlguidelines/principle1 for further elaboration.

UDL also involves seven features of teaching and learning (sometimes also referred to as UDL principles, see www.ncset.org/topics/udl/faqs.asp?topic=18) that facilitate the application of the three main principles:

- *equitable use* (e.g. having the same technology/resource available to, and useable by, everyone);
- *flexible use* (e.g. the same technology/resource is used for a number of purposes – arithmetic/social/language);
- *simple and intuitive application* (e.g. everyone knows how to look for a book in the library, or use the web to search for, or gain access to information);
- *perceptible information* (e.g. the technology communicates essential information to the user, regardless of the user's capabilities);
- *tolerance for error* (e.g. the learning process includes recovery processes when errors occur);
- *low physical effort* (e.g. the teaching process is accessible to students with sensory or mobility impairments); and
- *size and space* (e.g. accommodates students with particular needs, such as locating a student with a vision impairment at the front of the class).

At its most basic level, UDL is about using tools and resources that are usable by all students in a classroom with an emphasis on information and communication technology. Burgstahler (2001) distilled the initiatives achieved in design and architecture into a set of features relating to classroom application. These are:

- *inclusiveness*: a classroom environment that respects and values diversity;
- *physical access*: classrooms, resources and equipment that are accessible to all students;
- *delivery methods*: employment of varied delivery methods;
- *information access*: use of, for example, captioned videos, electronic copies of printed materials;

- *interaction*: different ways in which teachers and learners interact;

- *feedback*: effective and timely prompting and feedback;

- *demonstration of knowledge*: multiple ways for students to demonstrate their knowledge.

UDL focuses on adaptations to the way in which the curriculum is delivered and emphasizes information and communication technology. It promotes teaching practices that allow for equal access to information, student control of access to information, and facilitating learning through flexible teaching methods while recognizing that some students will always need individualized support. While there has been a significant evolution in UDL since its inception (evident in the expansive website: http://www.cast.org/udl/index.html) there remains a disposition toward the way in which the curriculum is delivered rather than what is delivered.

Curriculum differentiation provides additional propositions that augment UDL's principles. If there is a difference between UDL and differentiation, the latter emphasizes flexibility to accommodate students' cognitive capabilities.

Differentiation

Differentiation is a core element of responsive teaching and appears in the professional literature under several headings: curriculum differentiation, differentiated instruction and multi-level instruction. Differentiation refers to a flexible approach to teaching that addresses the different learning capabilities of individual students. It ensures that the teaching–learning context provides an appropriate fit for each student's cognitive needs while retaining a common instructional intent. For example, the goal might relate to arithmetic operations; the delivery might vary depending upon students' prerequisite knowledge. This can be achieved through adjustments to the curriculum so that students work toward slightly (or vastly) different goals in terms of content mastery (e.g. learning ideas and skills to be acquired), concept mastery (e.g. systems of knowledge to be acquired), and process mastery (e.g. research and information management skills to be acquired). Therefore, curriculum differentiation involves management of the:

- content: what is taught and learned (e.g. by focusing on activity-based tasks through to the conceptual and abstract);

- process or methods for acquiring content: how knowledge is delivered (e.g. accommodating preferred learning styles: visual, auditory, tactile, kinaesthetic);

- methods for assessment: how learning success is evaluated (e.g. using authentic tasks that involve real and relevant problems); and

- resources required: including material and human resources (e.g. equipment, ICT, aides, volunteers, experts).

Establishing a mindset that sanctions flexibility is the first step toward realizing responsive teaching. The second step has to do with managing the teaching–learning environment. This moves us on to considering some practical applications of responsive teaching ideas.

Practical applications

Over many years, I have had the privilege of observing teachers in early childhood, primary and secondary school settings. In each of these settings the overwhelming majority of teachers are sympathetic to students' individual needs, more so in small groups or during one-to-one interactions than in whole-of-class lessons. During conversation, however, many teachers have admitted that they are less than confident about how to respond effectively to their students' diverse capabilities, interests and motivations. Designing learning activities that respond to individual needs is a practice that parallels the development of individual education plans for students with serious learning difficulties.

On many occasions I have asked teachers if they have considered the factors that affect student achievement and then have talked to them about a simple way to begin their transformation to responsive teaching. The first consideration is the student, and the Student Log is a useful way of bringing together insights gained from an exploration of students' learning histories. The second consideration is the evaluation of the teaching–learning environment via an ecology assessment, ideally undertaken two to four weeks into a new teaching year. I have already given an example of one such assessment in Figure 7.2, prepared by a Year 8 teacher. Keeping Figure 7.2 in mind, what suggestions could be made?

Let's look at the setting first. There is useful ICT provided. The computers are in working order and have current software. The learning space can be converted into whole-class and small-group settings by planning how furniture can be moved quickly and efficiently to minimize congestion. The school has limited resources so the teacher would need to generate digital resources, perhaps in collaboration with a colleague. The aide and volunteers could also explore *Photo Story*, *The Le@rning Federation*, *Inspiration*® and *Kidspiration*® and pictorial resources for specific lessons and students. Toward this end, the teacher could identify two or three future lessons for which resources would be developed, taking into consideration the needs of students who experience learning difficulties. These lessons could become templates that might be stored with other resources for future lessons or classes. Templates flag the need for general goals, resources, expected teacher and student inputs, and target curriculum content (e.g. concept, skills, mathematical or scientific facts or formulae), examples of the application of the content, and ways in which students become familiar with, or practise operations related to content. Numerous examples of such lesson plans can be found in Ashman and Elkins (2012).

One teacher who uses ICT regularly reported that his teaching improved immeasurably by preparing templates that he could modify to deliver lessons and topics effectively and efficiently. Over two years, he set up an impressive collection of mini-lessons using *PowerPoint*, and web resources that included images and examples of learning and work products. His most telling comment was thus:

> As soon as I got settled using the templates, I found I was getting through much
> more content each term than I ever had. The kids really clicked with what was

happening and were much more motivated and innovative. It wasn't a silver bullet, of course. We still had some raggedy sessions and raggedy kids, but overall, the templates were a great success.

The key point here is the effectiveness of templates in reducing lesson planning time in a way that is responsive to all students in the classroom.

The teacher who prepared the material in Figure 7.2 is lucky to have an interactive whiteboard. This requires full use so the teacher, aide and volunteers must learn how to use it. An after-school exploration session might be an option or a demonstration by the supplier's representative. All personnel need to be present.

Students these days are digital savvy and digital still and video photography (e.g. using an inexpensive Flip™ video camera) is an excellent way to create learning resources and learning records. Photo presentations can be used to present information (via internet access, digital resources, PowerPoint) [think UDL Representation], record excursions, learning events [think Engagement], and also learning outcomes [think Expression]. The teacher or other adults need to be computer literate and inventive given limited ICT school resources. Digital resources can be stored on the school's server so that they are accessible to students and other teachers.

For classes in which there are students with limited capabilities, software like *Photo Story* could become popular. *Voicethreads* and a number of websites where there is access to images and sound clips might also provide resources that can support students who are visual/enactive learners. *Movie Maker* could be effective if students have an interest in multimedia, although this might be a whole-of-school initiative targeting a specific topic or theme.

As the teacher in this example is relatively inexperienced, access to professional development is essential. This will depend upon what programmes are available locally. There is a huge range of topics and programmes available each year via workshops in all jurisdictions and via the internet. The teacher might target programmes on curriculum differentiation.

Teacher confidence comes with experience and success. Experience provides teachers with knowledge about how to release some control over the teaching–learning environment. Co-operative learning and other peer-mediated learning approaches can be especially successful. As the teacher has links with a lecturer friend, enquiries about training in co-operative learning or relevant literature would be valuable (see e.g. Gillies 2007).

In terms of responsiveness to individuals, the Student Log can be an effective way of considering how teaching and learning approaches can be adapted to support individual students. Figure 7.3 sets out some identifying student characteristics. As brighter students can be overlooked when we consider inclusive education, this example deals with Sam, who is an above-average ability student.

Let's consider Sam. Sam is academically capable, easy to motivate, and can ignore distractions. He's inventive and prefers activity-based learning. He likes working alone but can work well in small groups. He's a creative computer user. Socially, Sam is liked by others, generous with his help, adaptable and easy-going. He has an already developed moral view about discrimination. Sam is emotionally stable and his teacher thinks that he has a flair for acting. His family circumstances are also stable. His

	Sam
	Strengths
Academic:	Performing near the top of the class; maths and science are best subjects, good general skills foundation.
	Reads well, understands content, answers questions readily; easy to motivate, works alone well, stays on-task and can dismiss distractions, task-focused, listens well, takes direction well, is inventive.
	Prefers activity to listening. Likes working alone but good in groups as well. Creative computer user.
Social:	One of the class leaders, well regarded by others, readily helps others (even when not asked). Pretty adaptable in all areas, easy going. Stands up for kids who are vulnerable to bullying.
Emotional:	Seems stable. Good actor, good sense of humour.
Family involvement:	Mother supportive. Thinks S is doing well. Hopes for professional career.
	Limitations
Academic:	Can be impulsive, especially when the lesson's dragging or when other 'aren't getting it'.
	Homework is not always 'up to speed'. Looks like it's hurried. Wants to spend more time on the computer than available. *(Use computer as a reward, maybe?)*
Social:	No problems.
Emotional:	Gets moody from time to time but short duration. Weary after lunch break.
Family:	Little other than PT nights. Would like to see more of mum at school (ex-teacher). Could use some help as a volunteer in the class *(if she was available)*.

Figure 7.3 A learning profile of Sam in Year 7

mother, who is the primary contact with the school, is very supportive of Sam and his parents are hoping that he will aim at a professional career, probably the law as his father is a barrister of some repute in the city. Sam's teacher generated the following plan based only on Sam's strengths.

Academic: extension activities; library and/or independent learning, focus on maths, science and ecology; probably a project focus that deals with the environment or sustainable energy; (external mentor could be found here?).

Social: tutor role but need to be careful to make sure Sam is not exploited; social mentor with other students, but again be careful.

Emotional: consideration of an extra-curricular drama programme.

Family: family involved in extension activities; holiday activities could encourage development of Sam's interests into the arts.

Academic: Extension activities;[4] library &/or independent learning, focus on maths, science & ecology;[1] project focus;[2] external mentor?[3]
Social: Tutor role (but carefully);[3] social mentor with other students?[5][6][7]
Emotional: Drama programme?
Family: Family involved in extension activities;[5] holiday activities to encourage interests.[2][7]

Universal Design for Learning principles
[1] Engagement – use of flexible options.
[2] Presentation – use different ways of presenting content.
[3] Expression – look for alternative ways of demonstrating mastery.
[4] Expectations – set them high but realistic.

Differentiation principles
[1] Focus on content, concept, process; continuity.
[2] Emphasize complexity and depth of learning.
[3] Respond to student as a learner.
[4] Ensure an appropriate curriculum fit and pace.
[5] Encourage the development of a community of learners.
[6] Emphasize higher-order thinking skills.
[7] Emphasize realistic expectations and provide examples that encourage achievement.

Figure 7.4 Sam's teacher's proposed response to Sam's learning profile

Sam's teacher drew on both UDL and differentiation principles when planning her response to the insights she had gained from her exploration of Sam's learning profile. The influences are shown via the superscripts in Figure 7.4.

Conclusion

Responsive teaching is hardly a new or novel set of propositions. The fundamentals of responsive teaching date back to the 1970s. It is curious, however, that inclusive education has been so hard to achieve given the legislative and policy imperatives and the educational initiatives and innovations that have been promoted over thirty years. Responsive teaching does not demand that a teacher learn new ways of doing his or her job. It offers simply a structured way of drawing together knowledge about students, the environment and the capabilities of the teacher. The only risk involved comes from trying something different. Teachers are not *required* to embrace every aspect of responsive teaching described above to achieve some teaching and learning gains.

Teaching is, itself, a learning process. As teachers gain experience, they learn to adapt to the changing environments of their classrooms and become comfortable with an ever-increasing diversity within the student population. It seems to me that the expanding body of literature on teaching models, approaches, hints, tips and tricks can entice teachers to explore alternative ways of teaching and move them out of their comfort zone. Responsive teaching is one key that will unlock the Pandora's box that we call inclusion. It may not be the only key as there are many described in Ashman and Conway (1997), in Buffum *et al.* (2010) and in other sources too numerous to report here. But it is one option and you are invited to consider it.

Taken in its entirety, responsive teaching is a way of empowering students. It involves deliberate planning, data collection and lesson presentation that accommodate all students' learning needs.

To close, I return to comments I made in the introduction to this chapter. It is questionable whether there has ever been a distinction between 'special' and 'regular' education in Australia's Indigenous communities. In those cultures, education has always been an all-of-life experience, rooted in an individual's perceptions of the world. It is my assertion that responsive teaching is consistent with traditional Australian Indigenous learning approaches. Those of us of Western/European ancestry still have much to learn from their genius and still much to reject from the rigid teaching and learning methods that are part of our heritage. It is concerning that the professional education literature has shown us that our efforts toward achieving full inclusion of students with special learning needs have been far less successful than we might have hoped (Ashman 2003, 2007).

References

ACARA (Australian Curriculum, Assessment and Reporting Authority) (2010) *The National Curriculum.* Available at: http://www.australiancurriculum.edu.au [Accessed 13 February 2011].

Algozzine, B. and Anderson, K.M. (2007) Differentiating instruction to include all students, *Preventing School Failure*, 51: 49–54.

Ashman, A. (2003) Peer-mediation and students with diverse learning needs, in R.M. Gillies and A.F. Ashman (eds) *Cooperative Learning: The Social and Intellectual Outcomes of Learning.* London: Routledge.

Ashman, A. and Elkins, J. (eds) (2012) *Education for Inclusion and Diversity*, 4th edn. Frenchs Forest, NSW: Pearson Australia.

Ashman, A.F. (2007) School and inclusive practices, in R.M. Gillies, A.F. Ashman and J. Terwel (eds) *The Teacher's Role in Implementing Cooperative Learning in the Classroom.* New York: Springer.

Ashman, A.F. and Conway, R.N.F. (1997) *An Introduction to Cognitive Education: Theory and Applications.* London: Routledge.

Bauer, A.M. and Kroeger, S. (2004) *Inclusive Classrooms: Video Cases on CD-ROM – Activity and Learning Guide.* Upper Saddle, NJ: Pearson.

Buffum, A., Mattos, M. and Weber, C. (2010) The why try behind RTI: Response to Intervention flourishes when educators implement the right practices for the right reasons, *Educational Leadership*, 68: 10–16.

Burgstahler, S. (2001) *Universal Design of Instruction.* Seattle: DO-IT, University of Washington. Available at: http://eric.ed.gov/ERICWebPortal/contentdelivery/servlet/ERIC Servletaccno=ED468709 [Accessed 7 October 2009].

Forlin, C. (ed.) (2010) *Teacher Education and Inclusion: Changing Paradigms and Innovative Approaches.* Abingdon: Routledge.

Gillies, R. (2007) *Cooperative Learning: Integrating Theory and Practice.* Thousand Oaks, CA: Sage Publications.

Hardy, I. and Boyle, C. (2011) My school? Critiquing the abstraction and quantification of education, *Asia-Pacific Journal of Teacher Education*, 39(3): 211–22. DOI: 10.1080/1359866X.2011.588312.

Hattie, J.A. (2009) *Visible Learning: A Synthesis of Over 800 Meta-analyses Relating to Achievement*. Abingdon: Routledge.

Howell, K. and Nolet, V. (2000) *Curriculum-based Evaluation: Teaching and Decision Making*. Belmont, CA: Wadsworth.

Jamieson-Proctor, R. and Burnett, P. (2006) ICT integration and teachers' confidence in using ICT for teaching and learning in Queensland state schools, *Australian Journal of Educational Technology*, 22: 511–30.

Mace, R. (1998) Universal design in housing, *Assistive Technology*, 10(1): 18–21.

Maker, J. (1982) *Curriculum Development for the Gifted*. Rockville, MD: Aspen.

National Curriculum Board (2009) *The Shape of the National Curriculum: A Proposal for Discussion*. Available at: http://www.acara.edu.au/verve/_resources/The_Shape_of_the_National_Curriculum_paper.pdf [Accessed 10 November 2010].

Poed, S. and Elkins, J. (2012) Legislation, policies, and principles, in A. Ashman and J. Elkins (eds) *Educating for Inclusion and Diversity*, 4th edn. Frenchs Forest, New South Wales: Pearson Education Australia.

Rock, M.L., Gregg, M., Ellis, E. and Gable, R.A. (2008) Reach: A framework for differentiating classroom instruction, *Preventing School Failure*, 52: 31–47.

Sattler, J.M. and Hoge, R.D. (2006) *Assessment of Children: Behavioural, Social, and Clinical Foundations*, 5th edn. La Mesa, CA: Jerome M. Sattler.

Tomlinson, C.A. (2003) *Fulfilling the Promise of the Differentiated Classroom: Strategies and Tools for Responsive Teaching*. Alexandria, VA: Association for Supervision and Curriculum Development.

Van Kraayenoord, C.E. and Elkins, J. (2012) Literacies and numeracy, in A. Ashman and J. Elkins (eds) *Educating for Inclusion and Diversity*, 4th edn. Frenchs Forest, New South Wales: Pearson Education Australia.

8

CHRISTOPHER BOYLE
Teachers make inclusion successful: positive perspectives on inclusion

Introduction

Part I of this book explores the theoretical issues of what inclusion is (also see Boyle *et al.* 2011), and these will not be repeated here. This chapter continues the themes in Part II about the 'how' of inclusion and considers teachers' perspectives of implementing inclusive principles in schools. It uses data from a range of interviews investigating secondary school teachers' attitudes to inclusive education, fully reported in Boyle (2009).

Policies of inclusion in schools now transcend national boundaries, but how teachers interact with each other in order to be successful in an inclusive environment is less well known. Studies that have been conducted in this area indicate the influence of teachers over other teachers and how they support each other in order to implement inclusive policies in schools (e.g. Goodman and Burton 2010; Boyle *et al.* 2012a). The decision to create an inclusion policy in a local authority or equivalent will obviously be determined within the current legislation of that country and will be refined to suit local circumstances. However, how much of this decision-making process will include involvement from the ground-level staff who are the de facto implementers of any new initiative? Policy makers can forget that there is a street-level bureaucracy (Lipsky 1980; 2010), and if people at the ground level who have to implement the policy are not in agreement with the philosophy underpinning the change, then the chances of success are naturally diminished. Lipsky's seminal work has been around for over twenty-five years, yet it is still a relevant factor even today.

This chapter will argue, with quotes from practising teachers, that they are the key players in the inclusion arena. It is, in essence, their will that makes or breaks inclusion policies in schools. Reporting some of the findings of a recent study of Scottish teacher attitudes to inclusion (Boyle 2009), the chapter will consider what teachers believe will help them to make inclusion successful – for themselves, for the school as a whole and, of course, for participating students. Mortier *et al.* (2010) conducted a study in Belgium where teachers gained in-depth knowledge of students who had special needs through community meetings with parents and other stakeholders. The teachers were able to provide input to the school's inclusion policy from a position of strength of knowledge, thus improving the quality of inclusion available.

In order for inclusion policies to be successful, teachers should be fully involved in the planning of policy in the school, as they are the ground-level workers who ultimately have the most power in the operation and ongoing success of a school's inclusion policy. As Subban and Sharma (2006) suggest, the teachers are generally supportive or at least neutral when it comes to attitudes about inclusion, but their concern lies with the implementation of the process and how much support is actually provided in order for them to do this effectively.

Teacher views of inclusion

Collecting practising teachers' views on how to be successful in an inclusive environment was done by structured interviews of 43 teachers across three schools in one Scottish education authority. The exploration of the interview data was by a thematic analysis, as described in Braun and Clarke (2006: 78): through '. . . theoretical freedom, thematic analysis provides a flexible and useful research tool, which can potentially provide a rich and detailed, yet complex, account of data'. Giving details of methodology is beyond the scope of this chapter, but is given in some length in Boyle et al. (2012) and Boyle (2009). The main question for the practitioners was to provide advice on how to implement inclusion, based on what they had learned through experience in teaching. Consideration was also given to what makes inclusion work in secondary schools for teachers – this tapped into the positive aspects of inclusion and how these were achieved (Avramidis and Norwich 2002).

What is it exactly that makes some teachers confident in working with children who have differing abilities and/or additional support needs? Why do some staff members embrace this type of work, while others could be described as being less than supportive in including children with difficulties in the mainstream classroom? Scruggs and Mastropieri (1996) conducted a review of the literature from 1958 to 1995 that indicated that the severity of the additional support need had an influence on whether the teacher's attitude was positive or negative towards inclusion. The authors recently redid this seminal study with similar results (Scruggs et al. 2011).

The next section of the chapter will focus on themes and highlight some pertinent comments from teachers with regard to implementing inclusion in their school. The question deliberately did not focus on specific conditions, but on general good teaching practice (as advocated in Bain 2005).

Direct experience of inclusion

Thirty-nine of the 43 respondents gave responses under this theme. Recognizing that teaching is about learning and self-improvement and that there will always be situations where you are able to reflect upon and improve practice for the next time is an important part of teaching (Loreman et al. 2011). This relatively new teacher (below) is reflecting that, despite four years being a reasonable period of experience in many occupations, this is not a lot in education and more learning and experience is required:

> I guess it is just being open to what their responses are. It is knowing that you might get something wrong now and again and you have to reflect upon that and improve it the next year and I certainly feel that way where four years is quite a long time but in education it is not because I still have tons of things to reflect upon, improve upon and implement.
>
> (Subject teacher of art, 4 years of teaching experience)[1]

A more experienced teacher believes that you have to continually change your classroom management strategy in order to accommodate students with additional support needs, but also that an understanding must be gained of the needs of all the students in the class:

> It's just about if you have a kid who comes to you with, whether it be behavioural or learning difficulties you've got to get to know that kid and you've got to again apply a range of strategies but always I think you need to have a clear idea of what is happening in your classroom and the kids need to be aware of all of them and then you look at the needs required.
>
> (Maths, 30 years)

As with the previous comment (and even with relatively little experience), the next teacher highlights the importance of basic good practice in the classroom and puts forward the point that it is not necessarily about putting in place strategies that may have come from elsewhere, but it is about your attitude to including students in the class:

> It's important that they understand it's not this horrendous huge job . . . it comes down to basic things that you do, the way you talk, the way you approach the class and things like that, the way you include the students in the class.
>
> (Science, Probationer)

Both teachers in the next examples refer to the importance of consulting with colleagues, as many teachers may have worked with a particular student with additional support needs and come up with effective strategies that work in their class. This is a valuable resource, which is readily available in schools, and it is possible that it is underused in some schools (c.f. Boyle *et al.* 2012a):

> But keep asking questions of other people and in departments where maybe another department has the same students – say 'How do you deal with this student? Have you found something that works?'
>
> (ICT/Business, 11 years)

Another teacher refers to the support of colleagues but also indicates that teachers should be prepared to try very different strategies in order to find the method that works across the range of students in the class:

Getting advice from other teachers and I think just trying things, even things you might initially think that's not going to work or that's going to lead to a disaster and that's going to lead to a riot, give it a try because sometimes the kind of out there things do actually end up being the most effective.

(Religious education, 6 years)

Another teacher discussed the subtlety that can be involved in including students in the class. It could be described as inclusion by stealth, but in some ways that seems sinister when it could also be described as good practice:

> . . . if you've got somebody who has got behavioural needs, or whatever, then try not to make them seem different and maybe bend the rules a wee bit so that it's not obvious to anybody else that you are doing that and not even obvious to the students themselves just that you're doing something different than you would normally do . . .

(Maths, 30 years)

This teacher recognizes that students learn differently and points out that you can use strategies to help, but ultimately it is only through directly working with students that an understanding of their individual learning needs can be fully gained:

> I think they have got to find out the needs of the student and they have to look at some of the strategies that are in place that are specific for that individual and I think that is ultimately where it starts and then it's taken from there because we have got such a broad spectrum of what the additional support needs are for that child.

(Guidance/Student Support, 9 years)

In a similar vein to the previous teacher's comments, another teacher reports that if lessons are not suitable for a particular child, then advice should be sought from other members of staff so that this can be rectified, which indicates that assistance received from other staff is important for lesson planning:

> You have got to find out what the support needs are to see whether or not your lessons cater for them already and if they don't, seek help from other colleagues or your faculty head or the additional support needs teacher staff.

(Art, 15 years)

Another teacher indicated the importance of teachers facilitating students with additional support needs to work in groups which contain students of all abilities (cf. Mallon 2005), so that there can be interaction among the students while they are learning:

> Just make sure that all the materials are differentiated; make sure that there is a lot of group-work happening and peer work, where they are working with other kids and communicating and talking to each other, lots and lots of

communication happening, not just standing in front of the class and talking
to them . . .

(Music, Probationer)

Assistance from Specialist Support[2]

Thirteen of the 43 respondents gave responses under this theme. There were
several teachers who directly mentioned Specialist Support, thus highlighting the
importance of this department with regard to supporting inclusion. In the UK
school academic departments are assisted by Specialist Support, which is usually
the source of information regarding what strategies are useful with which students.
However, there is evidence that some teachers do not properly consult information
documents that contain specialist details regarding what is effective with students
with additional support needs. If such details are not taken into consideration,
then it is fair to assume that opportunities to include those students properly will
be diminished:

> Always make sure you are aware of what is going on because there are clear
> guidelines from Specialist Support there. . .because some teachers maybe don't
> always take into account some of the difficulties that are going on because they
> haven't read the information . . .
>
> (ICT/Business, 14 years)

Furthermore, it is worth noting the importance of speaking with Specialist
Support staff so that teachers can improve their own teaching skills. There is recognition in this school that the Specialist Support staff are the most knowledgeable
in this area and should be accessed appropriately so as to support inclusion in the
class:

> Very important that teachers read the special needs document information on
> students with special needs. If they don't read it they don't know what strategies
> we propose to help these children. If they can't address them themselves then
> they have to come back to the special needs department or behaviour support
> and ask for our help.
>
> (Specialist Support, 32 years)

The point is that teachers should use their own skills first, but if they need more
help then they should come to the specialist staff for more support.

An experienced Specialist Support teacher has indicated that the most important
aspect in facilitating a student with additional support needs in an inclusive environment is for teaching staff to ensure that they have planned and thus adapted their
lessons in advance (particularly in relation to information supplied by the Specialist
Support department). Whether a teacher adapts his or her lesson may depend
upon the individual teacher's attitude towards certain students in the class, and
this can undermine the inclusion approach proposed by the management of the
school:

In the department we produce as accurate information as we can on all the individual children who are likely to be vulnerable in any way and I believe that it is very important to read carefully the information that is provided because I frequently find that you go into a class and information has not really been digested or observed so I think that is the first port of call – to read all the information they have available on that child and really use that information to support them as best they can and if there is something they don't understand or they need more advice on then to contact the department . . .

(Specialist Support, 34 years)

Attitudes to inclusion

Thirty-six of the 43 respondents gave responses under this theme. Students learn differently and it could be argued that *all* students are on a learning continuum, irrespective of additional support needs. Whether focusing on a label is positive or negative is a moot point and this is discussed fully in Lauchlan and Boyle (2007):

We've got a girl who is in a wheelchair and she actually is having to get one-on-one tuition . . . It was a self-conscious thing because she felt she couldn't do half of the things the rest of the kids were doing but maybe if another teacher had been in the room and was able to just focus with her and the group she was working in she might not have felt quite so self-conscious.

(Drama, 5 years)

This response embodies much about teaching in general but also about the importance of a positive attitude to inclusion in the classroom. If teachers do not have a positive attitude, then they may not put in the extra effort that is sometimes required to ensure students with additional support needs achieve success in the class:

Whether a child has additional support needs or not, every child is different, every child at some point in their lives experiences learning difficulties and I think we should learn and expect to anticipate to treat children as individuals, and when strategies don't work, whether these children have additional support needs or not, have a bank of alternative strategies up your sleeve, try different approaches, be flexible and versatile and be prepared to be led very much by the child, going back to the example of the wee boy without a hand who was so desperate to play the drum kit, let the young people guide you and just be open-minded.

(Music, 12 years)

A major theme has been the support from peers in the same department, peers in other departments, and the school management team. This makes a difference to how staff feel about inclusion in the school.

The following teacher puts forward a response from a Guidance/Student Support[3] perspective – the teacher would be more aware of some difficulties that certain students would be experiencing than the subject teacher. The simplest solution may be better communication, but with confidentiality being an issue permissions would have to be sought:

> Have an open mind and think of the big picture and think about the bits of the jigsaw that you don't know. We have a lot of teachers who are very What do you mean you've not got a pencil? What do you mean you've not got your PE kit? – and as a guidance teacher you feel that you are going to these members of staff a lot and you have to explain that you should be quite grateful that that child is here at all and this is probably the only normality and routine they are going to have in their day.
>
> (Guidance/Student Support, 12 years)

Another teacher's attitude is one of clear positivity to including students in the subject area with the call for *all* materials to be ready for *all* students. Specialist Support state that some departments are not willing to take responsibility for differentiating their own materials and think that this should be left to Specialist Support. It would be difficult to understand how non-subject specialists could effectively differentiate material in subjects where their knowledge is limited. However, it could be argued that if it was that easy, then there would be no need for subject specialists and teaching staff would become generalists:

> Again just what I was saying about making sure all materials are differentiated to all levels for students.
>
> (Art, 1 year)

Another statement here is controversial in that an experienced teacher is suggesting that younger teachers do not have such qualities as empathy and patience in dealing with students. Interestingly, that very suggestion is one that could equally have been levelled at older teachers who 'had been in the job too long':

> First thing that jumps out at me is having the right attitude. See having a bit of empathy, patience – these kind of professional qualities that perhaps some of the younger teachers don't have. They learn them as time goes on, you mellow a wee bit and as you mellow you see a bit of patience.
>
> (Technical, 25 years)

A further teacher suggests that being creative with lesson planning and delivery will help with teaching for all students (especially those with additional support needs) and also being able to share lesson resources with other staff members is an asset. The possibility of sharing resources whether within or outside the department seems to be a resource that teachers value – this was often repeated throughout the interviews:

> I think keeping your resources as varied, interesting and stimulating as possible – you can't rely on ICT but it is a huge benefit that once you have made it up you have it as a resource. Most notes I give to children are ones I made up last year, I'll edit them according to the student but it is a ten-minute job as opposed to two

hours from sitting from scratch so I think having a bank of resources and sharing them with your colleagues is a big benefit . . .

(Science, 2 years)

Similar to the advice provided by the Specialist Support teacher in an earlier theme, the emphasis is placed on the teacher making the effort to gain an understanding of what strategies work with a particular child. It is interesting that the new teacher, in the quote below, indicates the importance of the child as an individual and does not focus on particular difficulties or labels that the child may have:

The advice I would give is that they need to know their students even before they walk in the door. They need to know every piece of document that was written about these students from the previous year from the primary school and you need to know them inside out before they come in. Then obviously you need to get to know *them*.

(English, 1 year)

Getting to understand the student as a person is reinforced by another teacher who describes how s/he has interacted with a student with additional support needs and how that has helped the student participate in a subject area that may be difficult for the child.

Once you get over the fear that this one is different, just talk to these children. I have built up a great rapport with the boy in the wheelchair in my class. He doesn't like drama but I know he likes me and if I can control and encourage him then a lot of it is about that and giving these children self-belief – that's how I feel how you should approach it. Find out about their needs; don't ignore them and pretend they are not there – just embrace them.

(Drama, 14 years)

Inclusive views of the way forward

The quotations above provide a rich level of detail as to the perceptions and practical implications of inclusion in high schools. Irrespective of whether the staff felt supported by the management team, it was the focus away from student difficulties and more on the positive aspects which led to staff considering what they were able to do to support them. A topic that emerged from the interviewees was the emphasis given by some teaching staff to the possibility of co-operative teaching being afforded more prominence. This would be instead of having teaching assistants who are, by the nature of their position, not qualified teachers (discussed in more detail in Boyle *et al.* 2011). As a result of this they are restricted in what they can actually provide.

Salend and Whittaker, in Chapter 6 of this book, discuss the benefits of co-operative teaching. Interestingly Hattie (2009), in his extensive study of student achievement, indicates that the benefits attached to this approach seem to be small with a Cohen's d effect size of only 0.19. This is based on 136 studies across the world and can be regarded as a reasonably reliable statistical measure as to the efficacy of these programmes. However, there are several studies (e.g. Magiera *et al.* 2005; Scruggs *et al.* 2007) which suggest that co-operative teaching is successful in inclusive education programmes, although the robustness of measurement cannot compare with Hattie's analysis of meta-analyses.

It seems that this school was quite an encouraging place to implement inclusion policies effectively, with most staff feeling that they were supported either by their department head or the school management team. Appropriate senior management support was also found relevant in Leo and Barton's (2006) discussion on how to attain successful leadership when working with diverse school populations. As in Figure 8.1, the natural flow of support and thus influence of positive inclusion should come from the school leader and filter down to the teachers at the base of the pyramid. As has been indicated in the interview responses, if this does not take place then all is not lost, as 'teachers state that peer-support is crucial for working effectively with children who have special needs . . .' (Boyle *et al.* 2012b: 14). The crucial ingredients for ongoing success in inclusive education are the teachers themselves.

There were several mentions made of the assistance that should be provided by Specialist Support Staff. If all requests for direct support were to be accepted then it could be envisaged that the size of these types of departments would be huge and they may become difficult to orchestrate effectively. This indicates the importance of consultation within the support framework, where guidance is provided to staff so that they are best able to use their subject knowledge to support children in the class. The obvious benefits of this type of approach are that many more children and staff

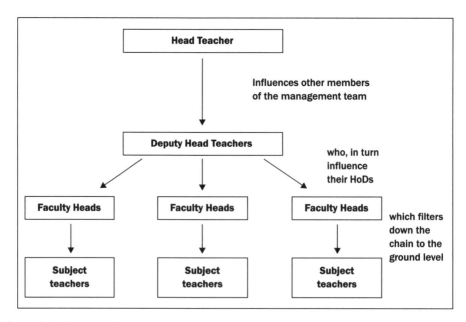

Figure 8.1 Expected flow of positive attitudes to inclusion

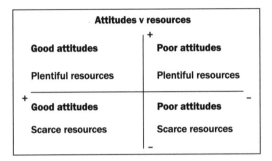

Figure 8.2 Attitudes v resources
Source: Boyle *et al.* 2012b

can be supported in an effective way, while freeing up time to work directly with the most educationally vulnerable children.

When this author worked as a School Psychologist there would often be mention made by parents and/or school staff that a student would require one-to-one support to access the mainstream curriculum. It was always interesting to note their disappointment when it was explained that it was not feasible to offer this level of support. No school can afford this, but it is interesting that the group of teachers interviewed for this chapter indicate that gaining knowledge to support their own practice is considered to be highly pertinent, as opposed to the cry for unattainable resources.

Resourcing and attitudes are factors that are related when considering the effect on implementation of inclusive education. The four quadrants are illustrated in Figure 8.2. The optimal position for a teacher is the top left quadrant, where there is a symbiotic relationship between 'good attitudes' and 'plentiful resources'. However, the antithesis of this is the bottom right quadrant, where there is a dearth of resources and also lacklustre attitudes. In the other two quadrants one aspect can directly affect the other. For example, in the bottom left quadrant the good attitudes aspect could mean that even though the resources are not available, attempts will still be made to be inclusive; whereas the converse is true for the opposite effect in the top right quadrant.

Conclusion

In an age of quantification of educational practice where results take precedence over the process of education (Hardy and Boyle 2011), this chapter has emphasized the importance of considering how teachers can make inclusion successful. It is argued that the teachers are the main players in the inclusion arena and that they are clearly resourceful and not against inclusion, as has been shown in several studies (e.g. Subban and Sharma 2006; Boyle, Topping and Jindal-Snape 2012b).

It seems that teachers can learn and have their practice strengthened by both colleagues and the students themselves. As Mortier *et al.* (2010) has suggested, by getting to know the students and understanding their individual strengths (and not their weaknesses or deficits), then successful inclusion is more achievable. This chapter has demonstrated that teachers are, indeed, more interested in what students can do than focusing on their deficiencies, which provides a useful base for successfully implementing inclusive practices. The teachers interviewed have indicated that this is something they recommend to colleagues and that this is despite the severity of the difficulty, which can affect the level of inclusion in some schools (Scruggs and Mastropieri 1996).

Teaching staff have shown that they regard peer support as crucial to the success or otherwise of inclusive education. Teachers supporting teachers seems to be the most powerful resource that ensures that staff have positive attitudes to inclusion and thus are motivated to be inclusive in practice. Good pedagogy is not about understanding categories *per se* or teaching to a general audience without showing cognizance of the individual, but it is about mastering appropriate classroom management that supports all students irrespective of a notional label.

Notes

1 From this point forward the subject of the teacher will be shown and a figure to represent the years of teaching experience e.g. (Art, 4 years).
2 Specialist Support refers to qualified teachers who were employed in the school to provide support to staff in any curricular department regarding children with additional support needs.
3 Guidance/Student Support is a promoted position where teachers are given extra responsibility to provide welfare and act as a contact point for all students in that school.

References

Avramidis, E. and Norwich, B. (2002) Teachers' attitudes towards integration/inclusion: a review of the literature, *European Journal of Special Needs Education*, 17(2): 129–47. DOI: 10.1080/08856250210129056.

Bain, A. (2005) A systems view of terminology, *Advances in Speech–Language Pathology*, 7(2): 94–7.

Billingsley, B. S. (2004) Special education teacher retention and attrition, *The Journal of Special Education*, 38(1): 39–55. DOI: 10.1177/00224669040380010401.

Boyle, C. (2009) The positive aspects of inclusion in secondary schools from the perspective of secondary school teachers. Unpublished PhD thesis, University of Dundee, Scotland.

Boyle, C., Scriven, B., Durning, S. and Downes, C. (2011) Facilitating the learning of all students: 'the professional positive' of inclusive practice in Australian primary schools, *Support for Learning*, 26(2): 72–8. DOI: 10.1111/j.1467-9604.2011.01480.

Boyle, C., Topping, K., Jindal-Snape, D. and Norwich, B. (2012a) The importance of peer-support for teaching staff when including children with special educational needs, *School Psychology International*, 32(3): 167–84. DOI: 10.1177/0143034311415783.

Boyle, C., Topping, K. and Jindal-Snape, D. (2012b) Teachers' attitudes towards inclusion in high schools. Manuscript submitted for publication.

Braun, V. and Clarke, V. (2006) Using thematic analysis in psychology, *Qualitative Research in Psychology*, 3(2): 77–101. DOI: 10.1191/1478088706qp063oa.

Goodman, R. L. and Burton, D. M. (2010) The inclusion of students with BESD in mainstream schools: teachers' experiences of and recommendations for creating a successful inclusive environment, *Emotional and Behavioural Difficulties*, 15(3): 223–37. DOI: 10.1080/13632752.2010.497662.

Hardy, I. and Boyle, C. (2011) My school? Critiquing the abstraction and quantification of education, *Asia-Pacific Journal of Teacher Education*, 39(3): 211–22. DOI: 10.1080/1359866X.2011.588312.

Hattie, J. A. C. (2009) *Visible Learning: A Synthesis of Over 800 Meta-analyses Relating to Achievement*. Oxford: Routledge.

Lauchlan, F. and Boyle, C. (2007) Is the use of labels in special education helpful?, *Support for Learning*, 22(1): 36–42. DOI: 10.1111/j.1467–9604.2007.00443.x.

Leo, E. and Barton, L. (2006) Inclusion, diversity and leadership: perspectives, possibilities and contradictions, *Educational Management Administration and Leadership*, 34: 167–80. DOI: 10.1177/1741143206062489.

Lipsky, M. (1980) *Street-Level Bureaucracy: Dilemmas of the Individual in Public Services*. New York: Russell Sage Foundation.

Lipsky, M. (2010) *Street-Level Bureaucracy: Dilemmas of the Individual in Public Services (30 Anniversary Expanded Edition)*. New York: Russell Sage Foundation.

Loreman, T., Deppeler, J. and Harvey, D. (2011) *Inclusive Education: Supporting Diversity in the Classroom*. Crows Nest, NSW: Allen and Unwin.

Magiera, M., Smith, C., Zigmond, N. and Gebauer, K. (2005) Benefits of co-teaching in secondary mathematics classes, *TEACHING Exceptional Children*, 37(3): 20–4.

Mallon, F. (2005) Peer and cross-age tutoring and mentoring schemes, in K. Topping and S. Maloney (eds) *The Routledge Falmer Reader in Inclusive Education*. Abingdon: Routledge Falmer.

Mortier, K., Hunt, P., Leroy, M., Van de Putte, I. and Van Hove, G. (2010) Communities of practice in inclusive education, *Educational Studies*, 36(3): 345–55.

Scruggs, T. E. and Mastropieri, M. A. (1996) Teacher perceptions of mainstreaming/inclusion, 1958–1995: a research synthesis, *Exceptional Children*, 63(1): 59–74.

Scruggs, T. E., Mastropieri, M. A. and McDuffie, K. A. (2007) Co-teaching in inclusive classrooms: a metasynthesis of qualitative research, *Exceptional Children*, 73(4): 392–416.

Scruggs, T. E., Mastropieri, M. A. and Leins, P. (2011) Teacher attitudes towards inclusion: a synthesis of survey, comparative, and qualitative research, 1958–2010. Paper presented at the annual meeting of the Council for Exceptional Children, Cumberland Maryland, 25–28 April.

Subban, P. and Sharma, U. (2006) Primary school teachers' perceptions of inclusive education in Victoria, Australia, *International Journal of Special Education*, 21(1): 42–52.

9

RICHARD A. VILLA AND JACQUELINE S. THOUSAND
Creating and sustaining inclusive schools

Introduction

In this chapter, the authors share what they have learned from their nearly three decades of advocating, creating and sustaining inclusive educational practices. Their experiences that inform the content of this chapter include:

- co-ordination of the first US federally funded project, 'Homecoming', to demonstrate that students with severe disabilities could be successfully included in general education classrooms in local neighbourhood schools (Thousand *et al.* 1986);

- the establishment of one of the first fully inclusive schools in the United States (Cross and Villa 1992);

- the development and delivery of an advanced leadership teacher preparation programme to prepare the first Integration Facilitator educators in the United States (Villa and Thousand 1996);

- work with advocacy and educational organizations to create inclusive education in rural communities, suburban settings and large urban centres (Villa *et al.* 2003a) through statewide systems change efforts in the United States (Villa *et al.* 2005; Villa and Thousand 2005); and

- teacher training and governmental support of systems change through university affiliations and non-government organisations (NGOs) in countries around the world including Scotland, the Czech Republic, Slovakia, Honduras, Vietnam and Laos (McNeil *et al.* 1995; Villa *et al.* 2003b; Villa and Thousand 2003).

This chapter defines inclusive education, briefly examines the rationales for inclusive education, and presents an overview of what research and experience have identified as critical variables necessary for inclusive schools to be established and maintained. Emphasized are administrative support, differentiated instruction, and collaborative planning, teaching and decision-making processes to support the education of all students in mixed-ability classrooms.

Inclusive schooling: what is it? Why do it?

Inclusive schooling defined

Inclusive schooling can be defined as welcoming, valuing, empowering and supporting the diverse academic, social, and language learning of *all* students in shared environments and experiences to facilitate the attainment of the goals of education. The authors have asked hundreds of thousands of parents, teachers, administrators, students, university professors and concerned citizens in multiple countries across the globe the following questions: 'What do you believe should be the goals of education? What are the desired outcomes, attitudes, dispositions and skills you want children and youth to acquire as a result of their schooling?' What we have noticed about the responses to these questions is that regardless of the divergent perspectives, vested interests or locales of the people queried, the responses fall within four categories – belonging, mastery, independence and generosity. These four categories of holistic well-being borrowed from the 10,000-year-old educational philosophy of Native American cultures appear to be universally desired goals of education today (Villa and Thousand 2005). Inclusive schools are the most promising learning communities in which to achieve these goals because they value the natural diversity of all students and are aimed at all students achieving academic and interpersonal development and success.

Rationales for inclusive schooling

There are multiple rationales for advocating inclusive schooling. As illustrated in the previous paragraph, a first rationale is that the goals of education appear to be universal and inclusive of all children and youth and that these goals are most achievable in inclusive rather than segregated settings (Villa and Thousand 2005). Second, contemporary international and national laws, policies and organizational position statements support inclusive schooling (IDEIA 2004; UN Convention on the Rights of Persons with Disabilities 2006). Third, inclusive education is perceived as a social justice issue, a basic human right (UNESCO 1994). Fourth, inclusive schooling already exists in both developed and developing countries. In countries such as Norway, Greece, Portugal, Spain, Estonia, Lithuania, Luxembourg and Italy 80–90 per cent of identified students are in inclusive environments (Ferguson 2008). Finally, as described below, research documents the sweeping benefits of inclusive schooling.

Research outcomes of inclusive schooling

As early as the 1980s, research showed that separate schooling experiences had little to no positive effects for US students with specialized needs (i.e. students eligible for special education) (Villa and Thousand 2005). Meta-analyses of effective special education settings have concluded that 'special-needs students educated in regular classes do better academically and socially than comparable students in non-inclusive settings' (Baker *et al.* 1994: 34). This outcome held true regardless of the type of disability or grade level of the student. The US Department of Education also has found that 'across a number of analyses of post-school results, the message was the same: those who spent more time in regular education experienced better results after high school' (1995: 87). Various other researchers also found that the inclusion of students with *severe* disabilities not only had no adverse effects on classmates' academic or behavioural success as measured by standardized tests and report card grades but, instead, enhanced classmates' as well as their own achievement, self-esteem, and school attendance (Sharpe *et al.* 1994; Straub and Peck 1994).

In a more recent large-scale study of over 11,000 students with disabilities, Blackorby and colleagues (2005) found that students with disabilities who spent more time in general education classrooms had fewer absences, performed closer to grade level than peers in pull-out settings, and had higher achievement test scores. This study confirmed that students with disabilities educated in inclusive general education settings outperformed their peers educated in separate settings on standards-based assessments.

In summary, US research findings to date overwhelmingly show that students with disabilities acquire greater mastery of academic and social content in inclusive settings. The United States federal legislation acknowledges this in the most recent 2004 reauthorization of the Individuals with Disabilities Education Improvement Act (IDEIA), stating that:

> nearly 30 years of research and experience has demonstrated that the education of children with disabilities can be made more effective by having high expectations and ensuring students' access in the general education curriculum to the maximum extent possible . . . [and] providing appropriate special education and related services and aides and supports in the regular classroom to such children, whenever possible.
>
> (IDEIA 2004)

Essential characteristics of inclusive schools and inclusive schooling

The *Working Forum on Inclusive Schools* (Council for Exceptional Children 1994), convened by ten of the leading US education organizations, summarized the characteristics of schools identified as successfully implementing the *least restrictive environment* (LRE) principle of the US IDEA legislation, with particular attention on inclusive education or schooling. This forum identified a dozen essential characteristics of schools implementing quality inclusive practices. These characteristics are as essential and relevant today as they were in 1994 and may be used as guidelines for educators, administrators, community members and social activists interested in forwarding quality inclusive schooling opportunities not only for students with identified learning needs, but for all children. What is educationally, socially and emotionally inclusive and healthy for students with special learning needs is inclusive and healthy for all children. The 12 characteristics of inclusive schools are as follows:

- *A sense of community*: an inclusive school has a philosophy and a vision that all children belong and can learn in the mainstream of school and community life.

Within an inclusive school, everyone belongs, everyone is accepted and is supported by peers and the adults in the school.

- *Visionary leadership*: the administration plays a critical role in an inclusive school by articulating the vision, building consensus for the vision, and actively involving and sharing responsibility with the entire school staff in planning and carrying out the strategies that make the school successful.

- *High standards*: within inclusive schools, all children meet high levels of educational outcomes and high standards of performance, which are appropriate to their needs.

- *Collaborative partnerships*: an inclusive school encourages students and staff to support one another with such strategies as peer tutoring, buddy systems, co-operative learning, team teaching, co-teaching, teacher–student assistance teams and other collaborative arrangements.

- *Changing roles and responsibilities*: an inclusive school changes the old roles of teachers and school staff. For example, teachers lecture less and assist more, school psychologists work more closely with teachers in the classroom, and every person in the building is an active participant in the learning process.

- *Array of services*: an inclusive school offers an array of services that are co-ordinated with the educational staff and designed to meet the needs of learners experiencing various cognitive, physical and/or emotional challenges.

- *Partnership with parents*: parents are embraced as equal and essential partners in the education of their children.

- *Flexible learning environments*: children in an inclusive school are not expected to move in lock steps, but rather they follow their individual paths to learning. Groupings are flexible, and material is presented in concrete, meaningful ways that emphasize participation. Although there is less reliance on programmes that pull children out of classrooms, there are still opportunities for students with and without disabilities to receive separate instruction if needed.

- *Strategies based on research*: research into how people learn is providing new ideas and strategies for teachers, and an inclusive school incorporates those ideas. Differentiated instruction, co-operative learning, a balanced approach to literacy instruction, interdisciplinary curriculum, authentic assessment of student performance, peer tutoring, direct instruction, reciprocal teaching, learning styles, Multiple Intelligence Theory, social skills training, positive behaviour supports, computer-assisted instruction and other forms of technology, and study skill training are some of the practices that have emerged from the latest research and are applied in inclusive schools.

- *Forms of accountability*: an inclusive school relies less on standardized tests, using new [and authentic] forms of accountability and assessment (e.g. portfolios, performance-based assessment) to make sure that each student is progressing towards his or her goal.

- *Access*: an inclusive school ensures that students have access to the general education curriculum and are able to participate in school life by making necessary modifications to buildings and by making available appropriate technology that makes participation possible.

- *Continuing professional development*: an inclusive school enables staff to design and obtain professional development on an ongoing basis so that there is continuous improvement in the knowledge and skills that they can employ to educate diverse students in shared environments and experiences.

Administrative support for inclusive education

Administrative leadership and support is foundational to facilitating change and success with any best practice initiative, of which inclusive education is one such initiative. Administrative support has five dimensions – vision, skills, incentives, resources and action planning. For an inclusive ethic and inclusive practices to take hold in a school community, the organizational leaders of the school organization – school principals, district central office administrators, grade-level team leaders, special education and related services directors, department chairs – must orchestrate attention to all five dimensions of change (Villa and Thousand 2005) by doing the following:

- building a *vision* for collaborative planning and problem solving to differentiate teaching;
- developing educators' *skills* and confidence to plan collaboratively, problem solve and differentiate instruction for diverse learners;
- creating and delivering meaningful *incentives* for people to take the risk to embark on a journey to educate diverse learners in mixed-ability groups in general education classrooms (e.g. building master schedules that provide common planning time);
- reorganizing, scheduling and co-ordinating human and other *resources*; and
- developing and activating an *action plan* of specific activities and sequence of steps.

Nine specific administrative actions seem to be essential for change toward inclusion to occur. Each is listed here along with the dimension or dimensions of change to which it attends.

- *Vision*: publicly articulate the rationale for inclusive education.
- *Resource*: redefine staff roles (i.e. in the job description of classroom teachers and support personnel) so that all are expected to participate in collaborative planning, problem solving and differentiated instruction.
- *Resources and incentives*: assess the staff's need for collaboration (e.g. With whom do I need to collaborate to adapt instruction successfully? From which colleagues can I acquire skills through modelling and coaching?)
- *Resources*: create a master schedule that allows for collaboration in planning and teaching (e.g. common prep and lunch periods).

- *Resources and incentives*: periodically provide additional meeting time for personnel who collaboratively plan and teach (e.g. hire substitutes, use in-service time for collaborative planning, provide release time for planning). Regularly provide time for instructional personnel to meet by relieving them from non-instructional duties that other staff that are not collaboratively planning and teaching are required to perform.

- *Skills and incentives*: establish professional support groups to help staff learn about and begin to practise problem solving, collaboration and differentiation and to analyse data.

- *Skills and vision*: institute staff development in order to create a common conceptual language and framework, a common skill set, and shared dispositions toward inclusive practice. Provide training in collaborative planning, problem solving, high-yield instructional strategies, differentiated instruction, authentic assessment, legal rights and responsibilities, data-based decision making, and the legal, philosophical, research and data-based rationales for change in educational practices (e.g. courses and workshops, mentoring and peer coaching systems, professional learning communities, book studies, job shadowing, clinical supervision, and the pairing of new teachers with veteran collaborators in planning and teaching).

- *Incentives*: educate school and community members about the successes of students who have been included.

- *Incentives*: provide incentives for collaboration in planning, problem solving and teaching. For example, publicly recognize the efforts and accomplishments of collaborators, offer additional training, provide release time to observe one another in action, support teams of teachers to attend conferences on inclusive practices, and arrange for teachers to deliver presentations about their accomplishments.

Planning for differentiated instruction

Two processes essential for successful inclusion are:

- processes for differentiating instruction; and
- collaboration processes.

Let us examine the process of differentiation first. Differentiated instruction is a teaching philosophy based on the premise that teachers should adapt instruction to student differences, because all students do not learn in the same way, at the same time, or at the same rate. Differentiated instruction begins with gathering facts about students so that instructional personnel can react responsively to students' varying background knowledge, culture, life circumstances, readiness, language, learning preferences, strengths and interests. Based upon this student-centred information, educators then may design multiple options for students at the three instructional design points of:

- content – what students will learn and how students can take in information (materials);
- process – what happens moment to moment in the classroom to assist students to make sense of information and ideas; and
- product – ways in which students can express and show what they know and have learned and how these products may be assessed (e.g. grading) (Thousand *et al.* 2007).

At each of the three instructional design points there are a series of questions for educators to consider in order to guide their thinking about differentiation.

Content differentiation questions

Among the questions to consider about differentiation of instructional content and materials are:

- What are the curriculum standards or objectives?
- What are the academic/social/language goals of the learners?
- What are recommendations from professional organizations?
- In what order will concepts/content be taught?
- What multi-level and multi-sensory materials will best convey concepts and content to each student?
- In what ways can we use technology (e.g. text-to-speech software)?
- Will we differentiate level of knowledge or proficiency?

Process differentiation questions

As any educator will tell you, how to deliver instruction in order to reach all students is an extremely complex set of decisions and actions. Questions to consider when planning how to differentiate the moment-to-moment instructional processes in the classroom are many and are presented in the four columns of Table 9.1. Each column illustrates an instructional process dimension. The first dimension, *instructional format*, concerns the overall design or structure of a lesson. The *instructional arrangement* dimension concerns student groupings during instruction. *Instructional strategies* are the instructional techniques, methods or applications of theoretical frameworks (e.g. Multiple Intelligences) employed during instruction. The *physical and social environment* process dimension has to do with the social, behavioural and physical norms and structure of the classroom as well as group and individual student behavioural and social/emotional supports.

Product differentiation questions

Questions to consider when thinking about differentiating ways in which students can show what they have learned include:

Table 9.1 Process options by format, arrangement, strategies and environment

Instructional formats	Instructional arrangements	Instructional strategies	Physical or social environment
Adapted lectures	Co-operative learning structures	Research-based teaching strategies	Strategic room arrangement
Activity-based	Same or cross-age peer tutors	Taxonomies	Establishing and enforcing social norms
Simulations or role plays	Independent individual work	Multiple Intelligence theory	Teach responsibility and decision making
Group investigation	Whole-group instruction	Integration of the arts	Positive behaviour supports
Discovery learning	Tutorial instruction		Behaviour support plan
Computer and web-based	Teacher-directed small groups		Environmental alterations
Self-directed			Use of spaces outside classroom
Centres and stations			
Integrated, cross-curricular thematic			
Community-referenced			

- What are the product options and how will they be assessed?
- What multi-level assessments and criteria will be used?
- Which authentic (e.g. real-life) products will be created?
- How will products be evaluated (e.g. a rubric or a set of criteria linked to learning objectives)?

Products that provide evidence of learning can be developed and presented by individuals, partners and/or groups of learners. Table 9.2 offers 20 examples of widely diverse ways in which students can show or demonstrate what they have learned.

Addressing mismatches between student characteristics and classroom demands

Despite every effort to differentiate the content, process and product of instruction, educators may still find a mismatch between a particular student's characteristics and

Table 9.2 Product differentiation ideas

Collage	Rap/Song	Mnemonics	Choral response	Podcast
Dance	Photo essay	Model	Simulation	Role play
Oral presentation	Written presentation	Teaching another	PowerPoint	Mural
Oral history	Diorama	Summary of interviews	Editorial	Commercial

Table 9.3 Mismatch problem-solving template

Facts about the student	Facts about lesson or classroom demands	Mismatches between the student and classroom demands	Potential solutions to mismatches
Strengths Background knowledge and experiences	**Content demands** How is the content made available to the learner?	1	1 a b c
Interests		2	2 a b c
Learning style Multiple intelligences	**Process demands** What processes do the teachers use to facilitate student learning?	3	3 a b c
Important relationships		4	4 a b c
Other:	**Product demands** How do students demonstrate what they have learned?	5	5 a b c
Goals	How are they graded?	6	6 a b c

needs and the demands of a lesson or classroom. Acknowledging this, we recommend the use of the template presented in Table 9.3 to address such mismatches (Thousand *et al.* 2007). The template prompts a comparison of a student's learning characteristics including strengths (Column 1) with the typical content, product and process demands of a lesson or classroom (Column 2) in order to identify content, process and product mismatches with the student's characteristics (Column 3). Column 4 prompts the brainstorming of multiple potential solutions for each mismatch in ways that not only acknowledge but also use the student's characteristics and strengths. We suggest generating a minimum of three potential solutions per mismatch so that there is a range of options from which to choose or integrate to remediate the mismatch.

As teachers become more adept at proactively differentiating the content, process and product dimensions of their lessons and more automatically vary materials, goals, instructional processes and assessment methods to accommodate the differences of all of the students in their classrooms, there will be less of a need to use a retrofit template such as this to resolve mismatches for individual students. The differentiation will already be built into lessons, the classroom design and the climate of the classroom.

Collaboration for and with students

Collaboration is the second essential process to successful inclusion. Most typically, we think of collaboration among school personnel, teachers and administrators. And yet, there are many other collaborative partners who are available and needed. Parents are essential partners. The positive impact of collaborating with parents is acknowledged in the most recent reauthorization of the federal special education law in the United States (IDEIA 2004). The law acknowledges that:

> nearly 30 years of research and experience has demonstrated that the education of children with disabilities can be made more effective by strengthening the role of parents and making sure that families of such children have meaningful opportunities to participate in the education of such children . . .
>
> (IDEIA 2004)

Educators often ask for more resources to be able to successfully meet the needs of the diverse students in their classrooms. We acknowledge that disparities in human and fiscal resources exist and will continue to exist among schools, school districts and nations. Yet, there is an often overlooked resource that always will be available in every school on the planet – the children themselves (Villa *et al.* 2010).

Collaboration with students in decision making and the design, delivery and evaluation of instruction involves students working in co-operative learning groups, as tutors and partners in partner learning (e.g. reciprocal teaching), and as co-teachers with their teachers. Collaboration with students means involving students as decision makers and problem solvers, as designers of their own learning and being self-determined in planning for their own futures. Collaboration with students means engaging students as mediators of conflict and controversy and advocates for themselves and others. Collaboration with students means fostering self-discipline and student learning and use of responsible behaviour.

Rationale for collaboration with students

There are multiple rationales for collaborating with students in instruction and decision making in order to forward inclusive practice. In addition to facilitating the goals of education of belonging, mastery, independence and generosity identified at the beginning of the chapter, collaborating with students serves as an example of democratic and inclusive schooling. It can increase student self-determination and academic and social competence as well as reap an untapped resource in times of limited fiscal and human resources (Villa *et al.* 2010).

There also are theoretical bases and rationale for student collaboration. First, from a zone of proximal development (ZPD) theoretical perspective (Vygotsky 1987), what children can do with the assistance of others is more indicative of their mental development than what they can do alone. Vygotsky (1978: 86) defined the ZPD as the distance between the actual developmental level as determined by independent problem solving and the level of potential development as determined through problem solving under adult guidance, or in collaboration with more capable peers. Further, cognitive psychologists have verified that when students become reciprocal teachers of one another (i.e. both students alternate being the teacher who coaches the comprehension skills they are learning), reading comprehension scores of poor readers increase (Palinscar and Brown 1984).

Finally, educational research supports students engaging in collaborative learning and teaching. For example, one variation of student instructional collaboration – co-operative group learning – has been identified as one of the top nine educational practices correlated with increasing student achievement on standardized tests (Marzano *et al.* 2001). Many positive social, communication and academic achievement outcomes have been reported in the research on peer tutoring, partner learning, reciprocal teaching and co-operative group learning – four variations of students serving as collaborators in instruction. For example, when students with disabilities have served as reciprocal tutors/tutees, they have shown higher achievement compared to when they were only recipients of tutoring (Elbaum *et al.* 2001). They also experience increased self-esteem as a result of being in the teacher role (Elbaum *et al.* 2001). Additionally, when children serve in teaching roles, they are increasing their own mastery of the content as well as learning valuable communication skills.

With regard to peer tutoring, it is critical that all students (e.g. students with learning differences and special educational needs) learn to serve as tutors and have the opportunity to learn as tutees from their peers. This is especially important for students who are considered gifted or talented, lest they become typecast as tutors only. They too can benefit from being tutored and receiving a challenging education filled with diverse activities and opportunities. Tutoring other students can be one exciting and challenging component of their day.

The 14 questions in the Student Collaboration Quiz presented in Table 9.4 summarize ways in which students can join adults in collaborative teaching, learning and decision making. With your own schooling experiences in mind, we invite you to take the quiz. We then invite you to challenge your own teaching practices by considering two questions: 'How might my own experiences as a student have influenced my teaching practices and the collaborative opportunities I make available to students today?' and 'How might the collaborative experiences suggested in the quiz facilitate student growth in academic, communication and social/emotional domains and thereby facilitate the holistic educational goals of belonging, mastery, independence, and generosity?'

Table 9.4 Student collaboration quiz

Directions: Please circle the rating that best fits your own experience as a student.

1 How often were you expected to support the academic and social learning of other students as well as be accountable for your own learning by working in co-operative groups?

Never Rarely Sometimes Often Very often

2 Were you, as a student, given the opportunity and training to serve as an instructor for a peer?

Never Rarely Sometimes Often Very often

3 Were you, as a student, given the opportunity to receive instruction from a trained peer?

Never Rarely Sometimes Often Very often

4 How often were you involved in a discussion of the teaching act with an instructor?

Never Rarely Sometimes Often Very often

5 Were you, as a student, given the opportunity to co-teach a class with an adult?

Never Rarely Sometimes Often Very often

6 How often were you taught creative problem-solving strategies and given an opportunity to employ them to solve academic or behavioural challenges?

Never Rarely Sometimes Often Very often

7 How often were you asked to evaluate your own learning?

Never Rarely Sometimes Often Very often

8 How often were you given the opportunity to assist in determining the educational outcomes for you and your classmates?

Never Rarely Sometimes Often Very often

9 How often were you given the opportunity to advocate for the educational interests of a classmate or asked to assist in determining modifications and accommodations to curriculum?

Never Rarely Sometimes Often Very often

10 How often were you asked to provide your teachers with feedback as to the effectiveness and appropriateness of their instruction and classroom management?

Never Rarely Sometimes Often Very often

11 Were you, as a student, given the opportunity and training to serve as a mediator of conflict between peers?

Never Rarely Sometimes Often Very often

12 How often were you, as a student, encouraged to bring a support person to a difficult meeting to provide you with moral support?

Never Rarely Sometimes Often Very often

13 How often were you given the opportunity to lead or facilitate meetings addressing your academic progress and/or future (e.g. Developing Personal Learning Plans, Student–Parent–Teacher Conferences, an IEP meeting)?

Never Rarely Sometimes Often Very often

14 How often did you participate as an equal with teachers, administrators and community members on school committees (e.g. curriculum committee, discipline committee, hiring committee, school board)?

Never Rarely Sometimes Often Very often

Conclusion

We, the authors, are hopeful that inclusive educational opportunities for children and youth with disabilities will continue to expand internationally. We are hopeful because numerous demonstrations currently exist worldwide. Whatever is (i.e. has already been demonstrated), is possible (somewhere else). We are hopeful because much of what is necessary to facilitate inclusive education has been documented. What is necessary are policies and laws; administrative leadership; collaboration among school personnel, families and students; professional development; a shift away from focusing on the perceived deficits within a child to an examination of the complex interaction between the learner and the content, process and product demands of the classroom; and the use of research-based, collaborative and differentiated instructional strategies to support learners in mixed-ability classrooms.

Schools do not change by imposing a model developed elsewhere; instead, they change through educators, policy makers and communities engaging with one another and sharing experiences (Wheatley 1994). Fortunately, experiences of schools attempting inclusive practices worldwide have been documented and continue to be discovered, refined and shared. The ultimate question is 'How do we expand inclusive schooling worldwide by borrowing from and massaging what we have learned to be common critical factors for success?' The obvious first answer is that, in order to influence others' beliefs about what is possible, those of us who have engaged in or been witness to the development of inclusive communities must continue to share learnings from our struggles in transforming ways in which schools operate. A number of these learnings and experiences have been shared in this chapter and other chapters in this book.

References

Baker, E., Wang, M. and Walberg, H. (1994) The effects of inclusion on learning, *Educational Leadership*, 52(4): 33–5.

Blackorby, J., Wagner, M., Camero, R., Davies, E., Levine, P., Newman, L. *et al.* (2005) *Engagement, Academics, Social Adjustments, and Independence*. Menlo Park, CA: SRI International. Available at: http://www.seels.net/designdocs/engagement/00_SEELS_TOC_10-04-05.pdf [Accessed 20 March 2012].

CEC (Council for Exceptional Children) (1994) *Creating Schools for All Our Students: What 12 Schools Have to Say*. Working Forum on Inclusive Schools. Reston, VA: CEC.

Cross, G. and Villa, R. (1992) The Winooski school system: an evolutionary tale of a school district restructuring for diversity, in R. Villa, J. Thousand, W. Stainback and S. Stainback (eds) *Restructuring for Caring and Effective Education*. Baltimorem, MD: Paul Brookes Publishing.

Elbaum, B., Moody, S.W., Vaughn, S., Schumm, J.S. and Hughes, M. (2001) *The Effect of Instructional Grouping Format on the Reading Outcomes of Students with Disabilities: A Meta-analytic Review*. Available at: http://www.ncld.org/research/osep_reading.cfm [Accessed 20 March 2012].

Ferguson, D.L. (2008) International trends in inclusive education: the continuing challenge to teach each one and everyone, *European Journal of Special Needs Education*, 23(2): 109–20.

IDEIA (2004) *Individuals with Disabilities Education Improvement Act*, 20 USC 1401. Public Law 108–446, Part B, Sec. 682 [c] Findings [5].

McNeil, M., Villa, R. and Thousand, J. (1995) Enhancing special education teacher education in Honduras: an international cooperation model in A. Artiles and D. Hallahan (eds) *Special Education in Latin America*. Westport, CT: Greenwood Publishing Groups.

Marzano, R., Pickering, D. and Pollack, J. (2001) *Classroom Instruction that Works: Research-based Strategies for Increasing Student Achievement*. Alexandria, VA: Association for Supervision and Curriculum Development.

Palinscar, A. and Brown, A. (1984) Reciprocal teaching of comprehension: fostering and monitoring activities, *Cognition and Instruction*, 1(2): 117–75.

Sharpe, M.N., York, J.L. and Knight, J. (1994) Effects of inclusion on the academic performance of classmates without disabilities, *Remedial and Special Education*, 15(5): 281–7.

Straub, D. and Peck, C. (1994) What are the outcomes for nondisabled students?, *Educational Leadership*, 52(4): 36–40.

Thousand, J., Fox, T., Reid, R., Godek, J. and Williams, W. (1986) The homecoming model: educating students who present intensive educational challenges within regular education environments (Monograph 7–1). Burlington: University of Vermont, Center for Developmental Disabilities.

Thousand, J., Villa, R. and Nevin, A. (2007) *Differentiating Instruction: Collaboratively Planning and Teaching for Universally Designed Learning*. Thousand Oaks, CA: Corwin Press.

United Nations (2006) *UN Convention on the Rights of Persons with Disabilities*. New York: United Nations.

UNESCO (1994) The Salamanca Statement and Framework for Action on Special Needs Education. Paris: UNESCO.

US Department of Education (1995) *Seventeenth Annual Report to Congress on the Implementation of the Individuals with Disabilities Education Act*. Washington, DC: US Department of Education.

Villa, R. and Thousand, J. (1996) Assembly: preservice and inservice personnel preparation to support the inclusion of children with disabilities in general education classrooms. Paper presented at Association for Supervision and Curriculum Development Annual Conference, New Orleans, 7–9 March.

Villa, R. and Thousand, J. S. (2003) Lessons learned from more than 20 years of research and practice in developing and sustaining inclusive education in developed and developing nations, in M.L.H.Hui, C. Robin Dowson and M. Gonzles Moont (eds) *Inclusive Education in the New Millennium*. Hong Kong and Macau: Education Convergence and the Association for Childhood Education International.

Villa, R. and Thousand, J. (2005) *Creating an Inclusive School*, 2nd edn. Alexandria, VA: Association for Supervision and Curriculum Development.

Villa, R., Falvey, M. and Schrag, J. (2003a) System change in Los Angeles: the city of angels, in D. Fisher and N. Frey (eds) *Inclusive Urban Schools*. Baltimore, MD: Paul Brookes.

Villa, R.A., Tac, L.V., Muc, P.M., Ryan, S., Thuy, N.T.M., Weill, C. and Thousand J.S. (2003b) Inclusion in Viet Nam: a decade of implementation, *Research and Practice for Persons with Severe Disabilities*, 28(1): 23–32.

Villa, R., Martinez, S., Keefe, L., Garcia, R., Hendrix, B. and Gallegos, A. (2005) New Mexico's LRE initiative: a collaboratively developed and implemented systems change plan. Paper presented at TASH Conference, The Heart of TASH – 30 Years and Still Beating Strong, Milwaukee, 9–12 November.

Villa, R., Thousand, J. and Nevin, A. (2010) *Collaborating with Students in Instruction and Decision-making: The Untapped Resource*. Thousand Oaks, CA: Corwin Press.

Vygotsky, L.S. (1978) *Mind and Society: The Development of Higher Psychological Processes.* Cambridge, MA: Harvard University Press.

Vygotsky, L. (1987) *The Collected Works of L. S. Vygotsky* (translated by R. W. Rieber and A. S. Carton). (Original works published in 1934 and 1960). New York: Plenum Press.

Wheatley, M.J. (1994) *Leadership and the New Science: Learning about Organization from an Orderly Universe.* San Francisco, CA: Berrett-Koehler Publishers.

10

JOANNE DEPPELER
Developing inclusive practices: innovation through collaboration

Coming together is a beginning; keeping together is progress; working together is success.

(Henry Ford)

Introduction

Diversity is a valuable asset that contributes to the richness and social capital of the inclusive school. *Collaboration* and *representation* are democratic processes that are critical for understanding diversity and for generating innovative solutions to the challenges of inclusive schooling. *Collaboration* enables teachers with diverse expertise to work together as equals with others in the school community and to share decision making to address the challenges in their school. *Representation* in inclusive schools means empowering all of the voices in the community to be heard and placing an equal value on all of the contributions. The knowledge and active involvement of every member of the school community is important for problem solving and building shared understandings. The school community includes local students, teachers, leaders, parents and professionals and business owners, policy makers and educational administrators, and others, in the wider educational community. All of these members have different perspectives, understandings and expectations with regard to the school and are potentially able to contribute to the collective knowledge and engage in the development of the school. *Genuine* collaboration must be based on common goals, voluntary engagement and parity among the participants and involve shared resources, decision making, responsibility, and accountability for outcomes (Friend and Cook 2007).

The expectation in much of the current international education is that educators will collaborate and share responsibility and accountability for the progress of *all* students, including those with disabilities and from diverse backgrounds. Often referred to as 'standards-based' reform, the central purpose is to ensure that *all* students achieve common educational standards. Despite the challenges associated with this reform agenda the emphasis on collaboration has expanded the ways that educators work with others and use evidence to develop unique solutions to meet the needs of the diverse learners in their school. Drawing on evidence and ideas from international literature, this chapter highlights a number of different forms of collaboration. These collaborative practices are intended to create equitable conditions for the generation and sharing of knowledge and for the active participation of members of the school community in inquiry activities that are focused on learning and success in inclusive schools.

Collaboration: working together in a professional learning community (PLC)

Decades of research have revealed that collaboration is essential for developing practices in schools and has been linked to:

- increased student achievement (Goddard *et al.* 2007);
- changes in teachers' practices (Desimone *et al.* 2002; Vescio *et al.* 2008);
- improvement in teachers' individual and collective self-efficacy (Cantrell and Hughes 2008).

Although collaboration can be highly effective, many collective efforts for educational progress have made little difference to the quality of teaching and learning (Hargreaves and Shirley 2009). There are complex challenges in bringing together and keeping together different professionals, families and teachers to work towards common goals. While schools are potential sites for shared practice, they often lack the structures or mechanisms for facilitating the active participation of the various members. Professional learning communities (PLC) have become increasingly popular as a structure to enable members of the school community to work together in systematic ways to achieve their collective purpose of enhancing student learning.

> A professional learning community is an inclusive group of people, motivated by a shared learning vision, who support and work with each other, finding ways, inside and outside their immediate community, to enquire on their practice and together learn new and better approaches that will enhance all pupils' learning.
>
> (Stoll *et al.* 2006)

Research evidence has demonstrated that there are positive benefits of PLCs as a structure for professional development (Stoll and Seashore Louis 2007; Dufour *et al.* 2008; Chappuis *et al.* 2009), for improving teacher practice (Grossman *et al.* 2001; Little 2002; Lachance and Confrey 2003) and as a strategy for school and system reform (Harris and Chrispeels 2008; Bryk *et al.* 2009). Further, it is generally acknowledged that strong PLCs support teachers not only to develop new content and pedagogical knowledge but also to critically examine and challenge existing assumptions about teaching (Little 2002) and result in higher student achievement (Lomos *et al.* 2011). While these benefits make this approach particularly valuable for developing inclusive practice, they are only realized when PLCs:

- are specifically focused on improving student learning (Stoll and Seashore Louis 2007);
- include appropriate pedagogical content and expertise (Bausmith and Barry 2011);
- are informed by evidence (Hargreaves and Shirley 2009); and
- are structured appropriately (Harris and Jones 2010).

In effective PLCs, everyone works together to investigate and solve the issues in the school and positive outcomes for teaching and learning are achieved. There are a number of features that characterize effective PLCs:

- There is a shared agenda and common values that are understood by all members.
- There is an explicit focus on effective teaching for student learning and equity.
- There is shared responsibility for student learning.
- There are high expectations for *all* students.
- There is a culture of openness, trust and respect.
- Leadership is distributed across the school and leaders are actively engaged.
- Parents, professionals and others from the wider school community all contribute.
- Student input is valued and student voices are frequently heard.
- Evidence and inquiry is valued and used to inform and improve teaching and learning.
- Appropriate pedagogical content and expertise informs teaching.
- There is a focus on risk taking and innovation and collective professional learning.
- Resources and organizational structures allow space and time for collaboration.
- Critical reflection and discussion of practices is common.

The active engagement of the leaders in the school supports and contributes to organizational conditions that build PLCs, which in turn influence teacher work and student outcomes (Mulford 2008). Ainscow and Sandill (2010: 404) argue that it is the organizational conditions that promote collaboration and problem solving that 'produce more inclusive responses to diversity'. School leaders who are deliberate in their efforts to support collaboration find creative ways to provide time (e.g. changes to the school timetable or by providing teaching relief; Deppeler 2006) and spaces for professional discussions (e.g. shared work spaces, strategic placement of the coffee machine; Stoll *et al.* 2006), and provide clear expectations and explicit support for learning how to work in teams (Thessin and Starr 2011). The introduction of these particular arrangements will not in itself build PLCs, nor will it develop inclusive practices. Leaders will need to create collaborative learning cultures that share a commitment to equity, voice and social justice (Riehl 2000) and provide long-term support to sustain them (Levine 2011).

Collaboration: using inquiry to inform shared decision making and change

PLCs create opportunities for teachers to work together in research *inquiry*. Various forms of inquiry have in common a search for solutions through systematic, reflective study of practice informed by evidence (Carr and Kemmis 1986; Cochran-Smith and Lytle 2009). When teachers work together in inquiry, they identify an issue or challenge, analyse and discuss relevant evidence, and then determine actions for further investigation. The term *collaborative inquiry* (CI) is sometimes adopted to refer to repeated cycles of action research conducted by a group of teachers as they attempt to understand an issue or question of importance to the school community (Bray 2000; Deppeler 2007; Ermeling 2010). 'Action research can provide the stimulus for changing and improving practice in order to make it appropriate for the unique individuals with whom we work' (Mertler 2008: 14). The cycle of action research typically involves a number of stages, for example the four-stage model described by Sagor (2011):

1   clarify visions and targets;

2   articulate theory and plan for implementation;

3   implement action and collect data; and

4   reflect on the data and plan informed action.

Forms of CI vary with respect to the focus for the work, with some emphasizing school-wide issues and others more explicitly focused on the improvement of teaching and student outcomes in specific curricular areas. The CI processes promote an appreciation of uncertainty and dialogue (Snow-Gerono 2005), risk taking and experimentation, which in turn has positive outcomes for teacher learning and students in schools (Deppeler 2007; Deppeler 2010; Miles and Ainscow 2011). These are powerful processes for empowering teachers and leaders not only to understand and demonstrate the effectiveness of their practices but to also generate new knowledge that is relevant to their school. There is little doubt that teachers and others who are directly connected with these issues are best placed to investigate the specific circumstances and to develop the unique solutions for improving their inclusive practices (Zech *et al.* 2000; Bray 2002; Burbank and Burbank 2003; Huffman and Kalnin 2003; Mariage and Garmon 2003).

Although research has demonstrated that teachers and leaders can become capable and confident with CI (Earl *et al.* 2003; Nelson and Slavit 2007), it has not typically been a feature of work in schools. Collaboration in inquiry does not occur naturally; it runs against the prevailing practice of teachers working individually, intuitively and in isolation. CI will not succeed if it originates from concerns of administrators and others outside the school or classroom (e.g. when teachers are expected to work together and confront school system improvement goals) or if there is insufficient support for the collaborative processes. Teachers' work in these circumstances is unlikely to lead to sustainable change in inclusive practices. Hargreaves (1994) has described this as "contrived collegiality" – where the internal politics of schools is ignored and decisions regarding collaboration are made centrally. In contrast, genuine CI is characterized by voluntary participation and shared interest in open dialogue about the investigation of practice-based issues. Long-term support should include specific training in collaborating skills as well as in conducting action research. Loreman *et al.* (2010) provide the following suggestions to guide CI processes in schools:

- Identify a specific focus for development.
- Establish the team with a range of stakeholders and include leaders and voluntary participation.
- Clarify expectations for roles and commitment.
- Schedule time and places for the collaborative work.
- Conduct an audit of practice, collecting a range of evidence relevant to student learning (e.g. performance on standard measures, teacher assessment, observations of classroom practice, student work, interviews with students, parents, attendance records).
- Critically analyse and discuss evidence.
- Use the results to select strategies for change and make decisions for an action plan based on the results and pedagogical practices.
- Plan and implement action and respond to resistance.
- Assess progress and share evidence and outcomes.
- Identify opportunities to implement successful practices more widely and for further development.

Collaboration: developing common quality assessments of student learning

Measuring the success of CI in terms of student outcomes can be challenging. There is increased accountability and pressure on schools to improve student performance on standardized measures of academic achievement. Standardized performance data, although readily available in schools, may be too narrowly focused or may not be sensitive enough to reflect other changes in student learning. Teachers can use a variety of evidence and data to understand better the issue being investigated as well as to inform decisions about what's working and where to go next. Lingo *et al.* (2011) suggest a number of practical assessment options for special and general education teachers working together, that can easily be incorporated into classroom activities, including: anecdotal recording, student work samples, and event, interval, duration and latency recording methods. Interviews and questionnaires with students, parents and others, policy documents, portfolios of teaching and student work along with systematic observations of classrooms (direct or video-recorded) are all potential sources of evidence that can be used as part of the processes of CI.

Many of the assessment techniques used as part of an *Assessment for Learning (AFL)* framework provide excellent alternatives for measuring student progress. In their now famous essay *Inside the Black Box,* Black and Wiliam (1998) made clear from a review of more than nine years of research that AFL has a powerful impact on student learning, and in particular for low-achieving students. An extensive body of research work has shown that four AFL assessment practices (questioning, feedback, shared criteria and peer and self-assessment) can frame teachers' CI work and are highly effective in documenting and monitoring student progress. All of the AFL practices emphasize the student's contribution as a source of evidence so that teachers can have detailed understandings about what students know and can do (Assessment Reform Group 2002; Clarke 2005). When used appropriately, there are enormous benefits for using these forms of teacher assessments as data to improve teaching and student learning (Wiliam *et al.* 2004; McMillan 2007; Boyle and Charles 2010).

> When teachers are provided with opportunities to use and interpret assessment data in order to become more responsive to their students' learning needs, the impact is substantive.
>
> (Timperley 2008: 24)

Teachers cannot, however, be expected to accomplish this on their own. Based on a synthesis of research and a number of projects with teachers engaged in inquiry in New Zealand, Helen Timperley and her colleagues have identified a set of conditions necessary for teacher assessment data to result in improved teaching practice and student outcomes:

- The assessment data needs to provide information that is relevant to the curriculum and that informs teaching and learning rather than being used to categorize or label students.
- Teachers need to be able to interpret the assessment data in ways that allow them to make changes to practice and to share and discuss this information with leaders.
- Teachers need relevant pedagogical content knowledge to inform decisions about changes to practice.
- School leaders need to know how to support members of the school community in cycles of evidence – informed inquiry.

> (Timperley 2008)

The accountability pressures exerted by current standardized testing require-ments are not fully consistent with teacher assessment practices. The increased emphasis on *good* test results can lead to valuing student work 'only in relation to a perceived link with their successes or failures in tests' (Black *et al.* 2010: 226). In many countries teacher assessment is often limited to local reporting, as opposed to the national testing at the system level, or international regimes such as PISA results (OECD 2010). Congruence between system-level accountability and teachers' assessment practices depends on the validity and reliability of teachers' interpreta-tions of assessment data. Many have argued that teachers' collaborative *moderation* of assessments can lead to closer alignment of assessment practices and can result in valid and reliable results comparable to external testing (Assessment Reform Group 2002; Harlen 2005).

Teacher moderation

Teacher moderation is a valuable collaborative practice that allows teachers to compare and discuss their assessments of student work with those of other teachers and to reach consensus about the quality of that work. It is the discussion of their different interpretations of the same work that helps to deepen understandings of what students have or have not learned. Teachers may need to debate their different understandings. The process challenges teachers to identify what teaching practices are working to support students' learning and to examine their beliefs about what individual students can and cannot do. Through the moderation process teachers develop common understandings and align their interpretations of the assessment criteria and standards they are using (see for example Cushman 2002; Ontario Literacy and Numeracy Secretariat 2007). The goal is to produce teacher assessments that are valid and reliable, and are consistent with the identified assessment criteria and with each other (Wilson 2004).

> When teachers work together to consider the work students have produced, . . . they bring the collective wisdom of all the people in the group to the exercise. More eyes (and consequently more brains) result in more reliable determinations of what students understand.
>
> (Earl 2004: 41)

Black et al. (2010: 228) suggest that communities of teachers need sustained support with assessment to 'work together to improve both their theories and their assumptions that underlie practice,' including support to:

- specify the agreed upon criteria in each subject area;
- use a portfolio composed of a diverse range of pieces of work to represent an overall measure of assessment of each student in a subject;
- develop procedures for moderation that develop common understandings of criteria and ensure overall consistency in assessment results;
- handle the interface between formative and summative assessment; and
- share assessment procedures with students and parents.

Moderation of assessment included as a part of teachers' routine collaborative practice can develop collective knowledge, common language and consistency in the application of assessment criteria throughout the school. As such, moderation is effective as a tool for improving teaching and the learning of a diversity of students. However, to maximize the impact of moderation, teachers need extensive opportunities to develop knowledge and skills in using assessment information to improve teaching in ways that benefit students. This means ongoing monitoring to ensure that any changes are having the desired impact.

Collaboration: sharing quality teaching practices

Teaching quality is critical and impacts student learning and the equity of student outcomes (Hattie 2003; OECD 2005; Field et al. 2007; Timperley and Alton-Lee

2008). It seems therefore that if inclusive schooling is to be achieved, including the equity of outcomes for *all*, then we must improve the quality of teaching. Improving the quality of teaching for *individual* teachers will not be sufficient to bring about the substantive and sustained changes needed to improve outcomes for *all* students. Quality teaching within inclusive schools requires focused attention on improving the *collective* professional knowledge and practices of teachers. This means teachers will need a deep understanding of both the content they teach and how students learn that content, as well as regular opportunities to incorporate and reflect on this *pedagogical content knowledge* (Shulman 1986) in collaboration with other teachers (Bausmith and Barry 2011).

Teacher collaborative discussion

Teacher collaborative discussion creates opportunities to share and critically reflect on practice. This is much more than friendly conversations about students and classrooms. When structured appropriately, collaborative discussion should support teachers to make explicit specific practices and then to examine the impact of those practices on students' learning. Studies have reported that when teachers have opportunities to examine and discuss the effectiveness of their practices they clarify the beliefs, and the theoretical and practical understandings they have about those practices and readjust the expectations they have for their students' learning and achievement (Desimone *et al.* 2002; Timperley and Phillips 2003; Groundwater-Smith and Dadds 2004; Deppeler 2007). Collaborative discussion of pedagogy supports a move from a focus on individual teacher practices to broader teaching and learning issues and collective purposes. Video or direct observations of classrooms are useful as a stimulus for prompting pedagogical discussions, and simultaneously can build trust for the process. Video in particular allows multiple viewing of an event, which can then be analysed from different perspectives. Teachers must be confident, however, that when they open their classrooms to others it is for the purposes of learning about pedagogical practices and not to judge or to evaluate teachers. In the *Learning Improves in Networking Communities* (LINC) projects in Australia, teachers observed each other in classrooms and used a tuning protocol (McDonald and Allen 1999) to structure 'warm and cool feedback' to each other regarding the effectiveness of a teaching episode.

> Trusting each other is very important and the tuning protocol helped start this practice ... there needs to be enough time to unpack the session to discuss feedback on an equal basis but it's the only way to understand real teaching and improve it.
>
> (Carrington *et al.* 2010)

Teachers attributed the improved outcomes for lower performing students to the changes in pedagogy. The collaborative discussion changed 'not only what teachers noticed but how they interpreted events', which then in turn influenced their daily classroom practices and raised their expectations for these students (Deppeler 2007). Parise and Spillane's (2010) study of elementary teachers indicated that teachers' on-the-job opportunities for professional learning, specifically collaborative discussion and advice seeking, were statistically significant predictors of changes in maths and English teaching practices.

'Expert' *coaching* has been advocated as a collaborative approach for developing *specific* pedagogical practices in the classroom. Yopp *et al.* (2011) have outlined a number of attributes that are considered important to enhance the effectiveness of the approach for both coaches and learners:

- include explicit targeted feedback;
- involve critical collaborative reflection;
- identify a teacher's professional needs;
- clarify expectations for processes and outcomes;
- be grounded in content-specific practices; and
- include a pre- and post-conference along with classroom observation.

Thus, the coaching processes should be consistent with social constructivist views of learning in a social community. It is essential that the coach engage in authentic dialogue and collaborative knowledge construction as opposed to acting in the role of the 'expert'. Coaching based on these traditional 'expert' practices can diminish 'the power and voice of teachers as agents for change – their own and that of their colleagues' (Crafton and Kaiser 2011: 104).

Collaborative discussions that are focused on teaching support teachers to align their pedagogical practices more closely and collectively can enhance the school's capacity to help every student succeed. Participating in discussions about teaching will be confronting for some teachers and quite different to their typical ways of interacting with colleagues. Some teachers may be reluctant and remain very uncomfortable in expressing their ideas and opinions about their colleagues' teaching. While protocols and structures can be useful for enhancing critical discussion about practices, genuine collaboration can be challenging to establish. Genuine collaborative discussions will work best when teachers participate voluntarily and feel safe in voicing their opinions, knowledge and reflective insights, and where it is clearly expected they will engage in debate.

Collaboration: home and school working together

Collaboration with families and between home and school is an essential component of the participatory processes critical to the success of *all* students. The term 'home–school' as opposed to 'parent' is used deliberately to reflect the range of other family members and other professionals that might represent and be engaged to support a student in school collaborative arrangements. Despite strong support for home–school collaboration, particularly for vulnerable students, who may be 'at risk' or disadvantaged because of social, economic or cultural factors or disabilities (Raffaele and Knoff 1999; Harry 2008), there is variation in the extent to which families and schools work together as 'genuine partners' (Christenson and Sheridan 2001). The gap between the rhetoric and the reality is said to be due to a number of barriers that centre on the differences between school and family beliefs, attitudes, perceptions and agendas regarding home–school collaboration (Hornby and Lafaele 2011). Traditional and hierarchical views of family involvement typically emphasize passive roles for parents. Educators in positions of authority decide on how home–school relationships will be structured, whose values they will incorporate, and what will be accepted in the way families are to be involved (Jordan *et al.* 2001). Although the language used to describe 'parent partnerships' may promote the 'enhancement of collaborative relationships', in reality the practices used by schools may be 'to groom and shape parents to ensure they meet the goals that the experts have developed' (Hornby and Lafaele 2011: 48). In contrast to this one-sided approach, schools can play an active role in establishing genuine home–school collaboration and 'work towards empowering parents' to voice their ideas and determine how they wish to be involved in their children's schooling (Ashdown 2010: 99).

Their contributions to knowledge provide unique and valuable insights that may not have otherwise been available to the school. This knowledge is then used to inform appropriate school-wide practices that promote success for all students. The challenges of building and maintaining genuine forms of home–school collaboration should not be underestimated. Success will depend on careful attention to:

- building relationships through respect, trust and understanding;
- developing mechanisms for eliciting perspectives and active participation;
- making certain families understand that their contributions are valued.

Conclusion

Inclusive schools value the multiple perspectives and contributions that collaboration within the school community can make to social capital and to finding creative solutions to complex issues. There is little doubt that collaborative investigations developed within the school community will have the most immediate and positive impact on developing practices to respond to learner diversity. Research has highlighted a number of common conditions of collaboration that are key to maximizing the impact for teachers and learners including trust and shared responsibility for students' learning, and the use of evidence based on sound pedagogic principles. Collaboration is socially complex and therefore depends upon shared leadership and structures that create collective action and that are respectful of diversity. Finally, each collaborative arrangement must be repeatedly and critically examined to ensure these conditions are maintained and in order to reap high-quality educational and social benefits, which arise from our efforts.

References

Ainscow, M. (2010) Achieving excellence and equity: reflections on the development of practices in one local district over 10 years, *School Effectiveness and School Improvement*, 21: 75–92.

Ainscow, M. and Sandill, A. (2010) Developing inclusive education systems: the role of organisational cultures and leadership, *International Journal of Inclusive Education*, 14: 401–16.

Ashdown, R. (2010) The role of schools in establishing home–school partnerships, in R. Rose (ed.) *Confronting Obstacles to Inclusion: International Responses to Developing Inclusive Education*. London and New York: Routledge.

Assessment Reform Group (2002) *Assessment for Learning: 10 Principles*. London: General Teaching Council for Northern Ireland. Available at: http://arrts.gtcni.org.uk/gtcni/handle/2428/4623 [Accessed 15 November 2011].

Bausmith, J. M. and Barry, C. (2011) Revisiting professional learning communities to increase college readiness, *Educational Researcher*, 40: 175.

Black, P. and Wiliam, D. (1998) *Inside the Black Box: Raising Standards Through Classroom Assessment*. London: School of Education, King's College.

Black, P., Harrison, C., Hodgen, J., Marshall, B. and Serret, N. (2010) Validity in teachers' summative assessments, *Assessment in Education: Principles, Policy and Practice*, 17: 215–32.

Boyle, W. F. and Charles, M. (2010) Leading learning through Assessment for Learning?, *School Leadership and Management*, 30: 285–300.

Bray, J. N. (2000) *Collaborative Inquiry in Practice: Action, Reflection, and Meaning Making*. Thousand Oaks, CA: Sage Publications.

Bray, J. N. (2002) Uniting teacher learning: collaborative inquiry for professional development, *New Directions for Adult and Continuing Education*, 94: 83–92.

Bryk, A. S., Sebring, P. B. and Allensworth, E. (2009) *Organizing Schools for Improvement: Lessons from Chicago*. Chicago and London: University of Chicago Press.

Burbank, M. D. and Burbank, D. (2003) An alternative model for professional development: investigations into effective collaboration, *Teaching and Teacher Education*, 19: 499–514.

Cantrell, S. C. and Hughes, H. K. (2008) Teacher efficacy and content literacy implementation: an exploration of the effects of extended professional development with coaching, *Journal of Literacy Research*, 40: 95–127.

Carr, W. and Kemmis, S. (1986) *Becoming Critical: Education, Knowledge, and Action Research*. London: Falmer Press.

Carrington, S. B., Deppler, J. and Moss, J. (2010) Cultivating teachers' beliefs, knowledge and skills for leading change in schools, *Australian Journal of Teacher Education*, 35: 1–13.

Chappuis, S., Chappuis, J. and Stiggins, R. (2009) Supporting teacher learning teams, *Educational Leadership*, 66: 56–60.

Christenson, S. and Sheridan, S. M. (2001) *Schools and Families: Creating Essential Connections for Learning*. New York: The Guilford Press.

Clarke, S. (2005) *Formative Assessment in the Secondary Classroom*. London: Hodder and Stoughton.

Cochran-Smith, M. and Lytle, S. L. (2009) *Inquiry as Stance: Practitioner Research in the Next Generation*. New York: Teachers' College Press.

Crafton, L. and Kaiser, E. (2011) The language of collaboration: dialogue and identity in teacher professional development, *Improving Schools*, 14: 104–16.

Cushman, K. (2002) *Looking Collaboratively at Student Work: An Essential Toolkit*. Available at: http://www.essentialschools.org/resources/list?search%5Btags_id_equals%5D=7 [Accessed 12 July 2011].

Deppeler, J. (2006) Improving inclusive practices in Australian schools: creating conditions for university-school collaboration in inquiry, *European Journal of Psychology of Education*, 21: 347–60.

Deppeler, J. (2007) Collaborative inquiry for professional learning, in A. Berry, A. Clemens and A. Kostogriz (eds) *Dimensions of Professional Learning*. Rotterdam: Sense Publishers.

Deppeler, J. (2010) Professional learning as collaborative inquiry: working together for impact, in C. Forlin (ed.) *Teacher Education for Inclusion: Changing Paradigms and Innovative Approaches*. London and New York: Routledge.

Desimone, L. M., Porter, A. C., Garet, M. S., Yoon, K. S. and Birman, B. F. (2002) Effects of professional development on teachers' instruction: results from a three-year longitudinal study, *Educational Evaluation and Policy Analysis*, 24: 81–112.

Dufour, R., Dufour, R. B. and Eaker, R. E. (2008) *Revisiting Professional Learning Communities at Work: New Insights for Improving Schools*. Bloomington, IN: Solution Tree.

Earl, L., Watson, N., Levin, B., Leithwood, K. and Fullan, M. (2003) *Watching and Learning 3: Final Report of the OISE/UT External Evaluation of the National Literacy and Numeracy Strategies*. London: Department for Education and Employment.

Earl, L. M. (2004) Collecting the evidence, *Network of Performance Based Schools*, 2: 41–3.

Ermeling, B. A. (2010) Tracing the effects of teacher inquiry on classroom practice, *Teaching and Teacher Education*, 26: 377–88.

Field, S., Kuczera, M. and Pont, B. (2007) *No More Failures: Ten Steps to Equity in Education*. Paris: OECD.

Friend, M. P. and Cook, L. (2007) *Interactions: Collaboration Skills for School Professionals*, White Plains, NY: Longman.

Goddard, Y., Goddard, R. and Tschannen-Moran, M. (2007) A theoretical and empirical investigation of teacher collaboration for school improvement and student achievement in public elementary schools, *The Teachers College Record*, 109: 877–96.

Grossman, P., Wineburg, S. and Woolworth, S. (2001) Toward a theory of teacher community, *The Teachers College Record*, 103: 942–1012.

Groundwater-Smith, S. and Dadds, M. (2004) Critical practitioner inquiry: towards responsible professional communities of practice, in C. D. J. Sachs (ed.) *International Handbook on the Continuing Professional Development of Teachers*. Maidenhead: Open University Press.

Hargreaves, A. (1994) *Changing Teachers, Changing Times: Teachers' Work and Culture in the Postmodern Age*. New York: Teachers College Press.

Hargreaves, A. and Shirley, D. (2009) *The Fourth Way: The Inspiring Future for Educational Change*. Thousand Oaks, CA: Corwin Press.

Harlen, W. (2005) Teachers' summative practices and assessment for learning – tensions and synergies, *Curriculum Journal*, 16: 207–23.

Harris, A. and Chrispeels, J. (eds) (2008) *International Perspectives on School Improvement*. London: Routledge.

Harris, A. and Jones, M. (2010) Professional learning communities and system improvement, *Improving Schools*, 13: 172.

Harry, B. (2008) Collaboration with culturally and linguistically diverse families: ideal versus reality, *Exceptional Children*, 74: 372–88.

Hattie, J. (2003) Teachers make a difference: what is the research evidence? *Building Teacher Quality: What Does the Research Tell Us?* Available at: http://research.acer.edu.au/research_conference_2003/4 [Accessed 7 July 2011].

Hornby, G. and Lafaele, R. (2011) Barriers to parental involvement in education: an explanatory model, *Educational Review*, 63: 37–52.

Huffman, D. and Kalnin, J. (2003) Collaborative inquiry to make data-based decisions in schools, *Teaching and Teacher Education*, 19: 569–80.

Jordan, C., Orozco, E. and Averett, A. (2001) *Emerging Issues in School, Family, and Community Connections*. Austin, TX: National Center for Family and Community Connections with Schools.

Lachance, A. and Confrey, J. (2003) Interconnecting content and community: a qualitative study of secondary mathematics teachers, *Journal of Mathematics Teacher Education*, 6: 107–37.

Levine, T. H. (2011) Experienced teachers and school reform: exploring how two different professional communities facilitated and complicated change, *Improving Schools*, 14: 30–47.

Lingo, A. S., Barton-Arwood, S. M. and Jolivette, K. (2011) Teachers working together, *Teaching Exceptional Children*, 43: 6–13.

Little, J. W. (2002) Locating learning in teachers' communities of practice: opening up problems of analysis in records of everyday work, *Teaching and Teacher Education*, 18: 917–46.

Lomos, C., Hofman, R. H. and Bosker, R. J. (2011) The relationship between departments as professional communities and student achievement in secondary schools, *Teaching and Teacher Education*, 27: 722–31.

Loreman, T., Deppler, J. and Harvey, D. (2010) *Inclusive Education: A Practical Guide to Supporting Diversity in the Classroom*. Crows Nest, NSW: Allen and Unwin.

McDonald, J. and Allen, D. (1999) *Tuning Protocol*. Available at: http://www.nsrfharmony.org/protocol/doc/tuning.pdf [Accessed 12 July 2011].

McMillan, J. H. (2007) *Formative Classroom Assessment: Theory into Practice*. New York and London: Teachers College Press.

Mariage, T. and Garmon, M. (2003) A case of educational change, *Remedial and Special Education*, 24: 215–34.

Mertler, C. A. (2008) *Action Research: Teachers as Researchers in the Classroom*. London: Sage Publications.

Miles, S. and Ainscow, M. (2011) *Responding to Diversity in Schools: An Inquiry-based Approach*: Abingdon: Routledge.

Mulford, B. (2008) *The Leadership Challenge: Improving Learning in Schools*. Melbourne: Australian Council for Educational Research.

Nelson, T. H. and Slavit, D. (2007) Collaborative inquiry among science and mathematics teachers in the USA: professional learning experiences through cross-grade, cross-discipline dialogue, *Journal of In-service Education*, 33: 23–39.

OECD (Organization for Economic Co-operation and Development) (2005) *Education at a Glance 2005: OECD Indicators*. Paris: OECD.

OECD (2010) *PISA 2009 Results: Executive Summary*. Available at: http://www.oecd.org/dataoecd/34/60/46619703.pdf [Accessed 12 July 2011].

Ontario Literacy and Numeracy Secretariat (2007) *Teacher Moderation: Collaborative Assessment of Student Capacity Building Series*. Available at: http://www.edu.gov.on.ca/eng/literacynumeracy/inspire/research/Teacher_Moderation.pdf [Accessed 12 July 2011].

Parise, L. M. and Spillane, J. P. (2010) Teacher learning and instructional change: how formal and on-the-job learning opportunities predict change in elementary school teachers' practice, *The Elementary School Journal*, 110: 323–46.

Raffaele, L. and Knoff, H. (1999) Improving home–school collaboration with disadvantaged families: organizational principles, perspectives, and approaches, *School Psychology Review*, 28: 448–66.

Riehl, C. J. (2000) The principal's role in creating inclusive schools for diverse students: a review of normative, empirical, and critical literature on the practice of educational administration, *Review of Educational Research*, 70: 55–81.

Sagor, R. (2011) *The Action Research Guidebook: A Four-step Process for Educators and School Teams*. Thousand Oaks, CA: Corwin Press.

Shulman, L. S. (1986) Those who understand: knowledge growth in teaching, *Educational Researcher*, 15: 4–14.

Snow-Gerono, J. L. (2005) Professional development in a culture of inquiry: PDS teachers identify the benefits of professional learning communities, *Teaching and Teacher Education*, 21: 241–56.

Stoll, L., Bolam, R., McMahon, A., Thomas, S., Wallace, M., Greenwood, A. *et al.* (2006) *What Is a Professional Learning Community?* Available at: http://networkedlearning.ncsl.org.uk/

knowledge-base/programme-leaflets/professional-learning-communities/professional-learning-communities-04-summary.pdf [Accessed 7 July 2011].

Stoll, L. and Seashore Louis, K. S. (eds) (2007) *Professional Learning Communities: Divergence, Depth and Dilemmas.* Maidenhead: Open University Press.

Thessin, R. A. and Starr, J. P. (2011) Supporting the growth of effective professional learning communities districtwide, *Phi Delta Kappan*, 92: 48–54.

Timperley, H. and Alton-Lee, A. (2008) Reframing teacher professional learning: an alternative policy approach to strengthening valued outcomes for diverse learners, *Review of Research in Education*, 32: 328–69.

Timperley, H. S. (2008) *Using Assessment Data for Improving Practice. ACER Research Conference 2009.* Available at: http://research.acer.edu.au/cgi/viewcontent.cgi?article=1036&context =research_conference [Accessed 7 July 2011].

Timperley, H. S. and Phillips, G. (2003) Changing and sustaining teachers' expectations through professional development in literacy, *Teaching and Teacher Education*, 19: 627–41.

Vescio, V., Ross, D. and Adams, A. (2008) A review of research on the impact of professional learning communities on teaching practice and student learning, *Teaching and Teacher Education*, 24: 80–91.

Wiliam, D., Lee, C., Harrison, C. and Black, P. (2004) Teachers developing assessment for learning: impact on student achievement, *Assessment in Education*, 11: 49–65.

Wilson, M. (ed.) (2004) *Towards Coherence between Classroom Assessment and Accountability. The 103rd Yearbook of the National Society for the Study of Education, Part 2.* Chicago, IL: Chicago University Press.

Yopp, D., Burroughs, E. A., Luebeck, J., Heidema, C., Mitchell, A. and Sutton, J. (2011) How to be a wise consumer of coaching: strategies teachers can use to maximize coaching, *Journal of Staff Development*, 32: 50–3.

Zech, L. K., Gause-Vega, C. L., Bray, M. H., Secules, T. and Goldman, S. R. (2000) Content-based collaborative inquiry: a professional development model for sustaining educational reform, *Educational Psychologist*, 35: 207–17.

11

RICHARD ROSE

Beyond the school gates: promoting inclusion through community partnerships

Introduction

Debates surrounding the inclusion of pupils who have previously been marginalized in schools have inevitably focused upon issues of school structure and management (Ainscow *et al.* 2006; Kinsella and Senior 2008), pedagogical approaches (Florian and Rouse 2001; Watkins and Meijer 2010) and access (Jha 2007; Egilson and Traustadottir 2009). These issues are at the core of those which are likely to impact upon the ability of schools to address the needs of a diverse school population. They have the advantage of immediacy in respect of considering the challenges faced on a daily basis by teachers and school leaders.

Schools have often taken a lead in promoting the inclusion of students described as having special educational needs and have played a major advocacy role on behalf of these and other marginalized individuals. Legislation in many countries, often in response to international initiatives such as the Salamanca Statement (UNESCO 1994) and Dakar Framework for Action (UNESCO 2000a) and reinforced by the Millennium Development Goals (UNESCO 2000b), has led to responses from educational policy makers which have required actions on the part of schools to promote inclusion. While it is clear that levels of response have varied and have often been determined by the socio-economic, political and social circumstances of individual countries, it is possible to see an international groundswell towards developing education systems that are more equitable and accessible than they may have been in the past.

Alongside a commitment towards the development of more inclusive schools has been a strengthening of the acceptance of social models of disability and need, and a move away from long-standing deficit views of individuals and provision (Priestley 1998; Connors and Stalker 2007). This has been important not only in promoting school environments and policies which are more accepting of diversity and committed to the provision of inclusive teaching approaches, but also in encouraging debates around the relationship of schools to the communities which they serve. While attendance at school is an important formative process that can shape the attitudes and understanding of all children, the overall impact of schools is likely to be limited if those attitudes and learning opportunities are not reinforced beyond the school gates. For some pupils it is only on entry to school that they experience learners who come from other cultures or who have disabilities or needs that are significantly different from their own. Such an experience often needs to be contextualized for them and examined in ways that enable them to gain positive insights into diversity. Teachers have a responsibility to interpret difference in positive ways that reinforce principles of equality and opportunity and there is evidence to suggest that in many instances they do so with considerable success (Shevlin 2000; Nowicki 2006). However, the influence of teachers and other professionals outside schools has often been limited and the positive messages received by students within schools are not always consistently reinforced. It may therefore be argued that a greater synthesis between schools and the communities that they serve is a critical component of ensuring that the inclusion agenda is more effectively delivered.

Schools and communities in England – exploring opportunities for partnership

In England initiatives to foster greater engagement between schools and local communities have often been centred upon areas of social deprivation. The concept of a range of services provided from a school which acts as a hub within a local neighbourhood has found particular currency through the government-initiated programme of 'extended schools' (DfES 2005). Within this initiative, extended schools are described as those providing activities and services, often beyond the school day, to address the needs of its pupils, their families and the wider community. Clearly influenced by the movement towards full-service schools in the USA (Dryfoos 1994; Cahill 1996), extended schools have developed services aimed at preventing social and educational exclusion and encouraging stronger partnerships between parents, community services and schools to address the needs of students. Implicit in this initiative is an increased opportunity to ensure that students who may otherwise find themselves marginalized are included not only in the core activities of schooling, but also within the communities in which they live and where in some instances they may have been excluded or rejected.

This chapter draws upon research conducted by the author and his colleagues in England, which has examined models of school provision aimed at encouraging greater cohesion across professional services and a stronger relationship with those communities served by the schools. This approach does have an important contribution to make in ensuring a greater synthesis of the social and educational aspects of inclusion.

Schools engaging with communities

The relationship between schools and the communities they serve is complex. The reputation of a school within a local neighbourhood is often forged upon the experiences of adults who may well have attended that school some years previously (Hill and Taylor 2004). For some parents of pupils currently attending a school, their own experiences and memories of their school days are less than positive and their willingness to associate themselves with an institution that may have been the source of previous discomfort or in some instances conflict may be limited. Research conducted into the development of extended secondary schools (pupils aged 11–16) in two areas of England (Rose *et al.* 2009; Griffiths and Smith 2011) found that schools located in areas of deprivation or with a record of low educational attainment and few school leavers moving on to post-compulsory education often had major challenges in establishing close working relationships with their local community. The image of a school within its immediate environs can have a significant impact upon the willingness of local individuals and groups to become associated. In the research conducted by the author and his colleagues it was clear that the negative attitudes of parents who had attended the schools were at times a barrier towards participation in initiatives emanating from these institutions.

The development of an open relationship based upon trust between professionals and parents has often been cited as a critical factor in developing inclusive schooling (Loreman *et al.* 2010). As the project continued it became evident that the investment of time in developing positive relationships was a critical factor in successfully raising the expectations of all parties. Some parents when interviewed spoke of their own negative feelings towards school and of their low expectations of what school could do for their own child. Often these were parents who did not attend school events such as parent evenings. They expressed the view that they were not convinced that the school was addressing areas of need which were relevant to their child. Over a number of years efforts to encourage such parents to attend school events had yielded few results. In some instances it had created a blame culture whereby teachers saw parents as being apathetic about the education of their children, while the parents perceived teachers as having little understanding of the needs of people living in the locality. Indeed, several of the parents interviewed as part of the research indicated that teachers within the school did not live in the community but travelled in solely for the purpose of their job. This was indeed true, with some teachers indicating that the school was located in a neighbourhood in which they would not choose to live.

The schools within the research had received additional funding in order to develop services aimed at raising school attainment, tackling disaffection, and encouraging increased community liaison and participation. Senior managers within the schools had specific responsibilities for the co-ordination of actions aimed at increasing communication with local agencies and for establishing firmer links with both parents and the general community. Among the actions taken was the appointment of family workers, often with a background in social work, who operated as a link between home and schools in attempting to build relationships and encourage greater understanding between parents and school staff. In addition the schools provided a home for professionals who had previously operated a service but from discrete bases detached from educational provision. The professionals included community police officers, community nurses and mental health service workers. In order to encourage members of the local community to become involved in the life of the school, sporting and leisure facilities were made available outside school hours to those living within the vicinity. The provision of these facilities was often supported through the making available of expertise from school staff such as teachers with computing skills or sports coaching experience. Equally important was the establishment of community-focused educational and health groups, such as healthy eating, stop smoking and parenting classes, which were made freely available to parents of pupils attending the school and their friends and family. Many of these activities were arranged in conjunction with local organizations, volunteers and groups who entered into partnership with school staff in order to facilitate wider community change.

This opening up of the schools and shift in their approach towards engaging with families and the local community entailed a radical reappraisal of the schools' purpose and functions. Rather than operating as a conventional school they became a focus for activity incorporating principles of care and community service as part of their core activity rather than an addendum to their everyday work. While teachers within the schools maintained a focus upon pedagogy and management of the curriculum, they found themselves engaging on a day-to-day basis with a wider range of professionals and community service providers than had traditionally been the case. This required a significant shift in the thinking of staff in respect of their responsibilities and the ways in which they might impact on the lives of their pupils beyond their educational role. Similarly, professionals who had previously been located outside the schools found themselves to be a part of a school community while supporting the local area. This change of location and an increased expectation of engagement with school staff and pupils required a different way of rationalizing their role and of fulfilling their duties.

A change of location or a different way of thinking?

In an effort to gauge the impact of developing schools that operate with an increased community focus, interviews were conducted with key individuals involved in the scheme. It is interesting to reflect upon the challenges and advantages which they perceived to emanate from the initiation of extended services based within the schools. It is of equal value to consider the impact of such initiatives upon the inclusion of pupils in danger of being marginalized both within school and in the local community.

Community police officers have operated in partnership with schools in England over many years; however, this has generally involved making occasional visits to school and has seldom seen them playing a major role in the classroom. In the schools visited for this study police officers are based within the schools for a significant part of the week and play a major role in working with pupils. One officer during interview intimated that when first given this brief he was far from pleased. He describes how he knew the reputation for trouble of the pupils at the school and that having been located in the area for some years he had a negative view of many of the families whose children attended. These were in his opinion youngsters who would need to be 'kept in view' as likely troublemakers. In particular he noted how there was a common belief that some of these youngsters were likely to perpetuate a family history of petty crime within the area.

Having been based within a school for more than a year this same police officer was asked about how he worked within the school and whether his views had changed. He was clear that in his opinion the move into school had brought benefits. His working days in school were divided into two distinct but complementary roles. These consisted of days when he was available to talk to groups of pupils or, in some instances, in confidence with individual pupils or staff and was visibly a police officer wearing his uniform. However, other days were spent when he would put on a track-suit and work alongside teachers and pupils in the classroom. Both aspects of the job were seen as important. In the first role he was seen as a police officer who had time to listen and was seen to respect the views of pupils, and through the second he was able to build relationships within the school through a direct participation in their day-to-day activity. The establishment of a trust that he perceived to be present in the school and which had proved over time to be a strength of the relationships developed was something which he saw as critical in enabling a more effective understanding of roles and responsibilities to be achieved:

> I mean, certainly one of the benefits of the extended schools that I can see is the fact that it gives you the ability to develop relationships with key members of staff, where you can happily exchange information knowing that it's not going to be misused.
>
> (School-based Community Police Officer)

Working within a school had changed his perception of the ways in which teachers, social workers and other professionals operated and had also caused him to reconsider his own role and that of the local police service:

> . . . no one agency can ever achieve everything themselves, you know, sometimes you need to sit down and say well I can do this . . . once you have identified what the issue is, you know, then you can say well this is what I can contribute towards it and people can contribute different things. As a cop I mean . . . I understand the value of it perhaps a lot more than some other agencies because for years we worked in isolation, we were the police, we could do everything, we were super human . . . we didn't need anybody else and that, you know, we operated in our own little world and not surprisingly we tended to do things very badly if at all and I think it was a great day of awakening for a lot of people when we said no, hang on a minute, perhaps we can do a lot more if we start linking with people and bringing other people into the equation.
>
> (School-based Community Police Officer)

This officer also reported a change in attitudes towards the young people attending the schools. In many instances this involved developing a greater awareness of the lives and experiences of these pupils and an increased understanding of the day-to-day challenges which they faced. The outcome of this change in perception was that these pupils were regularly seeking his counsel and initiating conversations with him about their difficulties and the ways they felt that he might be able to help.

Other professionals located within the study schools reported similar feelings with regard to gaining a more holistic view of professional relationships and operations:

> I think the great thing about working within the extended school is that you work much more closely with school and other agencies and because of the structure

to it and the referrals coming in. It's a way of making that contact with youth services and working together so that you have not got one service providing one line of care and then another service providing another line . . . you are working together in partnership.

(School Community Nurse)

Of particular significance was the perception of pupils within the schools that they were being helped not only in terms of their educational needs but in addressing personal problems which often manifested themselves beyond the school. For example, one teenager who had often been perceived as troublesome by teachers and whose academic attainment was significantly behind that of most of his peers was able to articulate how he worked in collaboration with a school-based social worker to provide support that enabled him to remain in school and focused on his own needs:

I have had outside help and inside help. Social Services helped me outside to get me through things; Mr — (form teacher) when he finds, he sees I am not in a very good mood because something has happened somewhere else he will take me out of the lesson, talk to me, calm me down and then say come on, get back, go on. And it is really helpful, it is useful, it is people helping you all the time telling you to get through things, you are going to do it, you are not going to fail.

(Pupil)

While the support described thus far was provided by established professionals who had adapted to new ways of working through a school base, the appointment of family workers was a venture that involved the creation of a new role. Family workers tended to come from a social work background and were appointed to the schools to act as a bridge between school and families. Much of their work was conducted in homes where they would listen to parents as they expressed their views about school and the challenges which were sometimes presented by their children. Acting in an empathic liaison capacity, the family workers would represent family views to the school while fulfilling a similar role in expressing the views of the school to parents. This role required a commitment of time to gain the confidence of all parties but was seen as critical in enabling both families and schools to build relationships and to begin to establish partnerships for the benefit of children. Teachers and families saw the strengths of this approach in enabling pupils to become better included in the daily life of the school. As an example, a teacher commented that a breakdown between the school and a family had resulted in a pupil feeling unsupported in her education, but the intervention of a family worker had re-established lines of communication and was enabling the pupil to feel that there was an emerging consensus between home and school:

She [the family worker] has actually been able to speak to mum. Her mum wouldn't speak to me and she wouldn't speak to any teachers because in her eyes we are a waste of time, you know?

(Teacher)

This same teacher recognized the potential for disaffection that might have resulted in a pupil dropping out from school had she not received the intervention from a family worker who had impacted upon pupil attendance and attitude through adopting a liaison role:

> She (student) now fits in and she is a lot happier and she attends well. And it has just changed her whole life in that sense, because she was going down the route of non-attending and that school held nothing.
>
> (Teacher)

Parents were also able to articulate the benefits that accrued from the involvement of family workers and saw this relationship with a professional who was from the school but perceived as different from others working at the school as important:

> Well what it was is my son, he wouldn't open up to no one, he wouldn't talk to no one. But (the family worker) managed to get through to him and it did, although it took a while with him, she did get through to him and he did find it helpful with her . . . I mean, you know, he wasn't seeing her like every week but she was there if he needed her and he did seem to open up to her, and at the moment one of my other children sees (the family worker) just on – it could be every month or so, just to see that she is alright, if she has got any problems in school. And (the family worker) has helped her to sort out a few things as well. So to me the whole project was really helpful because without it I didn't know where else to go.
>
> (Parent)

The co-ordination of services based within the schools was seen as a factor in enabling a swift response when difficult issues emerged or situations became critical. A deputy head teacher in one of the schools recognized the potential for pupils to fall out of the education system because of personal circumstances and family stresses and emphasized the value that school-based services could provide:

> Dad died quite tragically and he would have been . . . we wouldn't have had him here. He would have become one of the lost generations. I mean, we always have them, but students for whom something happens and they don't come in. Educational Welfare gets involved a bit and it goes on, and I mean fast track might have made a difference but I am not sure it would with (student). And we would have lost him and he would have had nothing. Without (the family worker) and the extended social worker based here that child would have been lost.
>
> (Deputy Head Teacher)

Similar messages with regards to the value of school-based services were a common feature of interviews with both professionals and families throughout the research. They often gave specific instances of the advantages of intervention:

> It has meant that we have been able to target support for a range of services a lot quicker. The particular deaf student was having problems being bullied on the

bus, he was making inappropriate friendships within the community and his mother was very, very worried about that. And it meant that we could, within about five days, we could target resources, human resources to actually solving the problem and getting support in for that student . . . the outside agencies that we would normally have to wait a long time to get access to are based in schools which meant that within a short space of time we have had access to those services that would have taken us a long time to do.

(Special Educational Needs Co-ordinator)

An equally positive response came from the support given to pupils and families beyond the normal school day through initiatives such as breakfast and homework clubs and holiday activities. A feature of these services included the making available of provision to pupils prior to their entry to school and the flexibility that enabled them to involve family and friends:

I know that he has particularly enjoyed the last six week holidays. Although he wasn't attending this school because he hadn't started, he got involved in an event down at Christchurch where they had the Sure Start football training, rounders, and also there was facilities there for my younger daughter who is five, she could come along. So we went down as a family.

(Parent)

I actually went to the trip along with my friend from Cambridge. He was coming down for the next day, he was coming over the Friday, so we rang my friend up, see if he wanted to come and he said yes, I would like to go quadding for the first time.

(Pupil)

The schools in the study came to be seen as a focus point for community activity where families were welcomed and provided with services that they wanted and were of immediate benefit to themselves. This was achieved only by changing the traditional image of the school to a place which could provide not only for the pupils on roll, but to the wider neighbourhood and those within it. Such a move inevitably requires a shifting in perceptions not only with regards to the fundamental purposes of schooling, but also the roles played by individuals within child-centred services. As the social worker cited below recognizes, many of these services come with a stigma attached which may be more readily breached within the locale of a school than in other vicinities:

I think it (the school) is one of the sort of fundamental places you can look at delivering the service because what you are looking for is a front door that people are happy to use and quite often people . . . well, certainly people wouldn't use the Social Services door because it has so much stigma etc. attached to it and it is not a universal service, it is an access service . . . so you look to an extent about where your front door might be. School is one of them, not everybody likes school, some people wouldn't choose to use school, but then you, if you then sort of thread it out that maybe the school also has different outlets as well so you might have an attachment from the school to the community centre or somewhere else, potentially you can build up links across the community, but if you have a core potentially that is legitimate I suppose then I think that is the way to go.

(Social worker)

Impacting upon inclusion

The findings of the research reported in this chapter concur with those of studies reported elsewhere. Blank *et al.* (2003) in their report of research into twenty community schools in the USA cited an increased sense of personal control within education, improved academic success, reduced dropout rates and an increased sense of school connectedness as common responses of students attending these schools. Students who had previously been seen as 'disconnected' with the schooling process valued the more holistic approaches adopted by these schools and became more included in both the academic and social aspects of learning. Within the UK, Statham *et al.* (2010) endorse the view that a positive impact upon students at risk of exclusion is more likely when greater cohesion between schools and the communities they serve is achieved. These researchers, both from the US and UK, would suggest that a failure to develop initiatives for the promotion of school and community cohesion is likely to have a limiting effect upon the attainment of goals associated with inclusion.

It is self-evident that, while schools can play a significant role in the development of an inclusive ethos and the fostering of positive attitudes and expectations, to do so in isolation is likely to have less impact than might be achieved from a co-ordinated response. The schools explored in the research that informed this chapter had made a commitment to endeavours that they hoped would benefit all pupils through the establishment of an inclusive learning environment. However, successes were limited until a more cohesive approach to engaging families and local communities was deployed and the schools became recognized as a central feature in the lives of those who have contact and responsibility for children but had not previously been associated directly with the schools. This finding accords with that of other researchers (Statham *et al.* 2010) who have recognized that those families who remain at a distance from schools are less likely to engage effectively in the learning of their children. The schools were based in areas of social deprivation and served a population that was rarely endeared to the fundamental philosophies associated with the education service. The efforts made by the joint services working with children to listen to the voices of members of the local community resulted in a considerable shift in the ways in which schools were perceived. Opening the doors of the schools and re-establishing their roles as providers of community-based activity beyond that traditionally expected was a critical factor in promoting successful engagement.

Conclusion

Moving towards changes of the type described in this chapter requires that professionals follow a difficult path. Personal professional barriers need to be broken and greater trust established with communities that may have previously been wary of the authority invested in professionals and institutions. Where this can be achieved greater empathy between all of the parties involved may well create an environment which is more conducive to developing understanding and thereby including everyone in the process of developing a more equitable education system.

Much of the research conducted into the promotion of inclusion has focused upon developments within schools (Ainscow *et al.* 2006). Research in this field, often responding to national legislation, has considered those pedagogical or school management factors that may encourage the participation of learners from diverse backgrounds within schools and wider educational initiatives (Watkins and Meijer 2010). However, any assessment of the effectiveness of inclusion must look beyond schools to consider how students are prepared for the communities in which they live. Local community engagement should become an essential feature of schools that wish to adopt the broader principles of inclusion and enable young people to feel that they belong within society as a whole. Schools should evaluate their responses not only to individual students labelled as having difficulties or special educational needs, but also to their families and other community members who have an essential role to play in fostering a more accepting society. Inclusive practices that are focused solely upon action in schools are unlikely to succeed. A greater cohesion across agencies and with families is required in order to move forward on this issue.

References

Ainscow, M., Booth, T. and Dyson, A. (2006) *Improving Schools, Developing Inclusion*. London: Routledge.

Blank, M., Melaville, A. and Shah, P. (2003) *Making the Difference: Research and Practice in Community Schools*. Washington, DC: Coalition for Community Schools.

Cahill, M. (1996) *Schools and Community*. Chicago, IL: Cross City Campaign for Urban School Reform.

Connors, C. and Stalker, K. (2007) Children's experiences of disability: pointers to a social model of childhood disability, *Disability and Society*, 22(1): 19–33.

DfES (Department for Education and Skills) (2005) *Extended Schools: Access to Opportunities and Services for All*. Nottingham: DfES Publications.

Dryfoos, J. (1994) *Full Service Schools. A Revolution in Health and Social Services for Children, Youth and Families*. San-Francisco, CA: Jossey-Bass.

Egilson, S. T. and Traustadottir, R. (2009) Assistance to pupils with physical disabilities in regular schools: promoting inclusion or creating dependency?, *European Journal of Special Needs Education*, 24(1): 21–36.

Florian, L. and Rouse, M. (2001) Inclusive practice in English secondary schools: lessons learned, *Cambridge Journal of Education*, 31(3): 399–412.

Griffiths, S. and Smith, A. (2011) Extended services in schools: developing resources to prepare student teachers for a rapidly changing working environment, *Support for Learning*, 26(1): 13–16.

Hill, N. E. and Taylor, L. C. (2004) Parental involvement and children's academic achievement, *Current Directions in Psychological Science*, 13(4): 161–4.

Jha, M. M. (2007) Barriers to student access and success: is inclusive education an answer?, in G. K. Gajendra, C. R. Bagley and M. M. Jha (eds) *International Perspectives on Educational Diversity and Inclusion*. London: Routledge.

Kinsella, W. and Senior, J. (2008) Developing inclusive schools: a systemic approach, *International Journal of Inclusive Education*, 15(5&6): 651–65.

Loreman, T., Deppeler, J. and Harvey, D. (2010) *Inclusive Education: Supporting Diversity in the Classroom*. New York: Routledge.

Nowicki, E. A. (2006) A cross-sectional multivariate analysis of children's attitudes towards disabilities, *Journal of Intellectual Disabilities Research*, 50(5): 335–48.

Priestley, M. (1998) Constructions and creations: idealism, materialism and disability theory, *Disability and Society*, 13(1): 75–94.

Rose, R., Smith, A. and Feng, Y. (2009) Supporting pupils and families: a case study of two English extended schools, *Management in Education*, 23(2): 57–62.

Shevlin, M. (2000) Fostering positive attitudes: reactions of mainstream pupils to contact with their counterparts who have severe/profound intellectual disabilities, *European Journal of Special Needs Education*, 15(2): 206–17.

Statham, J., Harris, A. and Glenn, M. (2010) *Strengthening Family Wellbeing and Community Cohesion through the Role of Schools and Extended Services*. London: Centre for Excellence and Outcomes in Children and Young People's Services.

UNESCO (1994) *The Salamanca Statement and Framework for Action on Special Needs Education*. Paris: UNESCO.

UNESCO (2000a) *The Dakar Framework for Action. Education for All: Meeting our Collective Commitments*. Paris: UNESCO.

UNESCO (2000b) Resolution 55/2 Adopted by the General Assembly. *The Millennium Development Goals*. Paris: UNESCO.

Watkins, A. and Meijer, C. (2010) The development of inclusive teaching and learning: a European perspective?, in R. Rose (ed.) *Confronting Obstacles to Inclusion*. London: Routledge.

Part III

Overcoming barriers to successful inclusion

12

MARGO A. MASTROPIERI AND THOMAS E. SCRUGGS
How can teacher attitudes, co-teaching and differentiated instruction facilitate inclusion?

Introduction

Inclusion has been practised in some form or another since the passage of the US federal law PL-94-142 or the Individual with Disabilities Education Act (IDEA) protecting educational rights of individuals with disabilities in 1975 and guaranteeing that special education should be provided in the 'least restrictive environment'. Some view inclusion as a basic civil rights issue for individuals with disabilities, meaning that all children regardless of severity of disabilities have a basic right to be involved in the general education classrooms all of the time. Others view inclusion as involving all students with disabilities whenever possible within general education classrooms (Mastropieri and Scruggs 2010). Finally, opinions exist all along a continuum of inclusive practices.

Inclusion has multiple meanings and appears in many different ways. As with any complex phenomena, multiple factors converge to influence inclusive practices. This chapter addresses some of the many factors influencing inclusive practices. First, a review of what is known about teacher attitudes toward inclusion is presented. Second, a review of co-teaching research and its impact on inclusion is discussed. Finally, recent research on peer-assisted learning with differentiated curriculum enhancements is described.

Teacher attitudes

Teachers and classroom environments can promote effective inclusion. In our research we have heard teachers openly promote individual differences as something beneficial for all students. A teacher told her fourth grade class that it was beneficial to have differences among students. She used an example of how good it was to have twins in their class because they were so different from everyone else (Scruggs and Mastropieri 1994). Another teacher had students take turns sitting in a big old barbershop chair during a 'hot seat' activity. While sitting in the hot seat, only positive comments were allowed about that individual (Mastropieri *et al.* 1994). Activities such as these were open demonstrations of supportive classroom environments and positive teacher attitudes toward inclusion.

It has long been hypothesized that teachers' attitudes can greatly influence the acceptance of individual differences. Scruggs *et al.* (2011) synthesized teacher attitudes research published during the fifteen years since a previous synthesis by Scruggs and Mastropieri (1996a) to determine whether teacher attitudes had shifted to more positive views. Forty survey reports were located that included over 8300 teachers from all over the United States, Italy, Serbia, South Korea and Greece. Overall 62.8 per cent supported the concept of inclusion while 61.4 per cent expressed a willingness to teach students with disabilities. There was higher agreement (70 per cent) for more generally worded items (e.g. 'Inclusion is a desirable educational practice') than for items worded with more intensity (40 per cent) (e.g. 'All students with disabilities should be educated in the general education class'). Teachers reported insufficient time, training and support for inclusion. Slight decreases in the amount of time were revealed from the previous synthesis (less than 22 per cent indicated they had sufficient time), while there were slight increases in the amount of training (less than 40 per cent agreement for having sufficient training) and support (less than 38 per cent agreement for having sufficient training).

Benefits of inclusion were also reported including:

- 50 per cent agreement for academic benefits;
- 72 per cent for social benefits;
- 60 per cent for general benefits; and
- 60 per cent for general education students.

As with the previous synthesis, teacher attitudes did not appear to be influenced by year of publication, geographic region, sample size, return rate or reliability of survey. However, again it was found that attitudes varied according to perceived severity of disability. For example, Ross (2002) reported a low of 40 per cent agreement for feeling competent at working with students with mental disabilities and 43.3 per cent for students with emotional disabilities. Hull (2005) reported a low of 36 per cent agreement for inclusion for students with emotional and behavioural disorders, but a high of 82 per cent for students with learning disabilities. It was also reported that elementary teachers were generally more supportive than secondary teachers.

Co-teaching

During co-teaching, special and general educators work together to meet the needs of all students better (Mastropieri and Scruggs 2010). Most co-teaching scenarios involve team teaching, station teaching, parallel teaching, alternate teaching, or 'one teach while one assists' models (Friend and Cook 2010). Team teaching refers to teachers working collaboratively and interacting during the teaching. Parallel teaching refers to teaching similar content simultaneously, but one teacher may be presenting higher level content than the other. Alternate teaching refers to teachers taking turns during class presentations. Finally, one teach one assist refers to one teacher taking the lead or dominant teacher role while the other teacher assists individual students on an as needed basis. Although extensively implemented, investigations documenting the efficacy of co-teaching are less widely available. Murawski and Swanson (2001) found only six out of 89 studies on co-teaching that reported sufficient quantitative data to include in a meta-analysis. An overall modest effect size of .40 was obtained on outcome variables ranging from attitudes, social, academic achievement and grades. Study effect sizes ranged from a low of .08 (Vaughn *et al.* 1998) to a high of .95 (Self *et al.* 1991). Nevertheless, this was a disappointingly small number of studies, only modest effects, and indicated a need for more rigorous research on co-teaching.

Recently more qualitative investigations on co-teaching have appeared. Although qualitative studies cannot produce efficacy data, they can shed needed insights into teachers' perceptions about the process of co-teaching. Scruggs *et al.* (2007) conducted a meta-synthesis of qualitative studies on co-teaching (see Scruggs and Mastropieri 2006 for a description of the synthesis procedures). Thirty-two studies were located that had examined co-teaching, involving 453 co-teachers, 142 students, 42 administrators, 26 parents, and five support personnel. Studies which were conducted across the United States, represented urban, suburban and rural districts, and across all grade levels. Schools had been selected to be representative or outstanding at implementing co-teaching. Scruggs *et al.*, who employed the constant comparative method using open and axial coding (LeCompte and Preissle 1993), identified 69 codes within the general categories of benefits of co-teaching, teacher roles in co-teaching, needs identified for co-teaching, and how instruction was implemented in co-taught classes.

The synthesis revealed some positive benefits for students with and without disabilities involved in co-taught classes. Specific benefits associated with co-teaching included increased individual attention for students with disabilities, improvements in self-esteem, and increased opportunities of social modelling from peers. Students without disabilities were reported to benefit both academically and socially. In these cases inclusion using co-teaching was reported as seen as beneficial for everyone in the class.

More cautious, challenging themes also emerged. Variability in students' skills and procedures for making co-teaching assignments revealed potential barriers. When students possessed significantly lower skill levels than the rest of the class, some teachers cautioned against placement in co-taught classes (Weiss and Lloyd 2002). Instances of students exhibiting tantrum behaviours because of lack of class prerequisites were described (Hazlett 2001). Some teachers believed administrators forced them to co-teach even when students with disabilities' skill levels were too low for their needs to be met in general education settings (Thompson 2001). Finally, due to administrative assignments of students, some teachers reported horror stories of classrooms heavily weighted with students with disabilities (Walther-Thomas 1997).

Highly similar co-teacher needs were identified. The themes of requiring more administrative support, having truly committed co-teacher dyads, compatibility between co-teacher dyads, and co-planning time were identified. Strong emotional feelings were voiced regarding being assigned to work with someone against your will. For example, one general educator commented: 'If I had known that I would have to defend the way I have always believed in teaching, I would not have agreed to co-teach . . . I have not been teaching for thirty years for someone else to tell me how to teach . . . I am furious' (Norris 1997: 107). Because of that type of sentiment many argued for voluntary co-teaching. However, if assignments were voluntary, others reported resentment from teachers who were free to opt out of co-teaching. For example, one middle school teacher said: 'There are people in my building – this really bothers me – that have the "Free from Special Ed" pass . . . So the special educator does *not* want to place students in those rooms' (Ward 2003: 110). A lack of co-planning time for co-teachers was also identified (e.g. Dieker 2001; Vesay 2004). Many teachers struggled to find sufficient co-planning time. Teachers linked insufficient planning time to a lack of administrative support (Buckley 2005).

Many teachers and administrators used a marriage analogy with co-teaching. The relationship was frequently described as very close but filled with compromises. For example, 'The teachers . . . described co-teaching as an unusually close partnership, or what one termed "a professional marriage", which, "like [a normal marriage], you have to work at"' (Rice and Zigmond 2000). In our own research (Mastropieri *et al.* 1998) we witnessed an extremely close relationship. For example, a general and regular educator worked so well together that during science classes they began to finish each other's sentences. If this relationship had not been so close it would be easy to see how such a style might irritate a co-teacher.

Overall the most prominent model of co-teaching observed was 'one teach, one support' or 'one teach and one assist'. Although alternative models were seen, they were much more limited. The role of the special educator was described most commonly as secondary to the general educator, who maintained the role of primary instructor (e.g. Magiera *et al.* 2005). Zigmond and Matta (2004) noted that special education teachers rarely assumed the primary instructor role. Although the definition of co-teaching involves a shared responsibility, few researchers observed all required components. For example, Rice and Zigmond (2000) did not find any co-teaching configurations that met all model criteria of shared teaching space, and planning and instruction by both co-teachers. Turf issues were also reported in some cases. For example, Wood (1998) reported that when special educators used specialized methods they were considered atypical and sometimes ignored by their general educator co-teaching partner. One special educator showed a general educator how she charted behaviour for students with disabilities. However, the general educator reported, 'I said "Well, OK", but I never did it because that's not the way discipline in the class runs' (Wood 1998: 191). Others reported friction between co-teachers due to sharing the classroom. One special educator reported that she had to raise her hand to talk with her co-teaching partner (Buckley 2005).

Many general educators believed that special educators' lack of content knowledge limited their roles in the co-taught classroom. Authors reported repeatedly, especially at the secondary levels, that special educators functioned more as classroom aides, providing secondary support, rather than providing primary instruction. As we observed in our study of secondary chemistry instruction, although both teachers had established an excellent rapport and working relationship, it was obvious that the general educator assumed the primary instructor role because of her superior advantage with content knowledge (Mastropieri *et al.* 2005). Evidently, in some instances the lesser role is preferred by some co-teachers. Other times, teachers resented the lesser role and status (Scruggs *et al.* 2007).

Differentiation of instruction is frequently touted as a major technique to involve students within inclusive classrooms because individual needs, background, motivation, requirements for learning and language differences are considered when planning instruction. Differentiated instruction attempts to maximize learning for all (Tomlinson 2001). However, equivocal findings were reported by Scruggs *et al.* (2007), especially with respect to general educators' differentiation of instruction. Many studies reported observing only whole-class instruction and whole-class activities, with all students using identical activities and materials all the time (e.g. Hardy 2001). For example, it was reported that 'teachers get into a lecture routine' (Magiera *et al.* 2005: 22). Another teacher reported that 'the regular education teacher said "There is no difference in the treatment of students with LD in my class."' (Norris 1997: 123). Feldman (1998: 89) reported that 'co-teachers are not likely to prepare individual lessons plans to accommodate students with disabilities'.

Special educators, conversely, were occasionally observed to differentiate instruction. For example, during a general educator's lecture, a special educator might write notes on the board to assist all students with key ideas and note taking (Trent 1998), or move things around to organize the room. However, special educators (or general educators) were never observed using specific teaching strategies to promote learning or memory and only rarely observed using any time of specialized learning strategy instruction (Scruggs *et al.* 2007).

Peer-assisted learning with differentiated curriculum enhancements

Mastropieri and Scruggs (2010) described differentiated curriculum enhancements (DCE) as one way of addressing the academic needs of all students in inclusive classes. DCE provides targeted practice in varied response formats, using a variety of strategies to be employed as needed by individual students. Moreover, DCE utilizes peer mediation in inclusive classes to maximize all student opportunities to respond and therefore increases relevant practice. The differentiated components are embedded with materials or procedures that are overall identical for all students. Three types of DCE have been investigated including class-wide peer tutoring with content sheets (Mastropieri *et al.* 2008), embedded mnemonic elaborations (Mastropieri *et al.* 2005) and differentiated activities (e.g. Mastropieri *et al.* 2006b).

Differentiated curriculum enhancements with content sheets

The first DCE approach involves class-wide peer tutoring on targeted content. Teachers identify and select the most important challenging content for students to learn and place that information on content sheets which are used during peer tutoring activities to maximize students' opportunities to practise and learn. Mastropieri, Scruggs, and Marshak (2008) taught 81 seventh graders (*N* = 15 with disabilities) in inclusive US history classes using a crossover design with alternating traditional and experimental units of instruction. During experimental instruction students were assigned partners, trained in tutoring rules and procedures, tutored and tested one another using the content sheets. Dyads also used self-monitoring to record when items were practised and when content was mastered. Instruction in the control condition included traditional teacher-led instruction and accompanying textbook worksheets. Students scored significantly higher in the experimental condition and a significant interaction indicated that students with disabilities gained more than general education students from the experimental materials. When students were interviewed post-treatment, the majority reported enjoying working together, described peer interactions as positive, and reported additional practice was beneficial.

In a follow-up study, Mastropieri *et al.* (2006a) randomly assigned 10 middle school inclusive classes, with 157 students ($N = 29$ with disabilities), to either the experimental or comparison conditions. Each condition received 18 weeks of instruction covering seven history units. The materials and procedures paralleled those used in the previous study. This time, however, the amount of content per unit was reduced to include fewer items based on teacher feedback. Again, significant differences were obtained favouring the experimental condition.

McDuffie *et al.* (2009) extended the research to middle school inclusive science learning. Eight classes containing 203 students ($N = 62$ with disabilities) were stratified by co-teaching or not and then randomly assigned to either DCE tutoring with life science content sheets or a traditional instructional approach for eight weeks. Materials and procedures replicated the history studies, but used science content over five units. Tutoring was the first ten minutes of the class and replaced the typical warm-up activities. Results revealed students in the experimental condition significantly outperformed control condition students, general education students significantly outperformed special education students, and co-teaching classes outperformed non co-taught classes on the identification items. These findings replicated the social studies results, but also indicated there may be value added with a co-teaching component. Students and teachers also reported enjoying using the DCE materials and tutoring.

Embedded mnemonic elaborations

Another type of DCE involves the use of materials containing embedded mnemonic elaborations within content sheets. Mnemonic instruction has been effective with students with disabilities (Mastropieri and Scruggs 1989; Scruggs and Mastropieri 2000). Mnemonic strategies were placed within chemistry materials to be used only when needed. For example, to practise the content associated with learning about 'moles', the first question on the content sheet was: 'What is a mole?' If students knew the correct response, they immediately proceeded to the subsequent elaborative questions, including, 'What else is important about moles? And what is an example of a mole?' However, when the response was unknown, partners provided an embedded mnemonic strategy containing an interactive illustration, in this case of a mole (the burrowing animal) sitting on a scale looking at the statement: 'Your weight in grams is . . .' with the strategy: 'Think of the word mole. Then think of this picture of a mole on a scale looking at his weight in grams, to help you remember that a mole is the atomic weight in grams of an element.' Partners provided peers with the strategy and the definition until mastered and then progressed to the next item. The provided strategies typically used the keyword method and taught students a concrete acoustically similar keyword for the unfamiliar word, and then displayed an interacting picture of the keyword and the definition.

Mastropieri *et al.* (2005) applied this approach in tenth grade inclusive chemistry classes, covering concepts such as thermic reactions, the periodic table, enthalpy, valence electrons and covalent bonding. After nine weeks of implementation, students in the experimental condition outperformed control students. Students with learning disabilities in the experimental condition appeared to benefit by gaining more (42.5 per cent) than average-achieving students (16.1 per cent).

Marshak, Mastropieri, and Scruggs (2011) replicated and extended these findings to US history content in eight inclusive seventh grade classes, with 186 students ($N = 42$ with disabilities), which were stratified by class status (team taught and general education) and randomly assigned to experimental or traditional instructional conditions. Both conditions used the same textbook and highlighted content according to the school district's benchmarks and state's high stakes tests. Materials for the traditional condition included teacher-developed graphic organizers and textbook-developed supplemental materials. Conversely, the DCE materials consisted of content sheets containing embedded mnemonic strategies to be used or skipped, depending upon student needs. For example, to teach that Rockefeller controlled the oil business, a picture was displayed of a rock (keyword for Rockefeller) with a pipe leaking oil on top. When partners asked their peers, 'Who is John Rockefeller?' they would proceed to the next item if peers responded correctly. If they were incorrect, partners would show the illustration and say: 'To help you remember that Rockefeller was a businessman who controlled the oil business, remember this picture of a rock with oil on top of it.' Tests contained targeted items as well as items not targeted within the content sheets. After 12 weeks of instruction, findings revealed significant differences favouring students in the DCE condition. Students in the DCE condition also learned significantly more non-targeted items. All students indicated they enjoyed using the materials and participating in tutoring, and identified other content area classes where materials would be helpful.

Differentiated curriculum enhancement activities

The final form of DCE activities included multiple activities to provide increasingly more intensive and challenging practice. The first level requires identifying a correct response from multiple choice or matching formats, with prompting as needed. The second level requires a production response that also contains prompts. The third level requires an unprompted production response. Mastropieri *et al.* (2006b) implemented these DCEs designed to teach an experimental investigation science unit for 213 ($N = 44$ with disabilities) eighth graders from 13 inclusive classes. To teach about qualitative and quantitative research design, a Level 1 activity required students to read a statement and identify whether the statement was qualitative or quantitative with prompting, using a board game-like activity. The Level 2 activities required students to produce three qualitative and three quantitative observations from illustrations, again with prompting as needed. The Level 3 activities required students to make unprompted qualitative and quantitative observations. Other units included:

- charts and graphs;
- experimental design;
- measurement;
- science; and
- liquid measurement.

Students worked with partners or in small groups to complete activities and completed self-monitoring and self-evaluation sheets on their daily performance. Findings on unit tests yielded a significant effect for treatment condition with experimental students outperforming their control condition counterparts. Findings on the end of year state's high-stakes testing also yielded significant effects favouring the treatment condition. Students also expressed positive attitudes toward the activities but indicated a stronger preference for those activities resembling game-like activities over those resembling more traditional workbook-like activities.

Simpkins *et al.* (2009) designed materials with two levels of differentiated activities in earth and space science and light and sound units for fifth grade students in three inclusive classes. Sixty-one students ($N = 18$ at risk or with disabilities) participated in the 10-week study. The Level 1 activities required identification responses with prompting when needed, while Level 2 required production responses. Content in the earth and space science units included content such as meteorologists, clouds, hurricanes, barometers and continental shelf; while the light and sound units included content such as chemical reactions, frequency, hertz, refractions, vibrations and visible spectrums. Findings revealed significant effects for the treatment condition over the traditional instruction. Students reported favouring the activities, found them interesting, felt they helped them with learning, and enjoyed working in small groups.

The current series of studies lend preliminary support to the use of supplementary materials and peer mediation. Content sheets, content sheets with embedded mnemonic strategies, and varying levels of hands-on activities all improved students' learning. Students of all abilities appear to enjoy the opportunity to work more closely with peers.

Conclusion

Effective inclusive education is important for the success of all students with and without disabilities; however, multiple variables influence any inclusive education practices. Such variables include teachers' attitudes toward inclusion, co-teaching and differentiated curriculum enhancements delivered with peer mediation programmes.

Teachers are generally positive with respect to their attitudes toward inclusion; however, teacher support for inclusion diminishes with respect to aspects of inclusion that teachers believe place additional burdens on their time. Co-teaching has been effective, but has revealed several complications in planning and practice. Peers have been seen to be very helpful in facilitating inclusion efforts; however, without specific training and monitoring, peers can also be seen to undermine inclusion efforts. Although differentiated curriculum enhancements delivered by peers have promising results, few teachers presently implement the practices. All these challenges, while significant, have been addressed, with varying degrees of success. For inclusion to become very effective, the field must listen to its teachers, provide necessary support and conduct further research on educational inclusion.

References

Buckley, C. (2005) Establishing and maintaining collaborative relationships between regular and special education teachers in middle school social studies classrooms, in T.E. Scruggs and M.A. Mastropieri (eds) *Cognition and Learning in Diverse Settings: Vol 18. Advances in Learning and Behavioral Disabilities*. Oxford: Elsevier, 153–98.

Dieker, L.A. (2001) What are the characteristics of 'effective' middle and high school co-taught teams for students with disabilities?, *Preventing School Failure*, 46: 14–23.

Feldman, R. (1998) A study of instructional planning of secondary special and general education co-teachers to accommodate learning disabled students in the general education classroom, *Dissertation Abstracts International*, 58(07): 4731A.

Friend, M. and Cook, L. (2010) *Interactions: Collaboration Skills for School Professionals*, 6th edn. Columbus, OH: Merrill.

Hardy, S.D. (2001) A qualitative study of the instructional behaviors of a dyad of educators in self-contained and inclusive co-taught secondary biology classrooms during a nine-week science instruction grading period, *Dissertation Abstracts International*, 61(12): 4731A.

Hazlett, A. (2001) The co-teaching experience: joint planning and delivery in the inclusive classroom, *Dissertation Abstracts International*, 62 (12), 4064A (UMI No. AAI3037002).

Hull, J.R. (2005) General classroom and special education teachers' attitudes and perceptions of inclusion in relation to student outcomes. Unpublished doctoral dissertation. University of West Florida, Pensacola FL.

LeCompte, M.D. and Preissle, J. (1993) *Ethnography and Qualitative Design in Educational Research*. New York: Academic Press.

McDuffie, K., Mastropieri, M.A. and Scruggs, T.E. (2009) Promoting success in content area classes: is value added through co-teaching?, *Exceptional Children*, 75: 493–510.

McDuffie, K.A., Scruggs, T.E. and Mastropieri, M.A. (2007) Co-teaching in inclusive classrooms: results of qualitative research from the United States, Canada, and Australia, in T.E. Scruggs and M.A. Mastropieri (eds) *Cognition and Learning in Diverse Settings: Advances in Learning and Behavioral Disabilities*, Vol. 20. Oxford: Elsevier Science/JAI Press.

Magiera, K., Smith, C., Zigmond, N. and Gebauer, K. (2005) Benefits of co-teaching in secondary mathematics classes, *TEACHING Exceptional Children*, 37(3): 20–4.

Marshak, L., Mastropieri, M.A. and Scruggs, T.E. (2011) Curriculum enhancements for inclusive secondary social studies classes, *Exceptionality*, 19(2): 61–74. DOI: 10.1080/09362835.2011.562092.

Mastropieri, M.A. and Scruggs, T.E. (1989) Constructing more meaningful relationships: mnemonic instruction for special populations, *Educational Psychology Review*, 1: 83–111.

Mastropieri, M.A. and Scruggs, T.E. (2010) *The Inclusive Classroom: Strategies for Effective Instruction*, 4th edn. Upper Saddle River, NJ: Prentice Hall.

Mastropieri, M.A, Scruggs, T.E. and Bohs, K. (1994) Mainstreaming an emotionally handicapped student in science: a qualitative investigation, in T.E. Scruggs and M.A. Mastropieri (eds) *Advances in Learning and Behavioral Disabilities* (Vol. 8). Greenwich, CT: JAI Press.

Mastropieri, M.A., Scruggs, T.E., Mantzicopoulos, P.Y., Sturgeon, A., Goodwin, L. and Chung, S. (1998) A place where living things affect and depend on each other: qualitative and quantitative outcomes associated with inclusive science teaching, *Science Education*, 82: 163–79.

Mastropieri, M.A., Scruggs, T.E., Graetz, J. and Conners, N. (2005) Inclusive practices in content area instruction: addressing the challenges of co-teaching, in T.E. Scruggs and M.A. Mastropieri (eds) *Cognition and Learning in Diverse Settings: Advances in Learning and Behavioral Disabilities* (Vol. 18). Oxford: Elsevier Science/JAI Press.

Mastropieri, M.A., Scruggs, T.E., Marshak, L., McDuffie, K. and Conners, N. (2006a) Peer tutoring in inclusive history classes: effects for middle school students with mild disabilities. Paper presented at the annual meeting of the American Educational Research Association, San Francisco, 7–11 April.

Mastropieri, M.A., Scruggs, T.E., Norland, J., Berkeley, S., McDuffie, K., Tornquist, E. H. *et al.* (2006b) Differentiated curriculum enhancement in inclusive middle school science: effects on classroom and high-stakes tests, *Journal of Special Education*, 40: 130–7.

Mastropieri, M.A., Scruggs, T.E. and Berkeley, S. (2007) Peers helping peers, *Educational Leadership*, 64: 54–8.

Mastropieri, M.A., Scruggs, T.E. and Marshak, L. (2008) Training teachers, parents, and peers to implement effective teaching strategies for content area learning, in T.E. Scruggs and M.A. Mastropieri (eds) *Personnel Preparation: Advances in Learning and Behavioral Disabilities*, Vol. 21. Bingley: Emerald.

Murawski, W.W. and Swanson, H.L. (2001) A meta-analysis of co-teaching: where are the data?, *Remedial and Special Education*, 22: 258–67.

Norris, D.M. (1997) Teacher perceptions of co-teaching in an inclusive classroom in a middle school: a look at general education and special education teachers working together with students with learning disabilities, *Dissertation Abstracts International*, 58 (06), 2162A (UMI No. AAG9735088).

O'Connor, R.E. and Sanchez, V. (2011) Responsiveness to intervention models for reducing reading difficulties and identifying learning disability, in J. Kauffman, D.P. Hallahan and J. Lloyd (eds) *Handbook of Special Education*. New York: Routledge.

Rice, D. and Zigmond, N. (2000) Co-teaching in secondary schools: teacher reports of development in Australian and American classrooms, *Learning Disabilities Research and Practice*, 15: 190–97.

Rosa, B.A. (1996) Cooperative teaching in the inclusive classroom: a case study of teachers' perspectives, *Dissertation Abstracts International*, 57 (7), 2968 (UMI No. AAG9638771).

Ross, S. (2002). Teachers' feelings of competency in educating children with special needs in the general education setting. MA thesis submitted to Touro College, New York.

Scruggs, T.E. and Mastropieri, M.A. (1994) Successful mainstreaming in elementary science classes: a qualitative investigation of three reputational cases, *American Educational Research Journal*, 31: 785–811.

Scruggs, T.E. and Mastropieri, M.A. (1996a) Teacher perceptions of mainstreaming/inclusion: a research synthesis, *Exceptional Children*, 63: 59–74.

Scruggs, T.E. and Mastropieri, M.A. (1996b) Quantitative synthesis of survey research: methodology and validation, in T.E. Scruggs and M.A. Mastropieri (eds) *Advances in Learning and Behavioral Disabilities: Theoretical Perspectives*, Vol. 10, Part A. Greenwich, CT: JAI Press.

Scruggs, T.E. and Mastropieri, M.A. (2000) The effectiveness of mnemonic instruction for students with learning and behavior problems: an update and research synthesis, *Journal of Behavioral Education*, 10: 163–73.

Scruggs, T.E. and Mastropieri, M.A. (2006) Summarizing qualitative research in special education: purposes and procedure, in T.E. Scruggs and M.A. Mastropieri (eds) *Advances in Learning and Behavioral Disabilities: Vol. 19. Applications of Research Methodology*. Oxford: Elsevier.

Scruggs, T.E., Mastropieri, M.A. and McDuffie, K.A. (2007) Co-teaching in inclusive class-rooms: a meta-synthesis of qualitative research, *Exceptional Children*, 73: 392–416.

Scruggs, T.E., Mastropieri, M.A. and Okolo, C.M. (2008) Science and social studies for students with disabilities, *Focus on Exceptional Children*, 41(2): 1–24.

Scruggs, T.E., Mastropieri, M.A., Berkeley, S. and Graetz, J. (2010) Do special education inter-ventions improve learning of secondary content? A meta-analysis, *Remedial and Special Education*, 36: 437–49. DOI: 10.1177/0741932508327465.

Scruggs, T.E., Mastropieri, M.A. and Leins, P. (2011) Teacher attitudes towards inclusion: a synthesis of survey, comparative, and qualitative research, 1958–2010. Paper presented at the annual meeting of the Council for Exceptional Children, National Harbor, MD, 25–8 April.

Self, H., Benning, A., Marston, D. and Magnusson, D. (1991) Cooperative teaching project: a model for students at risk, *Exceptional Children*, 58: 26–33.

Simpkins, P.M., Mastropieri, M.A. and Scruggs, T.E. (2009) Differentiated curriculum enhancements in inclusive 5th grade science classes, *Remedial and Special Education*, 30: 300–8. DOI: 10.1177/0741932508321011.

Thompson, M.G. (2001) Capturing the phenomenon of sustained co-teaching: perceptions of elementary school teachers, *Dissertation Abstracts Internation*, 63 (02), 560A (UMI No. AA13041129).

Tomlinson, C. (2001) *How to Differentiate Instruction in Mixed-ability Classrooms*. Alexandria, VA: Association for Supervision and Curriculum Development.

Trent, S.C. (1998) False starts and other dilemmas of secondary general education collaborative teachers: a case study, *Journal of Learning Disabilities*, 31: 503–13.

Vaughn, S., Elbaum, B.E., Schumm, J.S. and Hughes, M.T. (1998) Social outcomes for students with and without learning disabilities in inclusive classrooms, *Journal of Learning Disabilities*, 31: 428–36.

Vesay, J.P. (2004) Linking perspectives and practice: influence of early childhood and early child-hood special educators' perspectives on working collaboratively in the integrated preschool classroom, *Dissertation Abstracts International* 65 (03), 826A (UMI No. AAI3126498).

Walther-Thomas, C.S. (1997) Co-teaching experiences: the benefits and problems that teachers and principals report over time, *Journal of Learning Disabilities*, 30: 395–408.

Ward, R. (2003) General educators' perceptions of effective collaboration with special educators: a focus group study, *Dissertation Abstracts International*, 64 (03): 861A.

Weiss, M.P. and Lloyd, J.W. (2002) Congruence between roles and actions of secondary special educators in co-taught and special education settings, *Journal of Special Education*, 36: 58–68.

Wood, M. (1998) Whose job is it anyway? Educational roles in inclusion, *Exceptional Children*, 64: 181–95.

Zigmond, N. and Matta, D. (2004) Value added of the special education teacher on secondary school co-taught classes, in T.E. Scruggs and M.A. Mastropieri (eds) *Advances in Learning and Behavioral Disabilities: Vol. 17. Research in Secondary Schools*. Oxford: Elsevier.

13

LAUREL M. GARRICK DUHANEY
Understanding and addressing barriers to the implementation of inclusive education

Introduction

The latter part of the twentieth century has witnessed unparalleled momentum in modern societies in the transformation of special education from a segregated system, serving as a form of homogeneous grouping and tracking system with serious concerns about its programmatic efficacy, to a largely integrated system (Dunn 1968; McLeskey 2007). In the US, for example, various terms, beginning with normalization, followed by mainstreaming, then the regular education initiative (REI), and now inclusive education, where all students are educated together in the general education classroom, have emerged and reflect this transformation in philosophy and practices (Osgood 2005; McLeskey 2007; Salend and Garrick Duhaney 2007). A multidimensional philosophy, inclusive education is one of the most complex and controversial issues confronting educational professionals and policy makers worldwide (Mitchell 2005; Rose 2010). This chapter, however, embraces the principles of inclusion that improve the educational system for all learners by placing them together in age-appropriate, general education classrooms regardless of their learning ability, cultural, ethnic and linguistic backgrounds, economic status, gender, religious background and family structure (Sapon-Shevin 2003; Salend 2011).

Global shifts from segregated, categorically based schools where the medical model prevailed (i.e. perceived deficits in individual children) to more inclusive schools have been buttressed by the work of advocacy groups, researchers, special education legislation and international commitments, agendas, declarations and organizations (Forlin 2008; Rose 2010). For example, in 1994, at a world conference on special education, ninety-four countries and twenty-five international organizations, meeting under the aegis of the United Nations Educational, Scientific and Cultural Organization (UNESCO), adopted the ground-breaking *Salamanca Declaration and Framework for Action* (UNESCO 1994). The statement, which now significantly influences education policies worldwide, called upon *all* countries to educate *all* students in inclusive settings regardless of their unique characteristics, abilities, learning needs or other conditions (Wu and Komesaroff 2007). This call was strengthened by the Education for All agenda, which targets 2015 as the year to achieve univeral education (UNESCO 2008). Consequently, several nations have established inclusive education initiatives and policies aligned to their country's educational philosophy, history, and socio-political, cultural and economic dynamics (Brown 2005; Fletcher and Artiles 2005; Mitchell 2005; Mitchell and Desai 2005; Heng and Tam 2006; Alur and Bach 2008).

Although early efforts to advance inclusive education began in developed nations, developing and very poor countries also have made inclusive education a national priority (UNESCO 2008). China, Cuba, Indonesia, Laos, Lesotho, South Africa, Sri Lanka, Uganda, Vietnam, Yemen, Zimbabwe, and India all have made inclusive education a priority (Mittler 2005; UNESCO 2008). For example, India's efforts to implement inclusive education have centred on bringing students with disabilities into the education system (Singal 2010). Not surprisingly, there is considerable variation in commitments and rates of progress in implementing inclusive education worldwide (Mitchell and Desai 2005).

Despite greater global advancement towards inclusive education and research touting its academic, behavioural and social benefits to students (Black-Hawkins *et al.* 2007; Salend and Garrick Duhaney 2007), there are serious barriers that impede or otherwise prevent its implementation. This chapter therefore discusses barriers that obstruct the implementation of inclusive education and presents evidence-based approaches for overcoming them. It should be noted here that there is a slight degree of overlap among several of the barriers presented.

Socio-cultural and philosophical barriers

Cultural norms, social inequality and role of education

Cultural norms, social inequality and varied views of the roles of education in the society can serve to deter progress toward inclusive education. Many will agree that a key function of public schooling (state schooling in the UK) is to provide equal educational opportunities for students regardless of their ability, gender, social class, linguistic, cultural, religious and economic backgrounds. Public schools also are important instruments in educating an increasingly urban and heterogeneous school-age population (Nieto and Bode 2008; Taylor and Whittaker 2009). However, public schools are based on middle-class mainstream culture, are highly inequitable, and perpetuate a disparate social class structure that relegates low-income, disabled and culturally diverse students to a future that largely reflects their past (Orfield *et al.* 2004; Gollnick and Chinn 2009).

Thus, inclusive education confronts the major challenge of bringing about equity and educational success for all students within an increasingly multicultural and multilingual society. This entails more than affording students with disabilities an equal chance to attend inclusive schools. Once there, their teachers are challenged to make learning culturally relevant, interdisciplinary and rigorous for all students by addressing various ethnic and cultural alternatives and fostering a school culture and social structure that empowers students (Banks 2008). Teachers also are challenged to address cultural mismatches between the home and school in such things as child rearing practices, religious beliefs, social class, and values about schooling and education. How these disarticulations between the home and school cultures are managed by teachers will lead to equitable and excellent schools or inequitable and poor educational outcomes for students (Darling-Hammond and Friedlander 2008).

Schools can adapt a variety of learning activities and approaches to address socio-cultural and philosophical barriers to inclusive education. For example, multicultural education is an emergent educational philosophy, linked to inclusion, for restructuring schools to address the concerns of learners with disabilities as well as those from different nationalities, racial, ethnic, social class and socio-economic backgrounds (Banks 2008; Gollnick and Chinn 2009; National Council for the Accreditation of Teacher Education 2009). According to Salend (2011: 131), definitions of multicultural education 'range from an emphasis on human relations and harmony to a focus on social democracy, justice, and empowerment for *all students*'. To advance educational equity in schools, educational systems should strive to provide access and excellence for all students, recognize the importance of community and acceptance of individual differences, try to reduce prejudice, and foster an empowering school culture. Educators should try to ensure that instructional strategies and curricula are consonant with students' cultures, experiences and languages; address students' strengths and weaknesses; and demonstrate an awareness of cultural, religious, linguistic, experiential and economic factors that affect students (Obiakor 2007; Villegas and Lucas 2007; Banks 2008; Harry *et al.* 2008).

Fatalism and karma

Fatalism and karma are two examples of the ways in which cultural factors may impact beliefs about inclusive education. Fatalism assumes that an existing condition is unchangeable or fixed and is intended to remain so (Brown 2005). Parents and families who have fatalistic beliefs may consider a child with a disability punishment from God, which they must bear. Consequently, such parents may reject measures aimed at prevention, treatment and rehabilitation of their child's disability (Gupta and Singhal 2004; Brown 2005). Conversely, some parents who believe in fate may assume a proactive, hands-on, practical approach to managing their child's disability. In Kuwait, for example, some parents and families advocate for and accept educational intervention services to help their child with a disability achieve acceptable levels of functioning in school and society (Gupta and Singhal 2004; Raman *et al.* 2010). A characteristic of the Puerto Rican and Mexican American subcultures, fatalism is sometimes manifested in submissiveness and acceptance of a disability. Such fatalism may help parents cope with a child's disability (Seligman and Darling 2007).

A fair degree of fatalism is rooted in the philosophy of karma (Gabel 2004). Karma holds that disabilities may be attributed to retribution for sins committed in a previous incarnation or a curse from ancestors, and that attempts to improve the welfare of the disabled would hinder divine justice (Karna 1999; Gupta and Singhal 2004; Chiang and Hadadian 2007). Many followers of Hinduism, the main religion in India, believe in the doctrine of karma. There also is the tendency among Asians to attribute a child's disability to supernatural influences or to sins committed by the child's ancestors (Chiang and Hadadian 2007). Implications of this belief include neglect and exclusion of the disabled from society as well as fear, rejection, shame, dishonour, and feelings of obligation toward the child with a disability (Alur 2001; Gabel and Taylor 2004). Consequences may also include lowered expectation for achievement, lack of parental participation and co-operation with the school, and self-fulfilling prophecies of poor social behaviour (Brown 2005).

Fatalism and karma may be viewed as obstacles to inclusive education because they can impact the implementation of early intervention and other educational programmes and services offered to students with disabilities and their families. In addressing cultural beliefs, professionals working with parents and families of children with disabilities should:

- try to understand the parents and families' beliefs about disability and treatment, and the factors influencing those perceptions;
- tailor educational intervention programmes and services to the needs of students with disabilities, their parents and their families; and
- try to negotiate the tensions arising from clashes between the cultural beliefs of the home and the school. For example, professionals working with families from traditional Asian backgrounds should understand that requiring parents to participate in their child's educational planning may be threatening to some families who prefer to defer to the expertise of professionals (Gabel and Taylor 2004; Seligman and Darling 2007).

Institutional barriers

Funding inclusive education

Financing inclusive education is a primary concern for both developed and developing nations – more so for poor countries – because education must vie with other economic priorities such as healthcare, the AIDS pandemic, poverty, social welfare and defence budgets (Artiles and Dyson 2005). According to various reports, in 2007 there were 72 million children worldwide who were not in school, 150 million children dropped out of school before they could read or write, under 2 per cent of the disabled attended school in poor countries, and for every child killed in armed conflict three were injured or permanently disabled (Mittler 2005; UNICEF 2003, 2009; Bureau of Public Information 2010). Estimates are that it would cost US $16 billion annually to close the gap in meeting the Education for All goals in low-income countries; this, in an era of drastic cuts in aid for education from developed nations. For example, financial support for basic education fell by 22 per cent to US $4.3 billion in 2007 (Bureau of Public Information 2010).

In addition to cuts in education aid, overall education spending has been seriously restricted by the debt crisis that has engulfed the Latin America and Caribbean regions, the current global economic crisis, and the instability in food and fuel prices (UNICEF 2009). Economic policies from international donor agencies (e.g. International Monetary Fund, World Bank) have driven cutbacks in education thereby resulting in a lack of investment in schools, curricula and teachers, as demonstrated by lower teacher salaries, poorly trained teachers, lack of modern buildings and an overall decline in the quality of public schools (International Monetary Fund 2009). Further compounding this problem is differential access to educational resources with wealthier school districts receiving much more school resources than students in poorer, high-minority school districts (Nieto and Bode 2008).

But within a global context of shrinking economic resources, is it possible to achieve inclusive education for all? Both the Salamanca Statement of 1994 and research point to the cost-efficiency and cost-effectiveness of implementing inclusion by eliminating the inefficiencies of multiple systems of administration, organizational structures and services, and the financially unrealistic options of special schools (Peters 2003). International monetary agencies could reduce or even eliminate debt repayment on the condition that poor countries agree to invest the monies in social infrastructure, especially education (Mittler 2005). Furthermore, data from 120 developing countries for the period 1975–2000 revealed that a 1 per cent increase in education spending as a share of gross domestic product over 15 years could lead to universal primary school enrollment (UNICEF 2009).

Attitudes of educators, administrators, students and families

Because educators' support is the lynchpin for ensuring the success of inclusion, researchers also have investigated personnel-related barriers to inclusive education. Results of studies examining the attitudes of educators, administrators, students and families toward inclusion are mixed. Space limitations will allow only a brief summary of these findings. (See Elhoweris and Alsheikh 2006; Idol 2006; Black-Hawkins *et al.* 2007; Salend and Garrick Duhaney 2007; Silverman 2007; Ainscow 2008 for a more detailed discussion of the research on inclusive education.) Despite the progressively complex and restructured role of teaching and administering today's inclusive classrooms, there is general support among teachers and administrators for inclusion. Elementary education teachers tend to favour inclusion more than secondary teachers and special educators more positively than general education teachers (Salend and Garrick Duhaney 2007). However, there is some trepidation, apathy and rejection for inclusion. Teachers' concerns relate to professional competence, lack of support and resources, and questions about the effectiveness of an inclusive setting.

Variables that appear to be robust indicators of positive attitudes are

- shared accountability for educational outcomes;
- level of in-service and pre-service training;
- success in inclusive classroom settings;
- resources; and
- administrative support (Elhoweris and Alsheikh 2006).

Because administrative leadership is vitally important to successful inclusion, administrators should establish inclusion as a goal for all students, schedule time for school personnel to collaborate (e.g. special and general education teachers, teacher assistants, speech and language clinicians, school psychologist), and foster conducive working conditions (e.g. staffing ratios and caseloads) (Giangreco *et al.* 2010).

Like educators and administrators, the experiences of students with disabilities in general education classrooms also vary, ranging from isolation, fear, frustration and physical and emotional bullying to the development of friendships, increased social support, heightened self-esteem, greater intellectual challenges and improved academic performance (Salend and Garrick Duhaney 2007). Students without disabilities benefited from inclusion socially (e.g. made friends with and advocated for peers with disabilities) and typically performed as well as or superior to their peers in non-inclusive classrooms. Their concerns about placement of students with disabilities in inclusive classrooms were related to communication difficulties and physical and behavioural characteristics of students with disabilities (Idol 2006; Ainscow 2008).

Family involvement, empowerment, communication and collaboration also are essential to the success of inclusive education. Studies suggest that although the attitudes of families of students with and without disabilities toward inclusion were generally positive, they also had concerns about it (Garrick Duhaney and Salend 2000). Families of students with disabilities believed inclusion resulted in increased friendships, a more challenging curriculum, higher expectations and academic achievement, improved self-concept, and better language, motor, and social skills for their children. Families of students without disabilities reported that inclusion benefited their children by fostering greater tolerance of human differences and providing them with a good education. Concerns of families of students with disabilities about inclusive placements included loss of individualized special education services, quality of instruction, and fear that their children would be ridiculed, isolated, and verbally abused (Garrick Duhaney and Salend 2000; Hornby 2000). Educators can enhance families' perceptions of inclusion by engaging them in curriculum planning and individualized programme development; soliciting information from them about their children's strengths, challenges, and progress; advocating for students and families; resolving conflicts that may arise constructively; offering educational programmes to families; and by understanding and accommodating cross-cultural communication patterns and linguistic factors (Salend 2011).

Disproportionate representation

Disproportionate representation of culturally diverse students in special education poses a threat to inclusive education in the US. Disproportionate representation relates to the

> extent to which students with particular characteristics (e.g. race, ethnicity, linguistic background, socioeconomic status, gender) are placed in a particular type of educational program or provided access to services, resources, curriculum, and instructional and classroom management strategies.
>
> (Salend and Garrick Duhaney 2005: 213)

Culturally and linguistically diverse students are overrepresented in the high-incidence disability categories of emotional and behavioural disorders (EBD), learning disabilities (LD), mild mental retardation (MMR), and speech/language impairments (SLI) (US Department of Education 2006). Nationally, African American students are not only overrepresented in more restrictive educational settings but have a higher failure rate on state and national standards in basic subjects such as mathematics and language arts than their white peers (National Research Council [NCR] 2002). American Indian/Alaska Native students are disproportionately enrolled in the LD and EBD categories at the national and statewide levels (Donovan and Cross 2002; National Center on Culturally Responsive Educational Systems 2006).

A comprehensive intervention approach should be implemented to address disproportionate representation. Delivering a wide variety of effective, culturally sensitive educational services and practices within the general education classroom can help restrict the problem of disproportionate representation. These practices should address students' unique needs, strengths, opportunities, experiences, socio-cultural and linguistic needs as well as the relationships between teachers and families. Use of certified, academically competent and caring teachers; culturally sensitive and responsive teaching strategies; and culturally appropriate behaviour management strategies also can help to limit disproportionality (Salend and Garrick Duhaney 2005).

New standards-driven accountability demands for schools

Several governments have directed national priorities to standards-driven, highly accountable education systems (Dyson 2005). These priorities, that schools increase educational productivity and results as measured by assessed student performance, now rival or surpass discussions of inclusive education in some countries. For example, the *No Child Left Behind Act* (NCLBA), which is a driving force in US schools, reveals a new perspective of social equity, one centreing on equality of outcomes, not access (McLaughlin and Jordan 2005). NCLBA's goals focus on closing the educational achievement gap between traditionally high- and low-performing groups of students. It directs states to:

- establish challenging content standards in reading, mathematics and science, among other subjects;
- annually assess all Grades 3–8 students' performance;
- disaggregate assessment results by student subgroups, including students with disabilities; and
- establish an accountability system of sanctions and rewards centred on student results.

Based on NCLBA accountability requirements, schools create state- and district-level performance goals for each subgroup of students to ensure subgroups attain 'adequate yearly progress' (AYP) toward clear-cut achievement objectives on assessments. AYP calculations must include assessment results for 95 per cent of the students in each subgroup, including students with the most significant cognitive disabilities who may take an assessment based on alternate achievement standards (Salend 2011). Consequently, today's standard-driven educational priorities in the US require that all students have access to the same challenging curriculum, content standards and performance, assessments and accountability. So, although inclusive education remains a goal, the national priority and energy has shifted to standards-driven reform and the closing of the educational achievement gap between high- and low-performing students.

The escalating accountability mandates for meeting challenging performance targets not only intensify pressures upon schools but are at odds with student individuality and can weaken schools' commitment toward students with disabilities. Studies find that low-achieving students depress schools' performance and, in worse case scenarios, schools receiving poor reports may be placed on probation (Azzam 2008). Such schools may lose their autonomy and administrative positions, and could ultimately be closed. Under these scenarios, schools are cautious about including students with disabilities in their high-stakes testing as they may impede their performance, and teachers are reluctant to work in inclusive classrooms (Dyson 2005).

Strategies for addressing concerns about NCLBA's accountability demands that also could promote inclusive education include adopting multiple assessment measures for identifying students' progress instead of a one-size-fits-all standardized (or high-stakes) testing approach. These approaches could include classroom-based assessment strategies such as curriculum-based measurement, learning logs, error analysis, authentic/performance assessment and portfolio assessment. Offering students with disabilities testing accommodations including repeating directions as necessary, highlighting key words or phrases, placing fewer items on a page, presenting tests via signing or Braille, and providing an alternate testing environment would be consistent with the spirit of the Individuals with Disabilities Education Improvement Act (IDEIA) and benefit students. Ensuring that students have access to individualized instruction when needed and that the curriculum is varied to prevent narrowing of the curriculum are good practices to adopt. Providing highly qualified teachers for all students and employing scientifically based research educational practices are also useful strategies to employ (Salend 2011 provides detailed information on these strategies).

Need for highly qualified teachers

Widespread philosophical support for inclusive education has not abolished concerns about the inadequate preparation of and support for pre-service and in-service teachers. Consequently, what pre-service teachers need to know and be able to do to work successfully in inclusive classrooms has been discussed in the literature. Teachers should be able to diagnose learning difficulties and prescribe corresponding teaching approaches (Hodkinson 2005). However, questions have arisen with respect to whether only special education teachers need a specialized pedagogy, such as the diagnostic–prescriptive teaching approach, for teaching students with disabilities (Florian and Kershner 2009). Some believe both general education and special education teachers (i.e. *all* teachers) need to have extensive knowledge, technical and practical skills, and appropriate dispositions (i.e. attitudes, values and beliefs) for the inclusive classroom (Florian and Rouse 2010). The role of teacher training programmes should therefore be to help each teacher – not just the specialist/special education teacher – to develop the knowledge, skills and dispositions that support inclusion; thereby, reinforcing the viewpoint that *all* teachers have a major responsibility for meeting the needs of students with disabilities.

Both comprehensive pre-service training and ongoing in-service training are needed to maintain the success of inclusive education (Blanton *et al.* 2011). Teachers should have knowledge of what inclusion is, and of how to work with students with diverse learning needs, modify curriculum, use various instructional strategies, collaborate, communicate effectively, problem solve, design individual education plans, differentiate curriculum and pedagogy, and monitor students' programmes. Teachers should be able to use assessment as a tool for looking forward (assessment for learning) and not only backwards (assessment of learning). Practical training with students in high-poverty school districts and instructional practices constituting individualization and explicit instruction would also facilitate effective inclusion. Additionally, an understanding of how to use instructional technology, work with other professionals, develop age-appropriate goals, deliver one-to-one and large- and small-group instruction, and implement peer tutoring, strategy instruction, curriculum-based assessment, proactive behaviour management and peer supports would enhance inclusive education (Forlin 2010; Kaikkonen 2010; Salend 2011).

However, even when pre-service teachers possess the requisite knowledge, skills and attitudes to support inclusion, the inflexibility of some school systems to change the status quo impedes progress toward inclusion. Moreover, concern emerges in educational systems where the expectation is that teachers meet examinations and standards using a didactic traditionalist approach while attempting to implement an inclusive philosophy (Forlin 2010). Again, these situations thwart progress toward inclusive education.

Conclusion

The inclusive education philosophy has garnered unparalleled attention across the world as education systems come to accept that exclusion and isolation are no longer justifiable or defensible choices. More and more nations are restructuring their education systems to accommodate all students, including those with disabilities, as they address their belief in education as a fundamental human right for all children. But inclusive education for all is not an easy mission to accomplish and several barriers stand in the way of its attainment. Although inclusive education has progressed rapidly in many wealthy nations, elsewhere in the world progress has been less stable and in some cases non-existent. But even where progress toward inclusion has been rapid, barriers to inclusion remain. Those barriers, like the ones discussed in this chapter, must be confronted and eliminated if we are to attain inclusive education for all.

References

Ainscow, M. (2008) Making sure that every child matters: towards a methodology for enhancing equity within educational systems, in C. Forlin (ed.) *Catering for Learners with Diverse Needs: An Asian-Pacific Focus*. Hong Kong: Hong Kong Institute of Education.

Alur, M. (2001) Some cultural and moral implications of inclusive education in India, *Journal of Moral Education* 30(3): 287–92.

Alur, M. and Bach, M. (2008) *The Journey for Inclusive Education in the Indian Subcontinent.* London: Routledge.

Artiles, A. and Dyson, A. (2005) Inclusive education in the globalization age: the promise of comparative cultural–historical analysis, in D. Mitchell (ed.) *Contextualizing Inclusive Education: Evaluating Old and New International Perspectives.* New York: Routledge.

Azzam, A.M. (2008) Left behind – by design, *Educational Leadership,* 65(4): 91–2.

Banks, J.A. (2008) *An Introduction to Multicultural Education,* 4th edn. Boston, MA: Allyn and Bacon.

Black-Hawkins, K., Florian, L. and Rouse, M. (2007) *Achievement and Inclusion in Schools.* London: Routledge.

Blanton, L.P., Pugach, M.C. and Florian, L. (2011) *Preparing General Education Teachers to Improve Outcomes for Students with Disabilities.* Available at: http://www.ldaamerica.org/stateline/documents-2011/11July/AACTE-NCLD-Policy-Brief-05-11.pdf [Accessed 6 August 2011].

Brown, R.C. (2005) Inclusive education in Middle Eastern cultures: the challenge of tradition, in D. Mitchell (ed.) *Contextualizing Inclusive Education: Evaluating Old and New International Perspectives.* New York: Routledge.

Bureau of Public Information (2010) *Education for all Monitoring Report: Reaching the Marginalized.* Paris: UNESCO.

Chiang, L.H. and Hadadian, A. (2007) Chinese and Chinese–American families of children with disabilities, *International Journal of Special Education,* 22(2): 19–23.

Darling-Hammond, L. and Friedlander, D. (2008) Creating excellent and equitable schools, *Educational Leadership,* 65(8): 14–21.

Donovan, M.S. and Cross, C.T. (eds) (2002) *Minority Students in Special and Gifted Education.* Washington, DC: National Academy Press.

Dunn, L. (1968) Special education for the mildly retarded: is much of it justifiable?, *Exceptional Children,* 35: 5–22.

Dyson, A. (2005) Philosophy, politics and economics? The story of inclusive education in England, in D. Mitchell (ed.) *Contextualizing Inclusive Education: Evaluating Old and New International Perspectives.* New York: Routledge.

Elhoweris, H. and Alsheikh, N. (2006) Teachers' attitudes toward inclusion, *International Journal of Special Education,* 21(1): 115–18.

Fletcher, T. and Artiles, A.J. (2005) Inclusive education and equity in Latin America, in D. Mitchell (ed.) *Contextualizing Inclusive Education: Evaluating Old and New International Perspectives.* New York: Routledge.

Florian, L. and Kershner, R. (2009) Inclusive pedagogy, in H. Daniels, H. Lauder and J. Porter (eds) *Knowledge, Values and Educational Policy: A Critical Perspective.* London: Routledge.

Florian, L. and Rouse, M. (2010) Teachers' professional learning and inclusive practice, in R. Rose (ed.) *Confronting Obstacles to Inclusion: International Responses to Developing Inclusive Education.* New York: Routledge.

Forlin, C. (2008) Educational reform to include all learners in the Asia-Pacific region, in C. Forlin (ed.) *Catering for Learners with Diverse Needs: An Asia-Pacific Focus.* Hong Kong: Hong Kong Institute of Education.

Forlin, C. (2010) Teacher education for inclusion, in R. Rose (ed.) *Confronting Obstacles to Inclusion: International Responses to Developing Inclusive Education.* New York: Routledge.

Gabel, S. and Taylor, S.J. (2004) South Asian Indian cultural orientations toward mental retardation, *Mental Retardation,* 42(1): 12–25.

Garrick Duhaney, L.M. and Salend, S.J. (2000) Parental perceptions of inclusive educational placements, *Remedial and Special Education,* 21(2): 121–8.

Giangreco, M.F., Carter, E.W., Doyle, M. and Suter, J.C. (2010) Supporting students with disabilities in inclusive classrooms, in R. Rose (ed.) *Confronting Obstacles to Inclusion: International Responses to Developing Inclusive Education*. New York: Routledge.

Gollnick, D.M. and Chinn, P.C. (2009) *Multicultural Education in a Pluralistic Society*, 8th edn. Upper Saddle River, NJ: Merrill/Pearson Education.

Gupta, A. and Singhal, N. (2004) Positive perceptions in parents of children with disabilities, *Asia Pacific Disability Rehabilitation Journal*, 15(1): 22–35.

Harry, B., Arnaiz, P., Klingner, J. and Sturges, K. (2008) Schooling and construction of identity among minority students in Spain and the United States, *The Journal of Special Education*, 42(1): 5–14.

Heng, M.A. and Tam, K.Y. (2006) Special education in general teacher education programs in Singapore, *Teacher Education and Special Education*, 29: 149–56.

Hodkinson, A.J. (2005) Conceptions and misconceptions of inclusive education: a critical examination of final year teacher trainees' knowledge and understanding of inclusion, *International Journal of Research in Education*, 73: 15–29.

Hornby, G. (2000) *Improving Parental Involvement*. London: Cassell.

Idol, L. (2006) Toward inclusion of special education students in general education: a program evaluation of eight schools, *Remedial and Special Education*, 27: 77–94.

International Monetary Fund (2009) *Global Monitoring Report*. Available at: http://go.worldbank.org/AR2V89HT70 [Accessed 1 October 2011].

Kaikkonen, L. (2010) Promoting teacher development for diversity, in R. Rose (ed.) *Confronting Obstacles to Inclusion: International Responses to Developing Inclusive Education*. New York: Routledge.

Karna, G.N. (1999) *United Nations and Rights of Disabled Persons: A Study in Indian Perspectives*. New Delhi: A.P.H. Publishing Corporation.

McLaughlin, M.J. and Jordan, A. (2005) Push and pull: forces that are shaping inclusion in the United States and Canada, in D. Mitchell (ed.) *Contextualizing Inclusive Education: Evaluating Old and New International Paradigms*. New York: Routledge.

McLeskey, J. (2007) *Reflections on Inclusion: Classic Articles that Shaped our Thinking*. Arlington, VA: Council for Exceptional Children.

Mitchell, D. (ed.) (2005) *Contextualizing Inclusive Education: Evaluating Old and New International Perspectives*. New York: Routledge.

Mitchell, D. and Desai, I. (2005) Diverse socio-cultural contexts for inclusive education in Asia, in D. Mitchell (ed.) *Contextualizing Inclusive Education: Evaluating Old and New International Paradigms*. New York: Routledge.

Mittler, P. (2005) The global context of inclusive education: the role of the United Nations, in D. Mitchell (ed.) *Contextualizing Inclusive Education: Evaluating Old and New International Perspectives*. New York: Routledge.

National Center on Culturally Responsive Educational Systems (2006) *Disproportionality by Race and Disability 2003–2004*. Available at: http://nccrest.eddata.net/data/index.php?id=476fI=2003–2004&f2=Hispanic [Accessed 29 June 2010].

National Council for the Accreditation of Teacher Education (2009) *Professional Standards for the Accreditation of Schools, Colleges, and Departments of Education*. Available at: http://www.ncate.org [Accessed 20 July 2009].

National Research Council (2002) *Minority Students in Special and Gifted Education: Committee on Minority Representation in Special Education*, edited by M.S. Donovan and C. Cross. Division of Behavioral and Social Sciences and Education. Washington, DC: National Academy Press.

Nieto, S. and Bode, P. (2008) *Affirming Diversity: The Sociopolitical Context of Multicultural Education*, 5th edn. Boston, MA: Allyn & Bacon.

Obiakor, F.E. (2007) *Multicultural Special Education: Culturally Responsive Teaching*. Upper Saddle River, NJ: Merrill/Pearson Education.

Orfield, G., Losen, D., Wald, J. and Swanson, C. (2004) *Losing Our Future: How Minority Youth are Being Left Behind by the Graduation Rate Crisis*. Cambridge, MA: The Civil Rights Project at Harvard University.

Osgood, R.L. (2005) *The History of Inclusion in the United States*. Washington, DC: Gallaudet University Press.

Peters, S.J. (2003) *Inclusive Education: Achieving Education for All by Including Those with Disabilities and Special Educational Needs*. Washington, DC: Disability Group, The World Bank. Available at: http://wbln0018.worldbank.org/HDNet/hddocs.nsf/65538a343139aca b85256cb70055e6ed/8a1681957d70149f85256d7c004d9a61/$FILE/InclusiveEdEnglish. pdf [Accessed 23 July 2011].

Raman, S.R., Mandoda, S., Hussain, L.K., Foley, N., Hamdan, E. and Landry, M. (2010) Exploring the meaning of childhood disability: perceptions of disability among mothers of children with disabilities (CWD) in Kuwait, *World Health and Population*, 11(4): 49–60.

Rose, R. (ed.) (2010) *Confronting Obstacles to Inclusion: International Responses to Developing Inclusive Education*. New York: Routledge.

Salend, S.J. (2011) *Creating Inclusive Classrooms: Effective and Reflective Practices*, 7th edn. Columbus, OH: Pearson Education.

Salend, S.J. and Garrick Duhaney, L.M. (2005) Understanding and addressing the disproportionate representation of students of color in special education, *Intervention in School and Clinic*, 40(4): 213–21.

Salend, S.J. and Garrick Duhaney, L.M. (2007) Research related to inclusion and program effectiveness: yesterday, today, and tomorrow, in J. McLeskey (ed.) *Reflections on Inclusion: Classic Articles that Shaped our Thinking*. Arlington, VA: Council for Exceptional Children.

Sapon-Shevin, M. (2003) Inclusion: a matter of social justice, *Educational Leadership*, 61(2): 25–8.

Seligman, M. and Darling, R.B. (2007) *Ordinary Families, Special Children: A Systems Approach to Childhood Disability*, 3rd edn. New York: Guilford Press.

Silverman, J.C. (2007) Epistemological beliefs and attitudes toward inclusion in pre-service teachers, *Teacher Education and Special Education*, 30(1): 42–51.

Singal, N. (2010) Including 'children with special needs' in the Indian education system: negotiating a contested terrain, in R. Rose (ed.) *Confronting Obstacles to Inclusion: International Responses to Developing Inclusive Education*. New York: Routledge.

Taylor, L.S. and Whittaker, C.R. (2009) *Bridging Multiple Worlds: Case Studies of Diverse Educational Communities*, 2nd edn. Boston, MA: Allyn & Bacon.

UNESCO (1994) *The Salamanca Declaration and Framework for Action on Special Needs Education*. Paris: UNESCO.

UNESCO (2008) *Education for All: Global Monitoring Report*. New York: UNESCO.

UNICEF (2003) *The State of the World's Children 2003*. New York: UNICEF.

UNICEF (2009) *The State of the World's Children*. Available at: http://www.childinfo.org/files/ SOWC_SpecEd_CRC_EN_2010.pdf [Accessed 6 August 2011].

US Department of Education (2006) *26th Annual Report to Congress on the Implementation of the Individuals with Disabilities Education Act, 2004*. Jessup, MD: Ed Pubs. (ERIC Document Reproduction Service No. ED494709).

Villegas, A.M. and Lucas, T. (2007) The culturally responsive teacher, *Educational Leadership*, 64(6): 28–33.

Wu, C. and Komesaroff, L. (2007) An emperor with no clothes? Inclusive education in Victoria, *Australian Journal of Special Education*, 31(2): 129–37.

14

DIANE RICHLER
Systemic barriers to inclusion

Introduction

Inclusive education is good education. The United Nations (UN 1948, 2006), UNESCO (UNESCO 2008), the World Bank (World Bank 2011), the World Health Organization (WHO and World Bank 2011), the Organization for Economic Cooperation and Development (OECD 1999) and other multilateral and regional institutions advocate inclusive education as a right, a means to improved educational outcomes and economic and social development for students with and without disabilities. Yet despite repeated calls for the inclusion of students with disabilities in the regular education system and for major educational reforms that will both promote inclusion and improve educational outcomes for all learners, most children across the world who have a disability are not in school at all, and those who do attend school are not in the mainstream education system. At least one third of the world's children currently out of school have a disability (Peters 2004).

How is that possible? And why is it that despite national and international policies and laws supporting inclusion of students with disabilities in the regular education system, most who do go to school are in separate classes and separate schools (UNESCO 1994; Porter 2001; Peters 2004; UN 2006)?

It is important to consider both the exclusion of children with disabilities from education as a whole and inclusive education as a broader approach to education reform. In this chapter, inclusive education refers to the commitment of education systems to include and serve all children effectively. Inclusive education means that students with disabilities attend regular schools and classrooms with their non-disabled siblings and peers with the supports they require to succeed (Inclusion International 2009). This chapter will explore the systemic reasons for the continued exclusion of students with disabilities from education in general and from inclusive education in particular, and the barriers to be overcome in order to end this exclusion.

The global situation

Attempts to draw global attention to the worldwide exclusion of children with disabilities from education have been hampered by lack of data (Schulze 2009). Precise data on the number of school-aged children who have a disability are not available; there is similarly little data on the percentages of children with a disability who are in school or receiving an inclusive education. The invisibility of children with disabilities masks the extent of those who are being denied an education (Inclusion International 2009; Schulze 2009).

The problems start at birth. In many countries, birth registration is costly, and poor families with low expectations for the future do not see the advantage of registering their children who are born with a disability. This means that these children are never counted in population data and later have no rights as citizens to attend school or qualify for any other benefits. Stigma associated with disability often causes families to keep children with disabilities hidden even from their closest neighbours. This can be because of myths about disability being caused by sins of the parents or fears that having a disabled family member may reduce the eligibility of others to marry (Inclusion International 2009; UNICEF 2011).

The recently published World Report on Disability (WHO and World Bank 2011) rejects much of the existing data about the number of people around the world who have a disability. Previous WHO estimates (WHO and World Bank 2011) suggested that 10 per cent of the world's population had a disability. The new report claims that 15 per cent is a more accurate number. However, the numbers for children are much less clear. The report suggests that for children aged 0–14 years, 5.1 per cent have a moderate or severe disability and for those over 15 years, 19.4 per cent have a moderate or severe disability. However, the report states that 'there is substantial uncertainty about (these) estimates – particularly for regions of the world and for conditions where the data are scarce or of poor quality' (WHO and World Bank 2011: 29). UNICEF (2007) identified numerous reasons for the equivocal data. Especially in lower income countries, children with disabilities may be hidden; disability may only be identified at school entry, or never identified for children who do not attend school; illness, accidents and armed conflicts cause many disabilities during childhood. Milder disabilities affect learners who will have a special educational need at some point during their schooling, estimated to be between 15 and 20 per cent (OECD 1999; Jonsson and Wiman 2001). Students may have a disability but not have any special educational needs (Evans 2001), yet they are often denied access to education on the basis of their disability (Porter 2001; Peters 2004).

Research indicates that there is a close link between poverty, disability and school exclusion (WHO and World Bank 2011). The *World Report on Disability* states that 'persons with disabilities . . . are more likely to be poor than persons without disabilities' (WHO and World Bank 2011: 39). Because of extra costs for personal supports, medical care and assistive devices, individuals who have a disability and their families have less money for food, shelter, education, clothes or medical care than do others with similar incomes. Family income is also reduced when a family member – usually a mother, sister or grandmother – cannot generate income because of the need to care for a family member with a disability (Inclusion International 2006). Most children who are out of school live in the poorest countries of the world, and their families often live on less than $1 per day (Inclusion International 2006). Even if education is free, poor families often cannot afford the cost of texts, slates, notebooks or school uniforms for all their children, and the children with disabilities are least likely to go to school (Inclusion International 2009).

In other cases, when social rather than education ministries are responsible for children with disabilities, the disabled children may never be counted in education data (Inclusion International 2009). Furthermore, some children may be registered for school, and counted in data, but denied access because of lack of accessibility or other supports. For example, in Kazakhstan, students with severe disabilities may be registered in a school, but they actually receive their 'education' at home from infrequent visits by social workers who are not trained educators, while others receive no education at all (OECD 2009). Officially, however, the government of Kazakhstan reported that 99.5 per cent of children were attending primary school in 1998 (UNESCO 2006b).

As part of their obligations under the Convention on the Rights of Persons with Disabilities (CRPD), States that have ratified the convention must report regularly on their progress in complying with the convention to the Committee on the Rights of Persons with Disabilities of the United Nations Office of the High Commissioner for Human Rights (OHCHR) (UN 2006). The first submissions to this committee report a range in the numbers of persons with disabilities. Spain claims that 19.9 per cent of households have a person with a disability; Peru claims 8.4 per cent of the population has a disability; and Tunisia reported that 99 per cent of children of school age were enrolled in school, but claimed that only 1.5 per cent of the population had a disability (CRPD 2010).

The confusion over the number of children who have a disability and their invisibility in education data have resulted in a lack of accountability for their education and made it difficult for parents and other advocates to convince governments and donors of the extent of the current exclusion (Inclusion International 2009).

The study by Inclusion International (2009) pointed out several other systemic causes of the exclusion of children with intellectual disabilities from education in general and inclusive education in particular. Where education is available to students with disabilities, there is a dichotomy between systems that include those students in mainstream education and those that provide special supports, with few systems providing the necessary supports in an inclusive setting. When the mainstream system is the only option, but fails to provide supports, students are often not registered or drop out early (Inclusion International 2009). Organizations for persons who are deaf or blind have argued that regular systems have not provided the special supports required (ICEVI and WBU 2011; World Federation of the Deaf nd).

The Inclusion International 2009 study also called attention to the existence of separate systems of education for disabled and non-disabled students. In high- and middle-income countries the pattern is to have two parallel state-supported systems – often but not always within one education ministry: one for children without disabilities and one for children with disabilities. However, in emerging economies, where much of the funding for education comes through international co-operation funds, the most common pattern is for governments to provide a system that excludes students with disabilities and for donors to fund non-government organizations (NGOs) to provide special education in special schools for students who have a disability (Inclusion International 2009). A study by Human Rights Watch (2011) demonstrates that although the government of Nepal has a policy favouring inclusive education, it continues to invest in segregated systems. This pattern is similar to Lloyd's (2000) assessment of the situation in the United Kingdom, where budget allocations have not been adequate to support policy and legislative change in favour of inclusion.

The existence of parallel systems causes two main problems. First, it contributes to the invisibility of children with disabilities by keeping them out of mainstream education. Second, it increases the challenges of moving towards inclusion because the mainstream system has no responsibility for the education of students with disabilities and often is even prohibited from admitting students with disabilities (Muñoz 2007). Furthermore, inclusion may be hampered by inaccessible buildings, lack of transportation to school, or admission exams that preclude accommodation for deaf or blind students (Porter 2001; Inclusion International 2009).

Most of the pressure for inclusion has come from parents of excluded students with disabilities who fear that a segregated education will lead to a life of segregation (Inclusion International 2009). With little data to support them and ineffective law and policy, they have had little influence on mainstream systems.

Education for All

Since 1990, there has been global recognition that the lack of education of millions of people around the world is one of the greatest causes of poverty. The United Nations and several of its agencies convened a series of meetings designed to focus attention and investment on specific goals aimed at poverty alleviation in general and education in particular (UNESCO 1990; UN 1995, 2000). 'Education for All' became an objective and a slogan following the meeting convened by UNESCO in Jomtien, Thailand in 1990 which noted: 'The learning needs of the disabled demand special attention. Steps need to be taken to provide equal access to education to every category of disabled persons as an integral part of the education system' (UNESCO 1990, Article III, 5).

The commitment to Education for All (EFA) was reinforced with the adoption by the United Nations of the Millennium Development Goals (MDGs) in 2000, which laid out a set of eight goals for the reduction of world poverty to be achieved by the year 2015. The second goal is 'To ensure that, by (2015), children everywhere, boys and girls alike, will be able to complete a full course of primary schooling and that girls and boys will have equal access to all levels of education' (UN 2000: 5).

The reference to persons with disabilities in the Jomtien statement had set the stage for the UNESCO 1994 World Conference on Special Needs Education: Access and Quality. The resulting *Salamanca Statement and Framework for Action* (UNESCO 1994), agreed to by the representatives of 94 participating states, clearly articulated that the goal for students with disabilities was not simply to ensure that people with disabilities received an education. The goal was not inclusion *in* education but rather *inclusive education*.

The inclusion of the goal of primary education in the Millennium Development Goals gave Education for All a boost. However, the Millennium Declaration made no specific mention of disability, and efforts to achieve the goals have woefully ignored children with disabilities (Inclusion International 2009). The monitoring of the achievement of EFA has been done through annual Global Monitoring Reports published by UNESCO and based on a framework developed at the World Education Forum in Dakar, Senegal in 2000 (UNESCO 2009).

Given the number of out-of-school children who have a disability, neither EFA nor the MDGs can be reached if children, youth and adults who have a disability are ignored. In fact, the 2010 Global Monitoring report stated: 'The key message to emerge is that failure to place inclusive education at the centre of the EFA agenda is holding back progress towards the goals adopted at Dakar' (UNESCO 2010: 8). There is no accountability within the global monitoring frameworks to ensure that the commitments to provide quality inclusive education for persons with a disability are met. Data collected for the reports do not segregate information related to disability, so the invisibility of persons with disability is once again reinforced.

In its 2009 review of the education of children with intellectual disabilities, Inclusion International applied the Dakar goals to the current situation of children with disabilities and highlighted the following:

- *Early childhood care and education*: children with disabilities have little access; when services exist there is a predominance of a medical model in delivery.

- *Universal primary education*: policy and legislation are either lacking or not implemented; there is often separate responsibility for children with disabilities; children with disabilities are generally excluded from regular classes and regular schools; if students are in regular schools they usually receive few supports (and families often pay for the ones that exist); and special education systems fail both to provide quality and to reach most children.

- *Meeting lifelong learning needs of youth and adults*: there is very limited access to or flexibility in post-secondary education and what exists often provides training for 'dead-end' jobs (such as unskilled labour that has been replaced by machines in the labour market).

- *Adult literacy*: high rates of illiteracy were coupled with lack of access to quality programmes.

- *Gender equality in education*: a double disadvantage was found for girls and women and a lack of gender-sensitive approach in schools, education planning and monitoring.

- *Quality*: quality was compromised because of negative attitudes, lack of pre-service and in-service teacher training; inaccessible classrooms and schools; inflexible curriculum and assessment; and the fact that known success factors were not being adapted for inclusion.

(Inclusion International 2009: 55–85)

All of these points have been confirmed by the World Report on Disability (WHO and World Bank 2011). The Special Rapporteur on the Right to Education (Muñoz

2007) called for indicators and benchmarks in order to be able to monitor both the quantity of students with disabilities receiving an education and the quality of such education. Without such monitoring it is impossible to track progress in meeting the Dakar goals for children with disabilities.

The Convention on the Rights of Persons with Disabilities (CRPD)

In this chapter we have already seen that there is wide acknowledgement that children with disabilities are disproportionately excluded from education in general and inclusive education in particular; that the EFA and MDG goals cannot be reached if children with disabilities are ignored; and that monitoring of progress in reaching these goals has so far ignored children with disabilities. There are some positive signs that this situation is about to change.

In December 2006 the United Nations General Assembly adopted the CRPD (UN 2006). Article 24 of the Convention mandates States to 'ensure an inclusive education system at all levels'. As of May 2012 over one hundred countries have ratified the CRPD (UN 2011). Article 24 has several key elements. It guarantees the right to:

- an inclusive education system at all levels;
- quality and free primary education and secondary education on an equal basis with others;
- reasonable accommodation;
- effective individualized support measures such as Braille, sign language and an adapted curriculum; and
- equal access to post-secondary education and lifelong learning.

The CRPD is important because it is a legally binding instrument for countries that have ratified it. It provides the first legal obligation for States to provide an education to persons with disabilities in an inclusive way, to provide the necessary disability-related supports, and to report on their progress. Countries that have ratified must submit reports to the committee responsible for monitoring the convention within two years of ratification and at least every four years thereafter. This means that for the first time ever, countries are required to provide a public account of what they are currently doing to educate persons with disabilities, to meet the requirements of the Convention and to indicate their plans for achieving full compliance. While there are no penalties for non-compliance, the public nature of the reporting process provides a basis for active lobbying by organizations of people with disabilities and their families.

As of May 2012 the United Kingdom is the only country which, in ratifying the CRPD, issued an interpretive declaration on Article 24 indicating that it would continue to offer a choice between inclusion and special schools (UN 2011).

The rationale for the UK's interpretive declaration appears to be the government's desire to respect parental choice as evidenced in the written submissions to the Parliamentary Committee which reviewed it (Human Rights Joint Committee, nd). Both disability advocacy groups and the Equality and Human Rights Commission (nd) have criticized the interpretive declaration. It flies in the face of research by Ofsted (2006), which found that resourced mainstream schools provided better education than special schools. Porter (2001) raised the question of whether it is economically feasible to adequately fund two systems – a quality and inclusive main-stream system with supports for disabled students and a system of special and separate education. It remains to be seen whether the UK will continue to try to support both systems.

The Committee on the Rights of Persons with Disabilities (CRPD) receives reports from States that are parties to the CRPD – that is, they have ratified it – and is responsible for analysing their compliance with the Convention. The Committee is composed of independent experts and operates under the auspices of the OHCHR. It conducted its first review of State reports in 2011. In its Concluding Observations on the first report reviewed, from Tunisia, the Committee noted in particular the risk of exclusion of persons with psycho-social or intellectual disabilities and 'regrets the invisibility of children with disabilities in data related to protection of children' (CRPD 2010). With regard to Article 24, the CRPD committee reported:

> The Committee . . . notes with deep concern that . . . the inclusion strategy is not equally implemented in schools; rules relating to the number of children in main-stream schools and to the management of inclusive classes are commonly breached; and schools are not equitably distributed between regions of the same governorate; . . . that many integrated schools are not equipped to receive children with disabilities.

The Committee went on to recommend that the government:

> Increase its efforts to enforce inclusive education for girls and boys with disabili-ties in all schools; intensify training for education personnel, including teachers and administrators; (and) allocate sufficient financial and human resources to implement the national programme of inclusive education for children with disabilities.

These recommendations mark the first time ever that a national government has been held accountable for improving both the access and quality of inclusive education for children with disabilities. In its next report to the CRPD Committee, Tunisia will need to report on the progress made and all countries which have ratified will be subject to the same review.

While Article 24 of the CRPD deals specifically with education, several other elements and articles of the convention provide guarantees which are prerequisites to achieving inclusive education. For example, the Preamble recognizes that families require assistance so that they can help members who have a disability to exercise their rights. Other articles emphasize inclusion, non-discrimination, the need for awareness raising, eliminating barriers to accessibility, collecting data on the number of persons with disabilities, designating a focal point for implementation of the Convention, fully involving organizations of persons with disabilities and their representative organizations (such as family organizations of persons with intellectual

disabilities) to participate fully in this process and guarantees that international investments from donors in low- and middle-income countries support inclusive education.
Finally, the *Optional Protocol to the CRPD* (ratified by more than 60 countries) permits
individuals and groups to take complaints to the Committee after they have exhausted
national legal recourses (UN 2011).

This is the first time an article affecting donors has been included in a UN Treaty.
This means that not only the countries that receive funds from donors to support
education programmes but also donor countries will be reviewed by the committee to
ensure that they are supporting inclusion. Because UNESCO, UNICEF and other
UN agencies are bound by the CRPD, they also must now respect the letter and
intent of the convention in their implementation and monitoring of EFA. For the first
time, all UN agencies are working together to promote inclusive education (UNDG/
IASG 2010).

The fact that the World Bank must also respect the CRPD provides another
important step forward since its investment strategies will need to take the Convention
into account. The Bank's 2011 education strategy calls for 'investing for all ...' It
states:

> (L)earning for all means ensuring that *all* students, not just the most privileged
> or gifted, acquire the knowledge and skills that they need. This goal will
> require lowering the barriers that keep girls, people with disabilities, and ethno-
> linguistic minorities from attaining as much education as other population
> groups.
>
> (World Bank 2011: 56–7)

The Bank has made general statements like this before, but now one of the indicators
to measure progress will be the percentage of countries that have reduced schooling
or learning gaps for persons with disabilities since 2010. The multi-sectoral approach
promoted in the strategy recognizes the many systems that must be addressed to
make school inclusion possible (bad roads and limited transport services, poor health
and nutritional deficiencies, and shortages in clean water and power supply) and as
such addresses the holistic approach promoted by the CRPD.

In addition to the education strategy that will guide World Bank investments, the
Partnership for Education, formerly known as the Fast Track Initiative (FTI), can
provide important resources, both financial and technical, to promote inclusive
education. Initially under the auspices of the World Bank, the FTI was created in
2002 to assist those low-income countries furthest from achieving universal primary
education to move forward. The FTI has produced an 'Equity and Inclusion Guide'
designed to assist countries to include those most likely to be excluded, including
children with disabilities (FTI 2010).

National efforts to promote inclusion have also been helped by the recommendations of the Special Rapporteur on the Right to Education regarding the right to
education of persons with disabilities (Muñoz 2007). The Special Rapporteur
provided countries with a roadmap of the steps they should take in moving towards
inclusion, from constitutionally guaranteeing the right to free primary education and
ensuring that only one ministry be responsible for education of all children to the

transformation of existing special education resources to support inclusion, training, infrastructure and the provision of early childhood education.

But there is more to be done. The CRPD committee is supported by the OHCHR which reported that disability supports for 2010–11 represent 2.5 per cent of OHCHR's main programme budget (OHCHR 2010). With the committee meeting only two weeks per year to review reports from over 100 countries plus complaints from individuals, it will be difficult to monitor progress towards inclusion – although this process will be an important start. The UN General Assembly recognized this challenge and has extended the committee's meeting time by one week per year – still little time for such a daunting task (United Nations General Assembly 2012).

Conclusion

Much of the discussion about inclusive education focuses on immediate barriers such as school accessibility, teaching methods and discriminatory practices. However, if inclusion is to become a reality, more attention needs to be paid to systemic barriers, many of which extend far beyond education systems. The CRPD provides a framework for addressing those barriers and an accountability mechanism for doing so. The World Bank promotes inclusion as a means to economic growth. Moreover, it is a basic human right and basis for social cohesion (Meijer nd).

Today, children who have a disability are less likely than their non-disabled peers to start school or to complete a primary education. If they receive any education it is likely to be separate from their non-disabled peers, to be outside of the mainstream education system and to fail to prepare them for the labour market. For the situation to change, people who have a disability must move out of the shadows and overcome their invisibility. There are more than one billion people who have a disability (WHO and World Bank 2011). Taking their households into account, more than five billion people are affected by disability. These are too many people for the world to ignore.

Long-standing commitments to educate children with disabilities in the same systems and classrooms as their non-disabled peers have been strengthened by the CRPD. The force of the convention needs to overcome the invisibility of people who have a disability, to make inclusion of students with disabilities an issue in all aspects of educational reform and to mobilize the financial resources to implement the change. Doing so will not only mean justice for people with disabilities. It will improve education – and society – for all.

References

CRPD (Committee on the Rights of Persons with Disabilities) (2010) *Implementation of the International Convention on the Rights of Persons with Disabilities. Initial Report Submitted by States Parties under Article 35 of the Covenant: Tunisia.* Available at http://www.ohchr.org/ EN/HRBodies/CRPD/Pages/Session5.aspx [Accessed 5 August 2011].

CRPD (2011) *Implementation of the International Convention on the Rights of Persons with Disabilities. Initial Report Submitted by States Parties under Article 35 of the Covenant: Peru.* Available at: http://search.ohchr.org/search?q=cache:OFujPM2Q7_QJ:www2.ohchr.org/SPdocs/ CRPD/6thsession/CRPD.C.PER.1_en.doc+peru+%2B+disability&site=default_

collection&client=default_frontend&output=xml_no_dtd&ie=UTF-8&proxystylesheet=en_ frontend&access=p&oe=UTF-8 [Accessed 5 August 2011].

Equality and Human Rights Commission (nd) *Position Statement on UK Ratification of the Convention.* Available at http://www.equalityhumanrights.com/human-rights/international-framework/un-convention-on-the-rights-of-persons-with-disabilities/our-submissions-on-the-rights-of-disabled-people/position-statement-on-uk-ratification-of-the-convention/ [Accessed 21 November 2011].

Evans, P. (2001) Equity indicators based on the provision of supplemental resources for disabled and disadvantaged students, in W. Hutmacher, D. Cochrane and N. Bottani (eds) *In Pursuit of Equity in Education.* London: Kluwer.

Fast Track Initiative (2010) *Equity and Inclusion Guide*, 1st edn. Available at http://www.educationfasttrack.org/FTI-at-Work/vulnerable-groups/ [Accessed 20 October 2011].

G8 Information Centre (nd) *A New Focus on Education for All.* Available at http://www.g8.utoronto.ca/summit/2002kananaskis/education.html [Accessed 20 October 2011].

Human Rights Joint Committee (nd) *Written Submissions to the UN Convention on the Rights of Persons with Disabilities: Reservations and Interpretative Declaration.* Available at http://www.publications.parliament.uk/pa/jt200809/jtselect/jtrights/70/7010.htm [Accessed 21 November 2011].

Human Rights Watch (2011) *Futures Stolen: Barriers to Education for Children with Disabilities in Nepal.* New York: Human Rights Watch.

ICEVI (International Council for Education of People with Visual Impairment) and WBU (World Blind Union) (2011) *Joint Education Policy Statement.* Available at http://www.icevi.org/publications/ICEVI-WBU_Joint_Educational_Policy_Statement.html [Accessed 25 June 2011].

IDA (International Disability Alliance) (2010) *IDA Submission on List of Issues for Tunisia. Committee on the Rights of Persons with Disabilities, 4th Session.* Available at http://www.ohchr.org/EN/HRBodies/CRPD/Pages/Session5.aspx [Accessed 5 October 2011].

Inclusion International (nd) *The Implications of the Convention on the Rights of Persons with Disabilities (CRPD) for Education for All.* Available at http://www.inclusion-international.org/wp-content/uploads/ImplicationsCRPD_dr2_X2.pdf [Accessed 5 August 2011].

Inclusion International (2006) *Hear Our Voices. A Global Report: People with an Intellectual Disability and their Families Speak Out on Poverty and Exclusion.* London: Inclusion International.

Inclusion International (2009) *Better Education for All When We're Included Too.* Salamanca: Instituto Universitario de Integracion en la Communidad.

Jonsson, T. and Wiman, R. (2001) *Education, Poverty and Disability in Developing Countries*, World Bank Report. Available at http://www.congreso.gob.pe/comisiones/2006/discapacidad/tematico/educacion/Poverty-Education-Disability.pdf [Accessed 5 June 2011].

Jordan, L. and Goodey, C. (2002) *Human Rights and School Change.* Bristol: Centre for Studies in Inclusive Education.

Lloyd, C. (2000) Excellence for all children – false promises! The failure of current policy for inclusive education and implications for schooling in the 21st century, *International Journal of Inclusive Education*, 4(2): 133–51.

Meijer, C. J. W. (nd) *Inclusive Education: Facts and Trends.* Available at http://www.european-agency.org/news/news-files/cor-meijer.pdf [Accessed 20 June 2011].

Muñoz, V. (2007) *The Right to Education of Persons with Disabilities. Report of the Special Rapporteur on the Right to Education Vernor Muñoz to the Human Rights Council.* Available at http://daccess-dds-ny.un.org/doc/UNDOC/GEN/G07/108/92/PDF/G0710892.pdf?OpenElement [Accessed 5 June 2011].

OECD (Organization for Economic Cooperation and Development) (1999) *Inclusive Education at Work: Students with Disabilities in Mainstream Schools.* Paris: OECD.

OECD (2009) *Students with SEN in Kazakhstan, Kyrgyz Republic and Tajikistan*. Paris: OECD.

Ofsted (2006) *Inclusion: Does It Matter Where Pupils Are Taught?* Office for Standards in Education, Children's Services and Skills, HMI 2535. Available at http://www.ofsted.gov.uk/resources/inclusion-does-it-matter-where-pupils-are-taught [Accessed 18 November 2011].

OHCHR Office of the High Commissioner for Human Rights (2010) *OHCHR Report 2010*. Available at http://www2.ohchr.org/english/ohchrreport2010/web_version/ohchr_report2010_web/index.html#/home [Accessed 5 September 2011].

Peters, S. J. (2004) *Inclusive Education: An EFA Strategy for All Children*. Washington, DC: World Bank.

Porter, G. L. (2001) *Disability and Inclusive Education*, Paper prepared for the InterAmerican Development Bank Seminar, Inclusion and Disability, Santiago, Chile. Available at http://www.disabilityworld.org/05-06_01/children/inclusiveed.shtml [Accessed 5 June 2011].

Schulze, M. (2009) *Understanding the UN convention on the rights of Persons with Disabilities. A Handbook on the Human Rights of Persons with Disabilities*. New York: Handicap International. Available at http://www.handicap-international.fr/fileadmin/documents/publications/HICRPDManual.pdf [Accessed 20 October 2011].

Summit of the Americas (2001) *Declaration of Quebec City*. Available at http://www.summit-americas.org/eng-2002/quebeccity-summit.htm [Accessed 20 October 2011].

UN (United Nations) (1948) *Universal Declaration of Human Rights*. New York: United Nations.

UN (1989) *Convention on the Rights of the Child*. Available at http://www2.ohchr.org/english/law/crc.htm [Accessed 5 June 2011].

UN (1995) *Report of the World Summit for Social Development*. Available at: http://daccess-dds-ny.un.org/doc/UNDOC/GEN/N95/116/51/PDF/N9511651.pdf?OpenElement [Accessed 5 June 2011].

UN (2000) *Millennium Declaration*. Available at: http://www.un.org/millennium/declaration/ares552e.pdf [Accessed 5 June 2011].

UN (2006) *Convention on the Rights of Persons with Disabilities*. New York: United Nations.

UN (2012) Enable website. Available at http://www.un.org/disabilities/countries.asp?navid=12&pid=166 [Accessed 8 May 2012].

UNDG (United Nations Development Group)/Inter-Agency Support Group for the CRPD Task Team (2010) *Including the Rights of Persons with Disabilities in United Nations Programming at Country Level: A Guidance Note*. Available at http://www.un.org/disabilities/documents/iasg/undg_guidance_note.pdf [Accessed 5 June 2011].

UNESCO (1990) *World Declaration on Education For All*. Available at http://www.unesco.org/education/wef/en-conf/Jomtien%20Declaration%20eng.shtm [Accessed 20 October 2011].

UNESCO (1994) *The Salamanca Statement and Framework for Action on Special Needs Education*. Paris: UNESCO/Ministry of Education, Spain.

UNESCO (2000) *Education for All: Meeting Our Collective Commitments*. Available at http://www.unesco.org/education/efa/ed_for_all/dakfram_eng.shtml [Accessed 20 October 2011].

UNESCO (2006a) *Literacy for Life: EFA Global Monitoring Report 2006*. Available at http://www.unesco.org/new/en/education/themes/leading-the-international-agenda/efareport/reports/2006-literacy/ [Accessed 20 October 2011].

UNESCO (2006b) *Strong Foundations: EFA Global Monitoring Report 2007*. Available at http://www.unesco.org/new/en/education/themes/leading-the-international-agenda/efareport/reports/2007-early-childhood/ [Accessed 20 October 2011].

UNESCO (2008) *Inclusive Dimensions of the Right to Education: Normative Bases Concept Paper Prepared for the Eighth and Ninth Meetings of the Joint Expert Group UNESCO (CR)/ECOSOC (CESR) on the Monitoring of the Right to Education – 2008*. Paris: UNESCO.

UNESCO (2009) *The Six Dakar Goals*. Available at http://www.unesco.org/education/efa/ six_goals.shtml [Accessed 20 October 2011].

UNESCO (2010) *Reaching the Marginalized: EFA Global Monitoring Report 2010*. Available at http://www.unesco.org/new/en/education/themes/leading-the-international-agenda/ efareport/reports/2010-marginalization/ [Accessed 20 October 2011].

UN General Assembly (2012) Resolution A/RES/66/22. Available at http://www.un.org/ disabilities/default.asp?id=36 [Accessed 29 March 2012].

UNICEF (2007) *Promoting the Rights of Children with Disabilities*. Innocenti Digest No. 13. Florence: Innocenti Research Centre, UNICEF.

UNICEF (2011) *The Right of Children with Disabilities to Education: A Rights-based Approach to Inclusive Education*. Geneva: UNICEF Regional Office for Central and Eastern Europe and the Commonwealth of Independent States (CEECIS).

WHO (World Health Organization) and World Bank (2011) *World Report on Disability*. Geneva: World Health Organization.

World Bank (2011) *Learning for All: Investing in People's Knowledge and Skills to Promote Development*. World Bank Group Education Strategy 2020. Available at http://siteresources. worldbank.org/EDUCATION/Resources/ESSU/Education_Strategy_4_12_2011.pdf [Accessed 5 June 2011].

World Federation of the Deaf (nd) *Education Rights for Deaf Children*. Available at http://www. wfdeaf.org/policies/education-rights-for-deaf-children [Accessed 23 June 2011].

15

ROBERT CONWAY
Inclusive schools in Australia: rhetoric and practice

Introduction

Inclusive schooling is supported as a concept in all Australian educational jurisdictions, although practices vary across the six states and two territories in the way inclusion is supported and implemented (Rietveld 2008; Boyle *et al.* 2011). The chapter provides examples of the competing demands to ensure that, regardless of whether we argue for 'inclusion' or 'inclusive education' or 'inclusive schools' or 'education for all', all students have access to an education that caters for their educational needs.

What is the state of inclusion in Australian schools?

A well-developed literature on inclusion and inclusive practices exists in Australian education, embracing topics such as:

- teacher and school leader beliefs and attitudes towards inclusion and the inclusion of specific special needs (e.g. Center *et al.* 1985; Bain and Dolbel 1991);
- specific policies and practices in jurisdictions (see Berlach and Chambers 2011); inclusion practices across early childhood, primary and secondary settings (e.g. Pearce and Forlin 2005; Grace *et al.* 2008; Boyle *et al.* 2011);
- inclusion practices relating to specific special needs (e.g. Roberts *et al.* 2008); in-service and pre-service training needs (e.g. Sharma *et al.* 2011); and proposals to change the existing models (Forbes 2007) to cater better for the needs of all students and teachers.

While there are increasing numbers of students identified with disabilities in Australian schools (Dempsey 2011), it is difficult to obtain precise figures due to a lack of adequate data collection processes. Dempsey reported that the percentage of students with disabilities in Australian schools rose from 2.6 per cent in 1996 to 3.5 per cent in 2001 and 4.8 per cent in 2009. The percentage of students with disabilities in government schools has increased faster than in non-government schools. If students without special needs continue to leave the government school sector for the non-government sector, the percentage of students with special needs in the government sector will continue to rise. This places greater pressure on teachers in that sector to cater for the increasing percentage of students in their classes who will require differentiation in their learning and teaching. This pressure is often resisted.

A key difficulty in obtaining accurate data, and identifying needs, is the lack of a national definition of disability (Conway and Dempsey 2003). Hence, by including or excluding specific disabilities, jurisdictional data varies. In the Northern Territory prevalence levels are reported to be as high as 12 per cent while in other jurisdictions it is as low as 4 per cent. Some jurisdictions include socio-emotional categories (including behaviour disorders in some cases); others include, or exclude, communication difficulties and specific language disabilities. A nationally agreed set of disabilities (physical, sensory, cognitive, social/emotional) was agreed to in 2012.

Some low-incidence disabilities are eligible for some Australian government financial support to schools in order to obtain additional services such as some teacher aide support or additional materials. Support for the many students with disabilities who are not eligible for this funding must be catered for as part of unfunded mainstream differentiation.

Where a disability attracts considerable media and public attention, funding may be provided for professional learning. A good example is the considerable Australian government funding provided for teacher and parent training to support the inclusion of students with Autism Spectrum Disorder (ASD) in mainstream schools (DEEWR 2011a). Considerable resources are available that have not been allocated to any other special need. The training is provided to all levels of schooling from early childhood to secondary and to teachers and separately to parents. The professional development for teachers and school staff includes a five-day equivalent programme with a residential component of at least two days. Evaluation data (Kishida 2011) show that 68.9 per cent of teachers who attended the training could demonstrate at least one example of curriculum adjustment for students with ASD in their classroom, and 66.3 per cent could provide examples of increased teacher/parent collaboration. These data show that change in inclusive practices can occur at least in the short run and for one high-profile special need.

Such a resource across all areas of special education and inclusion would be a great asset in increasing staff self-efficacy. The question will be whether, at the end of this expenditure, students with ASD are more successfully included in mainstream schools in the long run. In the next round of funding (2012–14) for teacher and parent training in supporting students with ASD, there is a specific component of the tender allocated to research and evaluation on the effectiveness of the programme's content.

Key emerging issues

The current Australian educational environment has posed additional challenges to inclusion in practice. Among these are the Disability Standards for Education (2005), and the National Assessment Program – Literacy and Numeracy (NAPLAN). The Disability Standards for Education (DEEWR 2005) provided legislative support for students with disabilities to have access to curriculum, learning and teaching that met their specific needs. It clearly supports the necessity for teachers to make 'reasonable adjustments' to include students with disabilities in the same way as other students. The difficulty is that many teachers are unable or unwilling to comply with the requirements as these are seen as beyond their expertise. An undesired and unexpected outcome is that the requirements may result in increased disconnectedness between teacher and included students (O'Rourke 2011). A way to overcome this legislative requirement is to ensure that all schools have staff with teachers, and particularly school leaders, who are skilled in supporting students with special needs (Forbes 2007). The role of the principal is critical in any new initiatives in schools and in maintaining momentum during any initiative.

The establishment of the Australian Curriculum has been a major change in the implementation of curriculum in the country as eight state/territory curricula are replaced over time by one curriculum. As at 2011, there are only four subjects developed (English, mathematics, history and science) for Foundation to Year 10 with other curriculum areas to come as well as a senior years curriculum being developed for Years 11 and 12. The critical feature of the Australian Curriculum is that it contains content and outcomes for each year but no statements on pedagogy, which remains the responsibility of educational jurisdictions. Berlach and Chambers (2011) are critical of the current draft curriculum in that it does not address the issues of differentiation and inclusivity explicitly. The curriculum is designed for all students, and how students will be supported to achieve the outcomes for the year level is unclear. The other critical issue is how we address the needs of students unable to reach the year outcomes despite reasonable accommodations and differentiation. Given the difficulties that many teachers will have adjusting to the new curriculum with regular students, there is considerable concern that special needs will not be addressed, particularly in content not previously covered by the school. In addition, teachers may be reluctant to develop new differentiation activities for new topics.

If the Australian Curriculum causes concern for students with special needs in inclusive settings, the concerns related to national testing that occurs for all students at Year 3, 5, 7 and 9 in literacy and numeracy are greater. The National Assessment Program–Literacy and Numeracy (NAPLAN) has the same issues as the high-stakes testing regime in the USA and UK (Conway and Dempsey 2003) in that schools are rated on performance of students in each of the tested grades and the results published on the school's page on the MySchool website (www.myschool.edu.au). While schools which have a commitment to inclusive education will ensure all students attempt the tests and are part of the school's profile, many other schools, however, choose to quietly exclude students with special needs from the testing in order to produce scores as high as possible. Particularly in small schools, the involvement of students with special needs will alter the school's data considerably. The key issue in national assessment is that, for students with intellectual and cognitive disabilities, the assessment tasks are beyond their ability and hence participation only emphasizes their lower performance level.

Another key issue for students with special needs in mainstream settings is the move to remove or downplay sections of the curriculum in order to increase the time devoted to literacy and numeracy activities in preparation for NAPLAN assessments.

Of concern is the practice of teachers altering student responses to raise school performance, highlighting again the problems that testing is more about ranking of schools in terms of performance at the expense of inclusive practices. Teachers and their student with special needs are therefore caught between internal expectations and external pressures (O'Rourke 2011). Anecdotal evidence suggests that NAPLAN and curriculum challenges, particularly in secondary schools, are a driver behind increased secondary enrolment in special settings.

Difficulties in making inclusion a reality

Despite the strong rhetoric in favour of inclusion as a concept and a practice, there is recognition that there are practical difficulties relating to creating an inclusive educational model. It means that schools, not just individual teachers, have to face the reality of increasing numbers of students with special needs in their classes, and what this means in terms of learning and teaching to ensure success for all students in the class. This is a challenge that many teachers find difficult. As Hsien *et al.* (2009: 27) state, 'the successful inclusion of children with disabilities into the regular school setting is dependent on the attitude of teachers and their recognition of the child's right to participation'. Hsien *et al.* (2009) identify three key areas: lack of ability to implement inclusive practices successfully; lack of ability to plan and make instructional modifications in the classroom; and that special education teachers are better trained and have more effective methods of working with these students. In the first two areas, the need is for a specialist educator trained to work with mainstream teachers (e.g. a Support Teacher – Special Education) while the last requires a special education teacher trained as a vision, behaviour, hearing, ASD or other disability specialist.

The last point has always been of concern in the move of students from specialist settings to mainstream classes. In many jurisdictions funding for inclusion of students with special needs has been directed to the employment of teaching assistants (also known as teachers' aides, or support services officers in different states). In NSW schools, 90 per cent of the funding for students with special needs went to employing teachers' aides to work with the students (Parkins 2002, in Boyle *et al.* 2011). This has raised the possibility that the teacher's aide becomes the *de facto* teacher of that student.

A key issue raised by the work of Hsien *et al.* (2009) is the concept that special education teachers are better prepared and able to support the learning of students with special needs. Certainly studies exist in which special education teachers have reported having more positive and optimistic views of their ability to cater for students with special needs. Yet Hsien *et al.* (2009) cite studies showing special education teachers having expressed similar concerns to mainstream teachers. These common concerns are across issue such as: lack of sufficient materials, personnel resources and support shortages; insufficient training and knowledge; and lack of time for planning and collaborative teaching. Such concerns highlight special education staff with low levels of self-efficacy in terms of their ability to implement inclusive practices. Given that studies have shown that high teacher self-efficacy is a 'key ingredient to create successful classroom environments' (Sharma *et al.* 2011: 2) then we need to reconsider how we can change teacher self-efficacy through developing pre-service and in-service professional learning.

Differentiation, differentiated instruction and Universal Design for Learning approaches

Ensuring that all students in the classroom have a positive learning experience during the lesson should be the positive outcome of inclusive classroom practices. Yet for many teachers this is a concept rather than a practice. Much of the focus during both pre-service teacher education and in-service education has been based on the principles of differentiation of curriculum, teaching and learning. Differentiated instruction 'takes into account the individual differences and needs of an individual's experiences and contributions for learning in the classroom' (van Kraayenoord 2007: 3). Westwood and Arnold (2004) have argued that differentiation such as altering or watering down curriculum content is not effective. Yet differentiation does not have to mean watering down, but finding ways of presenting key concepts in accessible ways. Particularly in secondary school, students with special needs do not want activities that are different or which in any way highlight their inability to complete class tasks. Teachers point to problems in differentiating the curriculum because of lack of preparation time, large class sizes and teacher workloads. Certainly for many teachers, differentiation is a task that they are not prepared to invest time and effort on.

An alternative model for use in Australia has been proposed by a number of authors including Van Kraayenoord and Elkins (2005). Universal Design for Learning (see Van Kraayenoord 2007) is based on the premise that in planning the curriculum and teaching, the needs of all students are addressed during the preparation of the teaching content. 'Universal Design for Learning involves the conscious and deliberate creation of lessons and outcomes that allow all students access to, and participation in, the same curricula' (Van Kraayenoord 2007: 392). The model has been applied in a number of studies in Queensland schools (see Van Kraayenoord and Elkins 2005) with the teacher preparing two approaches to the learning of the same content and the students choosing which text version they wanted to access during an English curriculum topic. This reflected one of the key principles of the approach – that all students access the same curriculum. It could be argued that both differentiation and Universal Design for Learning are needed and not just one. Teachers need to ensure that the curriculum topics and teaching approaches accommodate all students during preparation and that teachers make specific differentiations to teaching and learning to accommodate students during the lesson if needed (see Conway 2011).

In reality all teachers will need to have skills both in designing curriculum activities that engage all students and in using specific differentiation activities in the classroom when a student requires additional support. The key point is to engage the whole class, not just the few.

Development of differentiation skills in schools – in-service professional learning requirements

Teachers continue to resist the placement of students with special needs in main-stream schools because of the perceived inability to differentiate learning and teaching strategies. The approach to changing this is not through one-off sessions within school staff development days. Change requires a sustained approach with sessions over an extended time, using a range of practical examples and strategies to develop self-efficacy in teachers to support inclusion. Pearce and Forlin (2005) present a series of additional challenges in secondary schools. These include: school structure based on discipline silos, teaching approaches that are heavily content-focused rather than student learning-focused; curriculum that is prescribed and dominated by external exams in the final year; subject-specialized teachers who are bound by content; and the difficulties of educating adolescents who are more socially motivated than curriculum motivated. All factors, individually and collectively, result in resistance by secondary teachers to make adjustments for any individual student and particularly for students perceived as being better placed in alternative settings. Inclusion may have a social equity basis but removal is focused on failure academically not socially.

Approaches that may work in secondary schools include structural changes to the layout of the school and changes to the operation of the school. An example is the establishing of year groupings with a set of teachers for that year, similar to the middle schooling model. In this way teachers have a more restricted set of adaptations and differentiations for students in that year. Teachers could change the year group they work with on a cyclical basis to ensure they remain in contact with the full secondary range of curriculum.

Collaboration between teachers is often uncommon in secondary schools and even in some primary schools, yet collaboration is a key strategy to support inclusive practices. As Pearce and Forlin (2005: 102) have observed, 'autonomy in the classroom, so long prized and part of the attraction of teachers to their role, is not necessarily conducive to the inclusive approach'. Where teachers are able to work in groups developing differentiation strategies for specific students and classes the responsibility is shared and the outcomes are available for a larger group.

Preparation of pre-service teachers for inclusive schools

There is strong support in the Australian and international literature for the incorporation of skills for including students with special needs in mainstream classes as part of pre-service training (see Subban and Sharma 2006). In Australia, this has not been compulsory in the past although many teacher education programmes have included a subject that refers to students with special needs and/or integration and/or inclusion concepts. A problem with such subjects is that often they have been optional or included as part of another more general subject on diversity. While diversity is an important area for teacher preparation, the specific need for skill development in the support of students with special needs cannot be overlooked. In the past, lectures and tutorials have traditionally focused on understanding the differing characteristics of specific disabilities (e.g. Ashman and Elkins 1990). This was replaced by a more generic approach to special needs that looked at the reasons behind the beliefs for integration. It also saw a move to focus on inclusion, and the strategies for teaching in diverse classrooms. These included differentiation of curriculum, teaching strategies and resources, where the needs of specific disabilities were not highlighted (e.g. Foreman 1996). Interestingly, both of these widely used Australian textbooks have, over various editions, changed to represent a more common approach in current editions (see Ashman and Elkins 2011; Foreman 2011). Their title terminology has also changed.

Studies have shown that engaging pre-service students in subjects on inclusive education can change their beliefs and practices, before they enter schools as teachers. A study of primary pre-service students from four universities in NSW (Woodcock and Vialle 2010) found that students had preconceived ideas about the differences in teaching strategies for students with and without a learning difficulty (LD). They believed that students with LD required more teacher-centred instructional strategies while those without LD could undertake more learner-centred strategies. Their decisions were based on a perception of the special need, not on knowledge. The authors argued that, uncorrected, the students could go into schools and deprive students with LD of the strategy that research shows works very effectively, teaching self-regulation. Why is this an important example? It demonstrates that unless there is effective teaching for inclusion in teacher education awards, students may leave with beliefs about teaching students with special needs that are extremely difficult to change. As Woodcock and Vialle (2010: 27) succinctly state, 'it is known that teachers form beliefs about the process of teaching during their pre-service training and also that once a belief has been held for a long time it is extremely difficult to change'.

A weakness of the approach to pre-service teacher education has been the tendency to have the subject taught exclusively by special education or inclusive education staff. This model only exacerbates the impression that it is different or separate. While we persist in teacher education with the concept that differentiation is separate, we will not engage lecturers in curriculum and pedagogy in considering differentiation as an automatic issue in all aspects of pre-service teacher preparation. The following content needs to be embedded within the academic programme for student teachers, across all topics:

- the educational reasons for inclusion;
- reasonable adjustment in learning and teaching across curriculum areas;
- strategies for specific special needs; and
- collaborative approaches to inclusive practices by teams of teachers and school leaders.

This needs to be balanced by a specific component in professional experience placements on inclusive teaching practices with direct reference back to the subject content taught in university settings. Engagement by all teacher education staff in teaching this content models inclusive practices (Conway 2011).

Pre-service preparation of special education teachers

There has also been a call for stronger preparation of special education teachers during teacher education awards (Forbes 2007). Until recently most special education teacher preparation has been through either a final year of an existing bachelor teacher preparation programme, or as an additional post-graduate qualification often as a Masters degree or at a Graduate Certificate level. A new model is the preparation of teachers in an extended and integrated undergraduate special education programme. These include the awards at RMIT University in Melbourne, the University of New England (UNE) in Armidale and most recently the Bachelor of Education/Bachelor of Disability Studies programme at Flinders University in South Australia. This four-year double degree is designed to prepare teachers to work in: traditional mainstream settings; as teachers supporting students with special educational needs in mainstream settings; and as special education teachers in settings from special classes to special schools. Importantly the 'discipline' in the other half of the double degree is Disability Studies, where the pre-service teacher works in a disability placement, as well as topics on disability across the lifespan taught by staff in the disability area. Students can undertake their studies focusing on early childhood and early intervention, primary or secondary settings. The key is to achieve what Forbes (2007), Thomas (2009) and others have argued, that we develop teachers, before they graduate, who understand the issues in inclusive settings as well as the specific needs of the students who are being included.

What then are the differences between preparing mainstream teachers and special education teachers? Hsien *et al.* (2009) highlight the differences as the key to self-efficacy in supporting students with special needs. Mainstream students are exposed to issues in inclusion and strategies that can be used to support students in a single subject (secondary) or across the curriculum (primary). Hence attitudes and skills are developed in isolation. Teachers in special education programmes have the added advantage that numerous topics address special needs, there is a much stronger coverage of disabilities and related learning needs, and they engage in a variety of professional experience placements that enhance self-efficacy in meeting student-specific learning needs.

What does this mean for pre-service students preparing to work in mainstream settings? As discussed earlier, there is a need to move to a more 'inclusive' teacher education programme that encompasses inclusion, differentiation and students with special needs in all subjects, and a deliberate focus on students with special needs in at least one professional experience placement. Such practices will ensure that pre-service teacher education is itself more inclusive.

A new approach?

The current approach to increasing self-efficacy in teachers to differentiate for students with special needs is based on professional learning activities that are often disjointed and short-term in nature. Particularly in secondary schools, the model will meet with limited success as resistance is often greater than the will of the professional learning session provider, who is often from outside the school or even the educational jurisdiction. In addition, school leaders are often not included in the professional learning even though their involvement is critical to showing and providing leadership in school change (Brigg 2008).

One model is to engage a range of special education staff as a resource to schools, working alongside teachers in supporting the actual differentiation strategies for teachers but with the teacher retaining the responsibility for the education of his or her student. Special education staff can be part of the school staff as in Support

Teacher positions attached to schools. They may be part of a district team working with a number of schools thus bringing strategies and ideas from one school to another, building up a network of resources and ideas. Forbes (2007) raises the prospect of special schools providing the base and expertise for students with a range of special needs, and staff working with a cluster of mainstream primary and secondary schools. Forbes (2007: 68) extends this concept to the possibility that students in an inclusive school model may move between mainstream and specialist education settings over time – 'inclusion should mean being involved in the common enterprise of learning rather than necessarily being under the same roof at a particular phase of education'. For those who believe in total inclusion, such a model would not be acceptable, but for many teachers and some parents, the opportunity to move between settings would be preferable. The problem with such a model is that primary schools will be more likely to work to support inclusion while secondary schools will support the concept of inclusion being in a separate but related setting.

A variation on the model has been proposed by Brigg (2008) with reference to students with ASD, although he sees this as a relevant model for the broader special education cohort. Brigg (2008: 5) argues that we need differing models across the student's schooling:

- evidence-based small group programs in the pre-compulsory years;
- adequate support for teachers in terms of professional learning and additional resources for students with autism in the mainstream;
- flexible programs in upper primary;
- the option of small group programs targeting individual need and focused on alternate pathways in secondary school.

The other model suggested by Forbes (2007) involves the co-location of special schools and mainstream schools on the one campus to provide staff and students with the ability to move between settings for different activities, thus having the benefits of both an inclusive setting and specialist support. Experience shows that the successful operation of this inclusion model depends largely on the ability of the two principals to make it work, rather than having inclusion defined by the proximity of two schools.

In late 2011 the Commonwealth provided a new round of funding support to educational jurisdictions to support students with special needs both in inclusive and mainstream settings. The More Support for Students with Disabilities initiative included the following outcomes:

- schools become more inclusive environments, in accordance with the Disability Standards for Education (DEEWR 2005), recognizing the diversity students with disabilities bring to the school;
- teachers are more capable of identifying and addressing the educational needs of students with disabilities;
- teachers of students with disabilities have better access to expert support.

Interestingly, the guiding principles include that the activities should:

- strive to support students in all settings in all sectors according to their level of need;
- recognize different schooling arrangements, including resourcing arrangements.

Experience shows that decisions on funded activities are often not made on research-based evidence, but on the needs expressed by pressure groups. Key priorities should be professional learning that:

- increases teacher self-efficacy in the ability to differentiate learning and teaching;
- demonstrates how to communicate and collaborate with others; and
- provides strategies to manage the behaviours of students who are not able to engage in the learning.

In the latter case awareness of the essential relationship between behaviour, learning and teaching would include awareness that misbehaviour by any student often occurs because the student is not actively engaged in the learning and teaching. Active engagement in academic tasks reduces behaviour problems. Hence differentiation and reasonable accommodation can be effective not only in including students with special needs; it can increase academic engagement by all students.

Conclusions

O'Rourke (2011: 23) cites the work of Roger Slee in saying: 'The challenge ahead is to appreciate that inclusion is less about disability and more about social change, school reform and educational restructuring.' We need to exert less emotion and energy debating existing issues such as who will fund inclusion, and focus more on the practical skills for the reality of inclusive classes and schools.

The National Professional Standards for Teachers (AITSL 2011) provide a great starting point for examining the changes we need to make. At each of the four levels of professional capabilities there are specific examples of how to implement Focus 1.5 'strategies to support the full participation of students with disability'. At each of the four levels: Graduate, Proficient, Highly Accomplished and Lead there are descriptors of how the focus looks in practice.

At the pre-service level where on graduation teachers must be at the Graduate level, this includes learning about, and implementing in professional experience placement, special needs accommodations and adaptations as part of teaching all students. In that way we see learning and teaching in schools as inclusive, not mainstream with special needs as an added issue. Beliefs and practices with which students leave teacher preparation programmes stay long into their teaching careers.

At the in-service level for the Proficient, Highly Accomplished and Lead teacher levels, whole-school approaches rather than individual teacher adaptations and adjustments are the key. The current national professional learning focus on teaching adaptations and adjustments for students with ASD needs to be modified and adapted by schools to address the broader range of students with special needs – commonalities are greater than differences in teaching and learning accommodations. In addition, using expertise from consultants, special schools and other lighthouse schools can provide a cross-school collegial approach to ensuring that all schools are inclusive.

References

ACARA (Australian Curriculum, Assessment and Reporting Authority) (2008) *National Assessment Program, Literacy and Numeracy* (NAPLAN). Available at: http://www.naplan.edu.au/home_page.html [Accessed 15 October 2011].

AITSL (Australian Institute for Teaching and School Leadership) (2011) *National Professional Standards for Teachers*. Melbourne: AITSL.

Ashman, A. F. and Elkins, J. (eds) (1990) *Educating Children with Special Needs*. Sydney: Prentice Hall.

Ashman, A. F. and Elkins, J. (eds) (2011) *Education for Inclusion and Diversity*, 4th edn. Frenchs Forest: Pearson Education Australia.

Bain, A. and Dolbel, S. (1991) Regular and special education principals' perceptions of an integration program for students who are intellectually handicapped, *Education and Training in Mental Retardation*, 26(1): 33–42.

Berlach, R. G. and Chambers, D. J. (2011) Inclusivity imperatives and the Australian national curriculum, *The Educational Forum*, 75(1): 52–65.

Boyle, C., Scriven, B., Durning, S. and Downes, C. (2011) Facilitating the learning of all students: the 'professional positive' of inclusive practice in Australian primary schools, *Support for Learning*, 26(2): 72–8. DOI: 10.1111/j.1467-9604.2011.01480.

Brigg, J. (2008) The approach to the education of students with autism in Australia, *Australasian Journal of Special Education*, 33(1): 1–5.

Center, Y., Ward, J., Parmenter, T. and Nash, R. (1985) Principals' attitudes towards the integration of disabled children into regular schools, *The Exceptional Child*, 32(3): 149–61.

Conway, R. N. F. (2011) Adapting curriculum, teaching and learning strategies, in P. J. Foreman (ed.) *Inclusion in Action*, 3rd edn. South Melbourne: Cengage.

Conway, R. N. F. and Dempsey, I. (2003) Development of a common definition of, and approach to, data collection on students with disabilities for the purpose of nationally comparable reporting of their outcomes in the context of the National Goals for Schooling in the Twenty-First Century. Report to the PMRT Disability Definitions Working Group, Canberra, ACT, Ministerial Council on Education, Employment, Training and Youth Affairs.

DEEWR (Department of Education, Employment and Workplace Relations) (2005) *Disability Standards for Education*. Available at: www.deewr.gov.au/Schooling/Programs/Documents/Disability_Standards_for_Education_2005_pdf [Accessed 12 October 2011].

DEEWR (2011a) *Helping Children with Autism*. Available at: www.deewr.gov.au/Schooling/Programs/Pages/helpingChildrenwithAutism.aspx [Accessed 5 August 2011].

DEEWR (2011b) *More Support for Students with Disabilities Initiative*. Canberra: DEEWR. Available at: http://www.deewr.gov.au/schooling/programs/pages/moresupportforswd.aspx [Accessed 5 September 2010].

Dempsey, I. (2011) Trends in the proportion of students with a disability in Australian schools, 2000–2009, *Journal of Intellectual and Developmental Disability*, 36(2): 144–5.

Forbes, F. (2007) Towards inclusion: an Australian perspective, *Support for Learning*, 22 (2): 66–71.

Foreman, P. (ed.) (1996) *Integration and Inclusion in Action*. Sydney: Harcourt Brace.

Foreman, P. (ed.) (2011) *Inclusion in Action*, 3rd edn. South Melbourne: Cengage.

Grace, R., Llewellyn, G., Wedgwood, N., Fenech, M. and McConnell, D. (2008) Everyday experiences of mothers and early childhood professionals negotiating an inclusive early childhood experience in the Australian context, *Topics in Early Childhood Special Education*, 28(1): 18–30.

Hsien, M., Brown, P. M. and Bortoli, A. (2009) Teacher qualifications and attitudes toward inclusion, *Australasian Journal of Special Education*, 33(1): 26–41.

Kishida, Y. (2011) Changes in teachers' practices following their participation in an autism-specific professional development program, *Special Education Perspectives*, 20(1): 29–39.

O'Rourke, J. (2011) The issue of inclusion, *Educational Review*, 16 June: 22–3.

Pearce, M. and Forlin, C. (2005) Challenges and potential solutions for enabling inclusion in secondary schools, *Australasian Journal of Special Education*, 29(2): 93–105.

Rietveld, C. M. (2008) Contextual factors affecting inclusion during children's transitions from preschool to school, *Australian Journal of Early Childhood*, 33(3): 1–9.

Roberts, J. M. A., Keane, E. and Clark, T. R. (2008) Making inclusion work: Autism Spectrum Australia's satellite class project, *TEACHING Exceptional Children*, 41(2): 22–7.

Sharma, U., Loreman, T. and Forlin, C. (2011) Measuring teacher efficacy to implement inclusive practices, *Journal of Research in Special Education Needs*. Available at: http://onlinelibrary.wiley.com/doi/10.1111/j.1471–3802.2011.01200.x/pdf.

Subban, P. and Sharma, U. (2006) Primary school teachers' perceptions of inclusive education in Victoria, Australia, *International Journal of Special Education*, 21(1): 42–52.

Thomas, T. (2009) The age and qualifications of special education staff in Australia, *Australasian Journal of Special Education*, 33(2): 109–16.

Van Kraayenoord, C. (2007) School and classroom practices in inclusive education in Australia, *Childhood Education*, 83(6): 390–4.

Van Kraayenoord, C. E. and Elkins, J. (2005) Differentiated instruction in inclusive classrooms. Paper presented at 50th Annual Convention of the International Reading Association, San Antonio, Texas, 1–5 May.

Westwood, P. and Arnold, W. (2004) Meeting individual needs with young learners, *ELT Journal*, 58(4): 375–8.

Woodcock, S. and Vialle, W. (2010) The potential to learn: pre-service teachers' proposed use of instructional strategies for students with a learning disability, *Contemporary Issues in Educational Research*, 3(10): 27–38.

CHRISTOPHER BOYLE AND
KEITH TOPPING
Conclusion: inclusion comes together piece by piece

The chapters of this book contain many suggestions by authors with different perspectives of inclusion based on their own interpretations and cultural experiences. In our concluding chapter we try to synthesize these important themes and ideas.

Theories of inclusion – what exactly is 'inclusion'?

Definitions of inclusion have been presented in many different ways by many different theorists (e.g. Topping and Maloney 2005; Boyle *et al.* 2011). In this section views about what inclusion entails from practical, educational, socio-political and fiscal standpoints are discussed. In Keith Topping's chapter (1), he advocated that the conception of inclusion should be regarded much more widely than is currently the norm. He considers that there are four levels of inclusion (see Figure 1.1 in Chapter 1) with the highest and most expansive being the complete social involvement of the student in the community, thus suggesting that effective inclusion cannot only be school-focused. In a similar vein, Fraser Lauchlan and Roberta Fadda (Chapter 3) refer to 1844 people with special needs where their involvement in mainstream schooling had a positive effect, in that they felt that they had a sense of belonging to the community. Not being separated from the mainstream population (whether physically or socially) seems to have a strong bearing on whether inclusion is seen to be a positive experience for the population with special needs.

Kim Michaud and Tom Scruggs in Chapter 2 provide a historical perspective of inclusion in the US, with a critique of major federal legislation which was intended to ensure inclusive education. The authors show that this is twofold, in that there are perennial debates about resourcing and whether teachers are supported adequately to perform their role in inclusive environments. The other area is that of inclusion being a civil right: '. . .an inherent right not to be denied. . .'. Michaud and Scruggs contend that the issue of whether students with special needs should be included has been won, but the argument has now shifted towards whether full inclusion is actually in the best interests of all students. The authors assert that the most powerful discussion in education (not just special education) is how to improve general education instruction and thus optimize learning and teaching experiences for all involved.

Roger Slee (Chapter 4) asserts that if inclusion is to work effectively, then there has to be a redistribution of resources between affluent area schools and those of lower socio-economic status. Slee suggests that academic failure stems from a lack of proper resourcing, which affects the success of inclusion programmes, as there is an 'insipid political will for making inclusion work'. There will continue to be issues about funding for specialist support in a mainstream environment.

The 'how' of inclusion

An eclectic mix of methods and strategies that have been proved to work within inclusive settings are put forward in this section. Brahm Norwich (Chapter 5) suggests that there will always be ideological debates about what should or should not be classified as inclusion. Norwich asserts that inclusion should be regarded as a continuum. At one end there will be the 'universalists' who advocate full inclusion without compromise, and at the other end are the 'moderates' who would allow inclusion to also enable some form of alternative placement. However, the inclusion debates should be in areas of agreed understanding, allowing productive discussion about what *can* work rather than what is or is not inclusion.

Spence Salend and Catharine Whittaker in Chapter 6 echo a point of Topping's that the degree of implementation of inclusion will vary according to various factors, such as the legal, economic and social. The challenge is bringing these different factors into a cohesive whole in order to facilitate a strong (and workable) policy on inclusion. Salend and Whittaker also suggest that there must be a 'comprehensive self-assessment' of implementation, to ensure effectiveness in going forward.

Chris Boyle (Chapter 8) and Adrian Ashman (Chapter 7) both focus on the importance of teachers as the main drivers for successful inclusion in general classrooms. Ashman introduces Responsive Teaching and suggests that this is not about teachers having to learn new knowledge or strategies, but it is about restructuring ways of using knowledge about the students and orchestrating interactions in the classroom environment. Peer support is an important aspect. Boyle explains that teachers supporting each other is by far the best support mechanism in ensuring good inclusive practice. As Boyle says: 'Good pedagogy . . . is about mastering appropriate classroom management and teaching practice that supports all students irrespective of a notional label'.

Richard Villa and Jacqueline Thousand (Chapter 9) put forward models that work in inclusion. The key is to understand your own institution and to adapt models and knowledge from various sources and apply them to the current context. Villa and Thousand suggest that many models should be incorporated, as each situation is uniquely different and programmes must take account of local nuances if success is to take place.

Jo Deppeler (Chapter 10) presents the case for collaborative working at various levels involving various professionals. Deppeler suggests that by distributing responsibilities for student learning then the best possible outcomes are achieved as good pedagogical principles are applied (c.f. chapters by Boyle, and Villa and Thousand). Following the theme of collaboration, Richard Rose (Chapter 11) considers the importance of community partnerships and shows that local community engagement is necessary for successful inclusive schools and communities. This links to the discussion of the Italian inclusion model by Lauchlan and Fadda (Chapter 3), which also emphasizes the social benefits of community inclusion. As Rose states, 'inclusive practices that are focused solely upon action in schools are unlikely to succeed'.

Overcoming barriers to successful inclusion

The final section of this book was designed to provide an understanding of and solutions to the types of barriers that may exist in successful inclusive processes and thus negatively impact on inclusion. Margo Mastropieri and Tom Scruggs (Chapter 12) reflect that there are multiple variables which can influence inclusion. These include whether there is a strong ethos of co-operative teaching in the school (c.f. Salend and Whittaker in Chapter 6) and how useful the differentiated curriculum is for supporting the teacher in adapting his or her teaching to accommodate the range of students in the class. As in Chapter 8 by Boyle, authors Mastropieri and Scruggs also assert that peer support is a positive way to enhance inclusion, while the converse is true in that poor peer support can act as a barrier to inclusion. It is therefore imperative that management teams listen to the teaching staff, as they are the ground-level staff who implement (or not) the inclusion programme.

Laurel Garrick Duhaney (Chapter 13) asserts that exclusion is no longer a justifiable concept. This echoes Michaud and Scruggs in Chapter 2, who considered it a civil rights issue for equality. Garrick Duhaney considers access to local mainstream education as a 'fundamental human right'. She is very clear that this is an issue of equity and supported by the Salamanca Statement (UNESCO 1994). Diane Richler (Chapter 14) considers barriers to inclusion to have a much wider focus than merely that of education, and takes a worldwide focus. She suggests that these barriers extend to different facets of society and governments, and are not an issue fixed to education systems. The Convention on the Rights of Persons with Disabilities (CRPD) is emphasized by Richler as being key, as it has built-in levels of accountancy that signatory countries must adhere to. As with Garrick Duhaney, Richler emphasizes that mainstream education is a basic human right for all. The barrier that needs to be overcome is that of the invisibility of the disabled in many facets of mainstream society across the world.

Finally in this section Robert Conway (Chapter 15) considers barriers from an Australian perspective. He advocates a moving away from a focus on the funding of inclusion to concentration on the reality of inclusion in classrooms. In this he is suggesting that quality pedagogical principles and effective strategies are the main means to achieve positive inclusion in the classroom. Conway believes that pre-service teaching should be targeted, so that inclusive teaching principles are universal in teacher education and not taught in solitary and sometimes optional modules.

Action for inclusion

So, if we want inclusion, how do we get there? A number of other publications offer advice. Advocates such as Ainscow (1999), Allan (1999), Cheminais (2001) and Lorenz (2002) give broad guidelines. Other authors suggest quite specific practical strategies, not only in the special needs area (e.g. Tilstone and Rose 2003), but also in other areas such as gender equity (e.g. Horgan 1995; Noble *et al.* 2001) and bilingualism (Gardner 2002; Smyth 2003). Continuing Professional Development (in-service training) for relevant staff (not only teachers) is obviously important (Hopkins 2002). Gross and White (2003) (among others) propose a whole-school inclusion audit leading to consideration of arrangements to train, deploy, support and effectively manage relevant staff. Daniels *et al.* (1997) propose the development of teacher support teams in both primary and secondary schools to facilitate peer support at the local level. Developing an inclusive school can be firmly set in wider issues of overall school effectiveness and school improvement (Boyle *et al.* 2011a, 2012b).

Turning to studies evaluating the effectiveness of interventions, Dyson *et al.* (2002) offered a systematic review of school-level actions for promoting participation by all students. Duchaine *et al.* (2011) found teacher coaching with written performance feedback effective in increasing behaviour-specific praise statements in high school inclusion classrooms. Robinson (2011) found modelling and video-based feedback effective in training paraprofessionals working with students with autism. Both systems of continuing professional development (CPD) were time-consuming, both to deliver and to receive. Osborne and Reed (2011) found that social–emotional behaviours were better facilitated in mainstream secondary schools with larger numbers of other kinds of children with SEN. Good teacher training facilitated social behaviours.

Do teacher attitudes to inclusion make a difference to their behaviour? Elliott (2008) found that teachers with a positive attitude toward inclusion provided all of their students with significantly more practice attempts, at a higher level of success. Do SEN pupils adversely affect the education of other children in the class? Manset and Semmel (1997) found that 'normal' pupils in mainstreamed environments were actually advantaged in terms of attainment by the presence of pupils with special educational needs – perhaps because their teachers were sensitized to the different learning needs of others in the class with challenges. Kalambouka *et al.* (2007) reviewed the evidence and reported that overall, there were no adverse effects on pupils without SEN, with 81 per cent of the outcomes reporting positive or neutral effects. In the UK, many special needs students are largely supported by teaching assistants. Unfortunately, Webster *et al.* (2010) found that teaching assistant support had a negative impact on pupils' academic progress, especially pupils with SEN. These findings render the current system of support for SEN highly questionable.

Turning from classroom practices to interaction with the peer group of students, intervention seems more reliably effective. Adibsereshki *et al.* (2010) explored the effectiveness of a programme on the acceptance of students with physical disabilities by their peers in inclusive schools. There was an increase of acceptance in the experimental group. However, acceptance was greater in girls than boys. The Circle of Friends Program widens the social network of students with disabilities by linking them to a social network of general education students. Calabrese *et al.* (2008) found participants felt involvement was a transformative experience whether they have disabilities or not.

Where improvements are made in inclusion practices, are these sustainable? Sindelar *et al.* (2006) found one middle school was notably successful, having built its inclusion model on a school culture characterized by shared decision making, collaboration and teaming. However, over four years, inclusion was not sustained. Three primary factors in this were: leadership change, teacher turnover, and state and district assessment policy change.

Conclusions

Roger Slee suggested in Chapter 4 that the inclusion project is ongoing. This whole book supports that theme. However, this book has attempted to concentrate on positive aspects. All the authors, while highlighting difficulties with the practicalities of the concept, embraced bringing solutions to the reader. This book contains many solutions and provides a unique understanding of inclusion from many different angles.

Inclusion is no longer limited to simple discussions about education at the school level. This is emphasized by Topping who proposes a four-level structure for inclusion with the community and social aspects as paramount. Rose, who discussed a community school project much wider than the school itself, reinforces this. Lauchlan and Fadda likewise suggest inclusion is a social responsibility and is not restricted to education.

From a worldwide perspective, Richler described barriers to inclusion from international missions and United Nations policy knowledge. Richler views the lack of social inclusion for many disadvantaged people as a blight on modern societies. In order to move forward, the invisible minority of the disenfranchised have to be properly recognized and supported. Michaud and Scruggs as well as Garrick Duhaney similarly believe that inclusive education is a basic civil right that cannot be denied to citizens. They link the inclusion 'struggle' to that of the 1960s civil rights movement in the US. In a different vein, Slee polemically suggests that to promote inclusivity there should be a redistribution of wealth between private and public schools, so that inclusion can be properly funded.

Norwich indicates that the labelling of students is always going to lead to an unhelpful system of categorization. He believes that we should be concentrating on what works in inclusion and not arguing about what inclusion is or is not. Conway supports the notion that practical inclusion in the classroom is based on good pedagogical skills, which should be emphasized on teacher training programmes. Boyle provides evidence to show that teachers see support from colleagues as paramount to successful inclusion. Mastropieri and Scruggs believe that management must do more listening to the teaching staff, if inclusion is to be successful at the school level. Ashman puts forward the Responsive Teaching approach for class teachers, where they restructure their teaching through gaining more knowledge about the students. Salend and Whittaker advance the suggestion that a comprehensive self-assessment of how inclusion is working in the school is essential to evaluate past successes and mistakes and plan forward in an orderly way. Villa and Thousand believe that the key is to understand your own institution, leading to the adaptation of models and knowledge that suit your own situation.

Coaching for teachers (Duchaine *et al.* 2011) is proposed as an effective strategy for inclusion – enabling teachers to value their own skills. Continuing Professional Development is obviously key to the future development of teachers, but the evidence is that methods that work tend to involve follow-up in the classroom and tend to be expensive. However, fiscal support is and has to be finite and extra resources are only a partial answer. Nonetheless, understanding and utilizing the strengths of the teachers to adapt and operate effectively in an inclusive environment is the real 'resource'. The evidence suggests that teaching assistant (TA) support does not have a positive effect, although this resource is currently widely used. Of course this may tell us something about how teaching assistants are trained (or not) and deployed, rather than about TAs *per se*. But there are many questions that need to be asked about how support is administered to many vulnerable students.

In relation to this, there is no evidence that special needs students in the classroom have a negative effect on the achievement or behaviour of the rest of the class. Indeed, where peer support for and from special needs students can be facilitated, it has an enormously positive effect.

There is no doubt that many schools in many countries are becoming more inclusive. But there are questions about whether and how such positive developments can be sustained. Even where excellent practice does exist, it may not necessarily continue to exist. We cannot be satisfied with cycles of better inclusion followed by worse inclusion, even though each successive period of worse inclusion may be better than the last period of worse inclusion. Future practice and research should seek to articulate strategies by which high-quality inclusive environments can be sustained and improved steadily and without regression.

The editors hope this book has been an exciting journey for the reader. Inclusion will remain an issue for debate in education circles, but you have been guided through chapters which provide the essence of how to work in an inclusive environment, as well as where pitfalls may lie. This book adds to knowledge in this area – reading it will enhance the wisdom of the reader – and then the reader must go forth into the world and actually *do* something different.

References

Adibsereshki, N., Tajrishi, M. P. and Mirzamani, M. (2010) The effectiveness of a preparatory students' programme on promoting peer acceptance of students with physical disabilities in inclusive schools of Tehran, *Educational Studies*, 36(4): 447–59.

Ainscow, M. (1999) *Understanding the Development of Inclusive Schools*. London: Falmer.

Allan, J. (1999) *Actively Seeking Inclusion*. London: Falmer.

Boyle C., Scriven, B., Durning, S. and Downes, C. (2011) Facilitating the learning of all students: 'the professional positive' of inclusive practice in Australian primary schools, *Support for Learning*, 26(2): 72–8. DOI: 10.1111/j.1467-9604.2011.01480.

Boyle, C., Topping, K. J., Jindal-Snape, D. and Norwich, B. (2012a) The importance of peer-support for teaching staff when including children with special educational needs, *School Psychology International*, 32(3): 167–184. DOI: 10.1177/0143034311415783.

Boyle, C., Topping, K. J. and Jindal-Snape, D. (2012b) Teachers' attitudes towards inclusion in high schools. Paper submitted for publication.

Calabrese, R., Patterson, J., Liu, F., Goodvin, S., Hummel, C. and Nance, E. (2008) An appreciative inquiry into the Circle of Friends Program: the benefits of social inclusion of students with disabilities, *International Journal of Whole Schooling*, 4(2): 20–7.

Cheminais, R. (2001) *Developing Inclusive School Practice*. London: Fulton.

Cigman, R. (ed.) (2007) *Included or Excluded? The Challenge of the Mainstream for Some Special Educational Needs Children.* London: Routledge.

Daniels, H., Norwich, B. and Creese, A. (1997) *Teacher Support Teams in Primary and Secondary Schools.* London: Fulton.

Demo, H. and Zambotti, F. (2009) Alcune relazioni tra percorsi di integrazione scolastica e percezione di integrazione sociale in contesti normali, *L'integrazione scolastica e sociale,* 8(5): 459–73.

Duchaine, E. L., Jolivete, K. and Frederick, L. D. (2011) The effect of teacher coaching with performance feedback on behavior-specific praise in inclusion classrooms, *Education and Treatment of Children,* 34(2): 209–27.

Dyson, A., Howes, A. and Roberts, B. (2002) *A Systematic Review of the Effectiveness of School-level Actions for Promoting Participation by All Students* (EPPI-Centre Review). London: Research Evidence in Education Library, EPPI-Centre, Social Science Research Unit, Institute of Education, University of London.

Elliott, S. (2008) The effect of teachers' attitude toward inclusion on the practice and success levels of children with and without disabilities in physical education, *International Journal of Special Education,* 23(3): 48–55.

Fullan, M. (2009) Large-scale reform comes of age, *Journal of Educational Change,* 10(2/3): 101–13.

Gardner, P. (2002) *Strategies and Resources for Teaching and Learning in Inclusive Classrooms.* London: Fulton.

Gross, J. and White, A. (2003) *Special Educational Needs and School Improvement.* London: Fulton.

Hopkins, D. (2002) *Improving the Quality of Education for All,* 2nd edn. London: Fulton.

Horgan, D. D. (1995) *Achieving Gender Equity: Strategies for the Classroom.* Boston and London: Allyn & Bacon.

Kalambouka, A., Farrell, P., Dyson, A. and Kaplan, I. (2007) The impact of placing pupils with special educational needs in mainstream schools on the achievement of their peers, *Educational Research,* 49(4): 365–82.

Lorenz, S. (2002) *First Steps in Inclusion: A Handbook for Parents, Teachers, Governors and Local Education Authorities.* London: Fulton.

Manset, G. and Semmel, M. I. (1997) Are inclusive programs for students with mild disabilities effective?, *Journal of Special Education,* 31(2): 155–80.

Noble *et al.* (2001) *How to Raise Boys' Achievement.* London: Fulton.

Osborne, L. A. and Reed, P. (2011) School factors associated with mainstream progress in secondary education for included pupils with autism spectrum disorders, *Research in Autism Spectrum Disorders,* 5(3): 1253–63.

Robinson, S. E. (2011) Teaching paraprofessionals of students with autism to implement pivotal response treatment in inclusive school settings using a brief video feedback training package, *Focus on Autism and Other Developmental Disabilities,* 26(2): 105–18.

Salend, S. J. (2011) *Creating Inclusive Classrooms: Effective and Reflective Practices,* 7th edn. Columbus, OH : Merrill/Pearson Education.

Sindelar, P. T., Shearer, D. K., Yendol-Hoppey, D. and Liebert, T. W. (2006) The sustainability of inclusive school reform, *Exceptional Children,* 72(3): 317–26.

Smyth, G. (2003) *Helping Bilingual Pupils to Access the Curriculum.* London: Fulton.

Tilstone, C. and Rose, R. (2003) *Strategies to Promote Inclusive Practice.* London: Routledge Falmer.

Topping, K. J. and Maloney, S. (2005) Introduction, in K. Topping and S. Maloney (eds) *The Routledge Falmer Reader in Inclusive Education.* Abingdon: Routledge Falmer.

UNESCO (1994) *The Salamanca Statement and Framework for Action on Special Needs Education*. Paris: UNESCO.

Webster, R., Blatchford, P., Bassett, P., Brown, P., Martin, C. and Russell, A. (2010) Double standards and first principles: framing teaching assistant support for pupils with special educational needs, *European Journal of Special Needs Education*, 25(4): 319–36.

Index

**CONTEMPORARY ISSUES IN
SPECIAL EDUCATIONAL NEEDS
Considering the Whole Child**

David Armstrong and Garry Squires

9780335243631 (Paperback)
2012

eBook also available

This thought-provoking and accessible book provides an overview of
key issues in the education of children with Special Educational Needs
and Disabilities. Written by highly experienced practitioners and
educationalists, the book explores a range of approaches for working
with this diverse group of learners and invites you to consider your
possible responses.

Key features:

- Encourages the reader to make rich and useful connections
  between concepts and approaches 'out there' and their own
  experience and approaches in the classroom
- Explores some difficult and highly conceptual notions such as
  'learner voice', 'diversity' or 'self-esteem' and what they actually
  mean in the context of complex and unique children with SEN
- Identifies the contributions psychology can make to developing
  and enriching educational practice

www.openup.co.uk

 OPEN UNIVERSITY PRESS
McGraw - Hill Education

INCLUSION
Developing an Effective Whole School Approach

Alison Ekins and Peter Grimes

9780335236046 (Paperback)
2009

eBook also available

This book examines and offers solutions to the challenges faced by schools in ensuring that all students are enjoying, participating and achieving in education. The authors argue that self evaluation lies at the heart of truly inclusive school development.

The book focuses on supporting schools in understanding and using school based systems and processes in a joined up, meaningful and strategic way to impact positively upon the progress and participation of all pupils.

Key features:

- Responds to the day to day needs of the SENCO, teacher, leader
- Provides case studies, examples, templates and models
- Focuses on supporting schools in understanding and using school based systems and processes in a joined up, meaningful and strategic way to impact positively upon the progress and participation of all pupils.

www.openup.co.uk

OPEN UNIVERSITY PRESS
McGraw · Hill Education

**TRANSFORMING THE ROLE
OF THE SENCO**
Achieving the National Award
for SEN Coordination

Fiona Hallett and Graham Hallett

9780335242412 (Paperback)
2010

eBook also available

This book offers an insight into the role of the Special Educational
Needs Coordinator (SENCO) at a time of transformation following the
recent legislative change and the introduction of the National Award
for SEN Coordination.
There are contributions from leading academics in the field of SEN
and inclusion, from NASEN and CSIE as well as from practitioners in
Local Authorities and educational settings.

Key features:

- A collection of keynote chapters outlining some of the issues and
  tensions of the role
- Five sections covering the main areas of the National Award:
  Professional Context; Strategic Development; Coordinating
  Provision; Leading, Developing and Supporting Colleagues; and
  Working in Partnership
- Friendly guidance on how the theory relates to the day to day
  practicalities facing the busy SENCO

www.openup.co.uk

OPEN UNIVERSITY PRESS
McGraw - Hill Education